Selling America

Selling America

Immigration Promotion and the Settlement of the American Continent, 1607–1914

Christina A. Ziegler-McPherson

BLOOMSBURY ACADEMIC

NEW YORK • LONDON • OXFORD • NEW DELHI • SYDNEY

BLOOMSBURY ACADEMIC
Bloomsbury Publishing Inc
1385 Broadway, New York, NY 10018, USA
50 Bedford Square, London, WC1B 3DP, UK
29 Earlsfort Terrace, Dublin 2, Ireland

BLOOMSBURY, BLOOMSBURY ACADEMIC and the Diana logo
are trademarks of Bloomsbury Publishing Plc

First published in the United States of America by ABC-CLIO 2017
Paperback edition published by Bloomsbury Academic 2024

Copyright © Bloomsbury Publishing Inc, 2024

Cover design by Silverander Communications
Cover photo: *Across the Continent: "Westward the Course of Empire Takes its Way."*
(Collection of Mr. and Mrs. Paul Mellon)

Bloomsbury Publishing Inc does not have any control over, or responsibility for,
any third-party websites referred to or in this book. All internet addresses given
in this book were correct at the time of going to press. The author and publisher
regret any inconvenience caused if addresses have changed or sites have
ceased to exist, but can accept no responsibility for any such changes.

Library of Congress Cataloging-in-Publication Data
Names: Ziegler-McPherson, Christina A., author.
Title: Selling America : immigration promotion and the settlement of the
American continent, 1607–1914 / Christina A. Ziegler-McPherson.
Description: Santa Barbara : Praeger, [2017] |
Includes bibliographical references and index.
Identifiers: LCCN 2016042572 (print) | LCCN 2017000567 (ebook) |
ISBN 9781440842085 (hardcopy) | ISBN 9781440842092 (eBook)
Subjects: LCSH: United States—Emigration and immigration—History. |Immigrants
—Recruiting—United States—History.
Classification: LCC JV6450 .Z54 2017 (print) |
LCC JV6450 (ebook) | DDC 304.8/700903—dc23
LC record available at https://lccn.loc.gov/2016042572

ISBN: HB: 978-1-4408-4208-5
PB: 979-8-7651-2626-4
ePDF: 978-1-4408-4209-2
eBook: 979-8-2161-4325-3

To find out more about our authors and books visit www.bloomsbury.com
and sign up for our newsletters.

Contents

Introduction

In 1607, the first Englishmen arrived in Virginia dreaming of gold and enslaved native servants. English separatists landed in Massachusetts 13 years later with a vision of a city on a hill populated by true believers and Christianized natives. But these Europeans found no gold and could neither convert the Native Americans nor force them to work as servants or slaves. A shortage of labor in a land populated by hundreds of thousands of people was the primary problem facing early European American communities. The solution was to import laborers from Europe and Africa. But the first colonizers of America approached the challenge of immigration promotion and labor recruitment very differently, depending on the source of that labor. Europeans, primarily from England, Scotland, Ireland, and the German-speaking states, were recruited to be both settlers and indentured servants (and future settlers). Africans, however, were always viewed as laborers and increasingly as slave-laborers for life. Since Indians refused to be servants or slaves, they had no place in the society Europeans were creating in North America, and so they were to be displaced and/or killed.

For more than 400 years, immigration has been central to the American economy, as Americans have sought to attract workers and settlers to conquer and develop the North American continent and build a new nation. To persuade Europeans to cross 3,400 miles of ocean to settle in a new country, American immigration promoters emphasized the ideals of hard work, upward mobility, and equality of opportunity in a New World. The idea of religious liberty was also an important selling point for many Europeans, especially those of minority religious sects, in the 17th, 18th, and 19th centuries. America, according to its promoters, was a richly fertile land of infinite resources and unlimited opportunity for anyone with enough ambition to reach out and grab it.

But this opportunity for upward mobility was only made available to certain people. From the beginning of American history, the desire to make and keep America as a "white man's country" has meant that Europeans, especially those from Northern Europe, would be welcomed as immigrant settlers and future citizens while Africans, Asians, and other non-whites would be either grudgingly tolerated as slaves or guest workers or excluded entirely.[1] And while for the first two centuries of American history, the central government was relatively weak in the area of immigration regulation when compared to the monarchies of Europe, state and local government were quite vigorous in their efforts to attract new residents, be they European immigrants or other Americans. Furthermore, the federal government could and did exert real power in pursuit of what its leaders perceived to be the national interest: conquering and occupying the North American continent and settling white European Americans on American Indian land.[2]

The story of the promotion of immigration to America between the 17th and 20th centuries intersects with three broad themes in American immigration history: immigration as labor policy; the relationship between immigration, citizenship, and race; and a central state that chose to cede oversight of immigration and citizenship matters to lower levels of government for most of the 19th century. Immigration promotion along with labor recruitment and contracting were among the most visible ways public and private actors sought to shape the nature and direction of immigration to America between the 17th and early 20th centuries.

The importation of labor, through either voluntary (immigration and indentured servitude) or involuntary (slavery and convict labor) means, has been the chief source of workers in America and central to the American economy from the beginning of settlement. When Europeans arrived in North America in the early 1600s, they discovered millions of native people who could not be forced to work for them, so the European conquerors had to import labor from Europe and then Africa. Most Europeans migrated to improve their economic opportunities and/or to escape downward mobility; desires for personal and religious freedoms were secondary motivations. Immigration in the 19th century was also driven mainly by economics, as economically displaced and increasingly impoverished Europeans were attracted to the United States by the opportunity to own land and by jobs created by a rapidly growing industrial economy. Chinese and Mexican immigrants also came to America in this period, but they were recruited as guest workers and were viewed as sojourners expected to leave once the job was done. Westward expansion across the continent and industrialization would not have been possible without the immigration of millions of workers from Europe, Asia, and Mexico.

Between 1607, when 104 Englishmen arrived in Virginia to establish the Jamestown settlement, and 1790, the year the new United States of America adopted its first naturalization act, approximately 484,000 Europeans and 388,000 Africans came to the eastern seaboard of North America. While Europeans came to America as free settlers, indentured servants, or convicts, Africans came as enslaved laborers, mainly to the Southern colonies of Virginia, Maryland, the Carolinas, and eventually Georgia.

Most of the Europeans were from the British Isles, but a sizable minority came from the Netherlands and the Rhineland region of what is now Germany. Virtually all of these Europeans belonged to one of the many Protestant sects, although there was a small number of Catholics and Jews. According to the first U.S. census in 1790, approximately 60 percent of the 3.9 million people living in the United States were of English descent; 9.5 percent were of Irish descent; 8.6 percent were of German descent, and 8 percent were of Scottish descent; 19 percent (760,000 people) were African American. So, colonial America was largely English-speaking and of English or British heritage, with sizable minorities of Africans, Germans, and Dutch.

The dominant myth of colonial settlement is that most immigrants came voluntarily, seeking religious freedom—that is, the Pilgrims, who landed at Plymouth Rock, Massachusetts, in 1620. In actuality, about 50 percent of European immigrants to America came as indentured servants, meaning they were contracted to work for several years for someone else who paid for their trans-Atlantic passage. Another 50,000 British convicts had been transported as a condition of punishment under the Transportation Act of 1718 by the time of the American Revolution. And most of the Europeans who arrived as free men migrated for economic, not religious, reasons, chiefly to escape downward mobility in Europe.

Behind every major colonization effort was a corporation specially organized by shareholders who intended to make a profit off their investment in the colonization company. English and eventually European investors saw colonization and settlement of the "New World" as a money-making venture, and immigrants were the means of achieving that profit, since most investors did not intend to do the hard work of colonization themselves.

Immigration in the 19th century was also driven primarily by economic forces as industrial capitalism both created new jobs and displaced old occupations. Between the end of the Napoleonic Wars in 1815 and the beginning of World War I in 1914, millions of Europeans decided to immigrate to both North and South America because of war; poverty; economic, political, and religious discrimination; and the hope of increased economic opportunities and upward mobility in the Americas. Between 1820 and 1920, 33,654,803 people came to the United States, most of them from Northern Europe and most arriving after the Civil War.

The high point of immigration before the Civil War was in the late 1840s and 1850s, when a fungus struck the Irish and then European potato crop and caused widespread famine in Ireland and Central Europe. After the Civil War, immigration from Europe increased and was only interrupted by economic depressions in 1873, 1893–1898, and 1907. Between 1860 and 1920, 28,773,029 people immigrated to the United States. In 1905, 1906, 1907, 1910, 1913, and 1914, more than 1 million immigrants entered the United States in each of these years, and the average annual immigration rate between 1900 and 1920 was 727,488 entries.

The largest groups to immigrate between 1820 and 1920 were Germans (5,494,690), Irish (4,348,759), Italians (4,100,735), Austro-Hungarians (4,068,451), English/British (3,857,038), Russians (3,179,254), and Scandinavians (2,134,415 from Norway, Sweden, and Denmark). Some groups, such as Germans, Irish, and British, immigrated in large numbers throughout the 19th and early 20th centuries. Other groups, such as Italians and people from the Austro-Hungarian, Russian, and Ottoman Empires, came in large numbers in the late 19th and early 20th centuries.

Compared to the millions of Europeans who immigrated in the 19th and early 20th centuries, the 223,100 Chinese who came between 1850 and 1880 and the 232,418 Japanese who arrived between 1880 and 1920 were much fewer, yet no less visible, and resulted in the first major diplomatic efforts by the federal government to restrict immigration in 1882 (from China) and then in 1907 (from Japan). Chinese and Japanese immigrants lived mainly in Western states and territories, where the movement for exclusion of these immigrants was the strongest.

Immigration in the 20th century is largely out of the scope of this study but was defined by increased bureaucratization and regulation, by ethnic and race-based restrictions, and then a dramatic surge in entries from new countries and regions, such as Latin America and Asia, after the Immigration Act of 1965. The distinctions between whites as immigrant settlers and non-whites as guest worker sojourners was both reinforced and lessened, depending on the immigrant group. Mexicans were increasingly defined as guest workers while Asians were eventually allowed to immigrate and naturalize after the Second World War.

The ethnic- and race-based restrictions on immigration instituted in 1924 and finalized in 1929 codified the long-standing presumption that Northern Europeans were desirable as immigrants because of their whiteness and their longer history of immigration, while Southern and Eastern Europeans were undesirable because of their questionable whiteness and their shorter history of immigration. In addition, because so many Southern and Eastern European men had engaged in circular or return migration, these groups were seen as guest workers, not permanent settlers.

At the same time, the restrictions on immigration from Europe allowed for unlimited immigration from the Western Hemisphere, which by 1924 meant primarily Mexico. Mexican immigrants were viewed as guest workers and allowed to cross the Southern border with almost no regulation. The image of Mexicans as temporary guest workers was reinforced during the Great Depression of the 1930s when hundreds of thousands of Mexican immigrants and their American-born children were expelled from the United States. The Bracero agreement between the United States and Mexico between 1942 and 1965 solidified the understanding of Mexicans as temporary guest workers, not permanent immigrants. Yet the abolishment of that program and the inclusion of Mexico into a Western Hemisphere quota in the 1965 Immigration Act ensured that hundreds of thousands and eventually millions of Mexicans would become permanent immigrants to the United States. Between 1970 and 2007, 10,128,528 Mexicans entered the United States legally, and an estimated 50 percent of the 11.3 million undocumented immigrants in the United States are from Mexico. In 2013, 11,584,977 million Mexican immigrants lived in the United States, and Mexicans are the largest immigrant group in the country.

The gradual lifting of discriminations against Asians in immigration and citizenship beginning in 1943 and then after 1965 has resulted in large numbers of immigrants from Asian countries, especially India, China, the Philippines, Vietnam, and Korea. Between 1970 and 2007, 9,293,141 million people from Asian countries immigrated to the United States, and in 2013, 10,425,640 Asian immigrants lived in America. These immigrants enter through an immigration regime that privileges education and job skills as well as family ties, and so many immigrants from Asia are better educated and more highly skilled than most native-born Americans.

The reasons most immigrants to the United States in the 19th century came from Europe (versus Asia or Africa) are complex, but they are directly tied to the relationship between immigration, American citizenship, and race.

The United States allows any legal immigrant to naturalize and become a citizen with the same rights and privileges as native-born American citizens, except the privilege of being president (which is limited to "natural-born" American citizens, meaning anyone who is a U.S. citizen by birth on American soil or birth to an American citizen). So who is admitted to the country is important. Yet the privilege of naturalization was limited to "free white persons of good character" ("persons" meaning men) until 1920, when white foreign-born women were allowed to naturalize, and then 1943, when Asian immigrants were allowed to become citizens.

Furthermore, American citizenship is based on the principle of *jus soli*, birth on soil, versus *jus sanguinis*, citizenship by blood, meaning that anyone born on American soil is a U.S. citizen, regardless of the citizenship of his or her parents. So while the American citizenship of American-born children of Asians immigrants was recognized by *U.S. v. Wong Kim Ark* in 1898, their parents were explicitly defined as "aliens ineligible for citizenship" because of their lack of whiteness. African American men were granted U.S. citizenship in 1868 by the Fourteenth Amendment to the Constitution, but few black men and women were able to exercise the rights of citizenship until the Civil Rights Act of 1964 and the Voting Rights Act of 1965. American Indians were not recognized as U.S. citizens until 1924 and were instead seen as citizens of their respective tribes, which were legally understood to be separate (although increasingly dependent) nations within the United States.[3]

The Naturalization Act of 1790 required a foreign-born white man to live in the United States for three years before he applied for citizenship; after this three-year period (changed to five years in 1802), the immigrant could then petition a court to make him a citizen.[4]

The fact that the new United States allowed European-born men to become citizens after a relatively short period of time and without any religious qualification was radical for the late 18th century. By the 1830s, property requirements for voting, office holding, and jury duty for white men had been abolished in all U.S. states and territories, making the United States one of the most generous nations in terms of political rights for male citizens.[5]

This relatively generous naturalization policy underlined the importance of the question of who was allowed to immigrate because an open immigration policy meant a *de facto* open naturalization policy, which, in turn, had important consequences for voting rights and American electoral politics. At various times, Americans have deemed certain kinds of immigrants—French in the late 1790s, Catholics in the 1840s to 1850s, Chinese in the 1850s to 1880s—to be political and/or socioeconomic threats and so have sought to limit their potential political influence by restricting their access to American citizenship.

But only hostility toward Chinese immigrants resulted in actual immigration restriction and the denial of the privilege of naturalization.[6] Significant democratic pressure existed in the mid-19th century in favor of limiting naturalization and/or immigrants' voting rights but anti-immigration activists never actually sought to limit immigration, in large part because the federal government lacked both the political will and the administrative means to effectively limit immigration. The ban on the African slave trade in 1807 was the first effort to restrict the importation of labor into the United States and was part of a larger compromise on slavery to get the Constitution adopted. To significantly restrict European immigration in the 19th century would have required a major investment of public funds to pay a government bureaucracy to enforce this restriction, and Americans were not willing to do this. Instead, the federal government chose to leave immigration relatively open and unregulated until the early 20th century, thus allowing for a wide variety of public and private actors to shape American immigration policy for most of the nation's history.

What regulation of immigration existed was handled primarily by states, especially those states with large ports, such as New York, Pennsylvania, and Massachusetts. New York created a Board of Commissioners of Emigration in 1847 to regulate conditions at the Port of New York and sought to impose a head tax on passengers, paid for by shippers, to pay for the social welfare services provided to newly arrived immigrants.[7]

But in 1849, in the *Passenger Cases*, the Supreme Court ruled that states could not impose head taxes on immigrants, and then in 1875, the Supreme Court ruled in *Henderson v. Mayor of New York* that existing state laws, such as the ones creating and governing the New York Board of Commissioners, were unconstitutional because they usurped Congress's exclusive power to regulate interstate commerce (and immigration was deemed part of interstate commerce). And yet the federal government was slow to develop a regulatory policy itself.

Only at the end of the 19th century did the federal government become increasingly involved in immigration policy, seeking to control and restrict who could enter the country, and this regulation was driven primarily by questions of race. The government targeted first Chinese laborers with the Page Act of 1875 and the Chinese Exclusion Act of 1882; contract laborers with the Contract Labor Law of 1885; and then poor, disabled, or criminal

Europeans with the Immigration Act of 1891, which established the inspection system at Ellis Island and other border stations.

But neither the Contract Labor Law nor the Immigration Act of 1891 excluded large numbers of people; rather, they were designed to facilitate the entry of millions of European workers at relatively low cost to the federal government. In fact, with the imposition of a federal head tax on immigration, which ballooned from fifty cents in 1882 to eight dollars in 1917, the federal government made money off European immigration.

The federal government also pushed regulatory costs onto the passenger shipping industry by requiring in 1882 that inadmissible immigrants be returned to their port of departure at the expense of the company that had transported them. This measure, and earlier efforts to limit ship overcrowding, forced the shipping companies to improve conditions on board ship and to develop facilities in Europe where they screened would-be immigrants to America for disease, disability, and criminality.[8]

Although the federal government did eventually begin screening immigrants for disease, poverty, and criminality at immigration stations such as Ellis Island, most of the filtering work had already been done by the steamship companies before the ships ever left Europe; only 2 percent of the 20 million immigrants who entered the United States between 1892 and 1924 were denied entry, mainly for health reasons.[9]

The federal government only developed an effective bureaucratic infrastructure to enforce the Chinese Exclusion Act of 1882; in fact, administratively, the federal government deemed Chinese immigration to be fundamentally different from European immigration.[10] For the most part, the federal government perceived immigration from Europe to be essential to the expansion of American power across the continent and the development of the nation's economy and refused to do anything to hinder the westward movement of people across the Atlantic.

Just as the federal government left immigration regulation mainly to states and private corporations, so did it leave naturalization to states and localities until the early 20th century, and these communities naturalized foreigners according to a wide variety of standards based on local needs and interests. Most U.S. states in the 19th century, in fact, did not require citizenship for voting, or allowed non-citizens who had expressed intention to naturalize (but had not completed the process) to vote and exercise other rights and privileges of citizenship. It was not until 1906 and the federal Immigration Act of that year that the federal government claimed jurisdiction over U.S. naturalization law.[11] Even then, voting by noncitizens was allowed under some circumstances in some locales as late as 1926.[12]

Although the federal government was largely unwilling to directly regulate immigration for most of the 19th century, the federal state did play an indirect, but important, role in encouraging westward expansion and population growth through immigration in several ways. First, the federal government ignored significant democratic pressure, especially in the 1840s and 1850s, to limit immigrants' political mobility by changing the naturalization requirements from five years to twenty-one years as nativists demanded. The federal government also refused to restrict access to public land to U.S. citizens only through the Homestead Act of 1862. Instead, the government created an incentive for European immigrants to naturalize by allowing immigrants who had declared an intention to naturalize to file homestead claims.

Second, and most importantly, the federal government, regardless of which political party was in charge, was committed to a long-term policy of removing Native Americans from their lands, by either treaty or military force or both, and resettling white Americans and European immigrants on this territory.[13] The federal government spent nearly $260 million between 1776 and 1890 on Indian wars, with annual expenditures of $1 million to $9 million occurring every year after 1832.[14] The government also spent millions of dollars compensating Indian tribes for land purchases through dozens of treaties.[15]

This policy of Indian removal began early after the United States defeated the Western Confederacy of several Northwestern tribes at the Battle of Fallen Timbers in 1794. President Thomas Jefferson first developed a policy of removing American Indians west of the Mississippi River to the newly purchased Louisiana Territory. This unofficial "Indian Territory" was gradually and then rapidly reduced in size to what is now the state of Oklahoma between 1834 and 1854, as various Midwestern territories and states were created and Indians were forced farther west and/or segregated onto shrinking reservations.[16]

Yet the western lands to which the United States removed Eastern tribes was by no means empty, and so the removal policy resulted in increased intra-Indian violence as tribes competed with one another for rapidly decreasing resources.

This work operates under the assumption that all of the territory making up what is now the continental United States once belonged to American Indian tribes, which had established border lines and use rights among themselves over hundreds of years of negotiation and warfare. All "public land" in the United States was once Indian land, and the federal government devoted significant time and resources to gain control of this property for white settlement.

At the same time that the federal government was giving millions of acres of Indian land to white settlers and railroad corporations, it was refusing to redistribute confiscated Confederate property in the occupied South to freed slaves on the argument that it would foster black dependency. While the federal government did pass the Southern Homestead Act of 1866, which opened 46,398,544.87 acres in Florida, Alabama, Louisiana, Mississippi, and Arkansas to homesteading, only 6,500 black farmers claimed homesteads, and of these, only about 1,000 of them became farm owners.[17] Homesteading, and the redistribution of now public land in general, was for whites, including European immigrants, to ensure their economic independence. Blacks, Mexicans, and Asians, who would be denied the right to property ownership through state laws, lack of access to credit, and extralegal violence, were expected to be farm workers.

The federal government also took active, and sometimes aggressive, steps to ensure American control of as much of the North American continent as it could obtain. With strong powers, such as France and Great Britain, the U.S. government bought land and negotiated boundary treaties, such as the Adams-Onís Treaty that settled the boundaries of the Louisiana Purchase in 1821 and the Oregon Treaty of 1846 that put the boundary between U.S. and British territory in the Pacific Northwest at the 49th parallel. With weaker powers, such as Mexico, the United States militarily seized 650,000 miles of territory in the Mexican-American War of 1846–1848.[18]

Ever since acquiring the Louisiana Territory from France in 1803, Americans had dreamed of a continental empire. Elites' study of Roman history reassured them that there was no conflict between republic and empire, while more ordinary Americans desired access to virtually unlimited land and other natural resources. Thomas Jefferson might have viewed the interior as a place to hold troublesome Indians until they assimilated into white culture, but most Americans saw all of North America as future white territory, and it was their manifest destiny to conquer and settle it.[19] The United States' weak immigration policy and its aggressive foreign policy toward American Indian nations and Mexico were two sides of the same project of national expansion and economic development.

The federal government's reluctance to regulate and restrict immigration in the 19th century allowed state and territorial governments and private, often corporate actors to develop promotional policies to attract certain kinds of immigrants to populate and develop the interior of the continent. Among the states, immigration promotion was the domain of the new Midwestern and Western states, which wanted white settlers, and of Southern states, which wanted to replace their troublesome freed black workforce with whites after the Civil War. Eastern states were well settled, urbanizing, and industrializing; anti-immigration sentiment or nativism on the part of native-born white workers was centered in the East. Thirty-five states passed laws and/or developed policies to encourage immigration to their territories between 1845 and 1911; of these, nine were in the Midwest; nine were in the West, and fifteen were in the South.[20] The few Midwestern states that did not develop immigration promotion policies—Ohio, Indiana, and Illinois—had industrializing economies that attracted enough immigrant workers without state effort. The only Eastern states to pass immigration promotion laws were Maine and Delaware, which wanted to redistribute undeveloped timber and agricultural lands, respectively, in the late 19th century.

Unlike states, which, not surprisingly, had provincial promotional programs focused only on their areas, railroads had regional and even continental approaches to their promotional efforts and desired people who would establish farms and communities along their lines and become permanent customers. The railroads aggressively marketed their land grants to mostly Northern Europeans who had enough capital to make the passage across the Atlantic, travel across much of the American continent, buy land, and develop it. The railroads also recruited labor, especially in China and among immigrants living in Eastern cities, but this work was understood to be temporary, and labor recruitment was separate from immigration promotion in railroad corporations' organizational charts.

Many religious groups immigrated as congregations, but few achieved the level of organization and scale of Mormon converts from Great Britain and Scandinavia, and Jews fleeing religious persecution in Russia. By the 1850s, the new Church of Jesus Christ of Latter-day Saints (LDS) had a well-organized office that helped converts emigrate and travel to first Ohio, Illinois, and then Utah. This immigration experience was an important part of the conversion process for European LDS converts. In the late 19th century, German Jewish charitable organizations in the Northeast feared that a concentration of poor Jews in American cities would spark anti-Semitism, and so these organizations encouraged newly arriving Eastern European Jews to disperse themselves and settle in small towns and in rural areas in the Midwest. Zionists also promoted the idea of Jewish farming as a way of practicing for the colonization of Palestine.

Just as important as the "push-pull" factors that caused Europeans to immigrate in the 19th and early 20th centuries is the role of means and processes, the "how" of migration. It was the how—the long western flowing rivers, the sailing ship and steamship routes, the canals, roads, and railroads—that facilitated the movement of thousands and then millions of Europeans to North America and then westward across the continent. Means and processes also explain why it was English, Irish, Germans, and Scandinavians who immigrated in the largest numbers in the 19th century rather than Spaniards, Italians, or Russians. All across Europe people suffered from poverty, too little land or unproductive land, rigid class systems, political and/or religious discrimination, and legal barriers to immigration. It was not that Irish, Germans, or Norwegians, for instance, suffered these problems more than people in Southern or Eastern Europe (and, in fact, these "push factors" were often greater in Southern and Eastern Europe than in Northern Europe). But unlike Eastern or Southern Europeans, Northern Europeans had the means to immigrate in the early to mid-19th century and so did so in the millions, following the trade routes across the Atlantic that had been established in the 17th and 18th centuries.

These Europeans faced not just the question of whether to emigrate, but equally important, the question of where to immigrate. The most important factor in determining where a migrant goes is whether he or she knows someone in the destination place. People are much more likely to immigrate to a particular place if they know someone there and/or have information from a trusted source about a place. Such networks and information sharing establishes a chain of migration in which people follow pioneering immigrants.

But how does this chain get started? Pioneering immigrants wrote letters home and these letters were widely circulated, often published in local newspapers.[21] Most people did not immigrate solely because of the information they received in a pamphlet published by a state immigration agency or railroad. But these promotional campaigns did help influence pioneers, those eager for new opportunities, the first immigrants to establish a chain.[22]

Immigration promotion also played an important role in encouraging immigrants to move to rural, agricultural areas by advertising the opportunity to own land in the Midwest and West. Although New York, Boston, Philadelphia, Chicago, and St. Louis developed large immigrant communities in the 19th century, the majority of immigrants to the United States moved west upon arrival and settled in rural areas, since many of them had been farmers or farm laborers in Europe.[23] Many artisans also moved to farm communities because these areas provided more opportunity for independence and had less competition than in the big cities.

The first immigration promoters tended to be immigrants themselves from Great Britain, Germany, the Netherlands, and Scandinavia, and these individuals not surprisingly focused their recruitment efforts on their former countrymen, because they were familiar with the language, customs, and conditions in those countries. These early immigration promoters were excellent advertisers of the opportunities existing in America because they could present themselves as examples of success in the United States and could speak knowledgeably about life in America.

But whether they were foreign-born or native-born Americans, immigration promoters were also influenced by the prejudices of their times: by the assumptions that Northern Europeans were more hardworking, more productive, and more adaptable to new environments than other ethnic groups; the pseudoscience that claimed that people were attracted to climates similar to the ones they had left (the so-called isothermal theory of migration); and the racial biases that asserted that white people could flourish in any environment.

The vast majority of promotional material was produced in the 19th century and was created to advertise the Midwest. Midwestern states devoted considerable resources to immigration promotion and were rewarded for their efforts with a surge in population, particularly after the Civil War. Western states and territories lagged in developing promotional policies and often relied heavily upon the railroads to market Western land to both Eastern Americans and Europeans. The message of opportunity on the Western frontier also clashed with the realities of extreme weather and hostile Indians resisting removal. The South also encouraged European immigration after the Civil War, but this effort was half-hearted and was more about attracting white workers to replace freed slaves than about attracting large numbers of immigrants who might change Southern society or cultural mores about race. Railroads were also successful in their promotional efforts, if land sales are used as a measurement of success. Some religious groups, particularly the Church of Jesus Christ of Latter-day Saints, were successful in promoting immigration among their members, while Jews were less so, mainly because of the incompatibility between the goals of promoters and the people they were attempting to resettle in America.

The United States was not unique or exceptional in this effort to encourage immigration from Europe. The colonial possessions of the United Kingdom, particularly Canada, Australia, and New Zealand, encouraged migration from the Mother Country and benefitted from Imperial citizenship policies that encouraged British migration to those colonies. Argentina, Brazil, Peru, and Uruguay also promoted immigration from Europe through advertisement and transportation subsidies. Just as the United States was not exceptional in being a destination for European immigrants, so too were American immigration promotion policies part of a larger trend in the 19th century of frontier states trying to attract Europeans to settle and develop territory being seized from indigenous peoples.

Another major trend of the 19th century was labor recruitment and contracting. Railroads, mining companies, and private contracting businesses recruited unskilled workers in Southern and Eastern Europe and Asia and transported them to developing countries such as the United States, Canada, and South America, as well as to industrialized Northern Europe, to be cheap, temporary labor. Chinese immigrants were contracted to work on American railroads and on plantations in Peru, Italian immigrants were contracted to be farm laborers in Louisiana and Brazil and miners in France, while Poles were recruited to be railroad workers in western Canada and miners in the German Ruhr. This international labor market developed as steamships made ocean transit faster and cheaper. Even the passage of laws against contract labor adopted in the United States in 1885 and in Canada in 1897 did not end the practice of companies recruiting foreign short-term workers. Individuals and companies that hired contracted labor sought to profit off labor shortages in developing regions and had little interest in whether the immigrants they hired stayed or left a place once the work was finished.

The focus of this work is on immigration promotion, not contracted labor recruitment, and it examines contract labor and labor recruitment only as a means to juxtapose which groups were desired as immigrants and future American citizens and which were not. Labor contracting was one of the ways in which unskilled workers, particularly Asians and later Mexicans, but also Southern and Eastern Europeans, came to America. Immigration promotion was one of the ways in which Europeans who had capital to buy land or start businesses, were skilled, and were indisputably white were encouraged to immigrate, settle, and become Americans. But racial understandings of American citizenship meant that even Southern and Eastern Europeans who had been recruited as temporary workers, not as immigrant settlers, could nonetheless naturalize, unlike Asian immigrants. The role of government at multiple levels in shaping the national community by promoting and/or regulating immigration is at the heart of this story.

The methods of immigration promotion and labor recruitment changed surprisingly little from the 17th century to the 19th century. Both early colonial and 19th-century promoters and recruiters relied heavily on the written word but also sometimes used speeches as a means of disseminating information about America. Although labor was always the primary reason for encouraging migration, the literature written in the 17th century justified English colonization of North America in terms of spreading (Protestant) Christianity, overcoming native barbarism, and spreading English national greatness. Promoters in the 19th century justified migration in terms of developing supposedly unused Indian land in more productive ways, spreading American Christian civilization and democratic republican government across the continent, and preventing the overcrowding and decadent urbanization that was supposedly unhealthy for an agrarian society.

While 17th-century promotional material often used religious language to explain or justify colonization, 19th-century promotional literature relied heavily on the presentation of "facts" as truth, and, in particular, used statistics as a form of information.[24] But 19th-century promoters were just as likely to call America the next Garden of Eden as 17th-century authors were, and writers in both periods sought to inspire and motivate their readers as much as inform them.

The methods of 17th- and 19th-century immigration promotion would be unrecognizable to anyone today involved in advertising, sales, or marketing. Pamphlets and advertisements were text (pictures did not appear in advertisements until the 1870s, photographs not until the 1890s) and in the 19th century were generally associated with disreputable products, particularly patent medicines. The purpose of advertising was also understood to be to bring the potential customer to the salesman, who would do the actual selling, not actually selling a product or service itself.[25] Promoters of America were pioneers in advertising and salesmanship, selling the country as others sold goods or services.

This campaign to sell America to Europeans began with the first colonization efforts in the early 17th century, as English investors in colonization corporations recruited laborers to do the hard physical work of conquering Indian peoples and developing their land for the colonization companies' shareholders. The image of America as an excessively fertile place where a comfortable livelihood could be achieved without much difficulty or labor was first propagated in England in the early 17th century, and promoters would repeat this theme without significant variation for the next 200 years.

CHAPTER ONE

Tenants Wanted: The Promotion of Immigration to the New World, 1607–1776

Approximately 467,000 Europeans and 282,000 Africans migrated to North America in the 17th and 18th centuries.[1] Thanks to the work of many scholars, we know a fair amount about these people: where they came from, where they settled, and their experiences in the "New World." But we know less about what attracted these people to America versus other places. Despite the myth of the Pilgrims and Plymouth Rock, the motivation for most Europeans to migrate was economic opportunity, not religious liberty.

Furthermore, behind every major colonization effort in North America was a corporation specially organized by shareholders who intended to make a profit off of their investment in the colonization company.[2] European investors saw colonization of the Americas as a money-making venture, and immigrants were seen as the means of achieving that profit. Many of the investors in these early colonization schemes never left Europe but recruited others to go in their place as employee laborers. How to recruit these tenants and servants was the primary challenge of 17th-century colonization corporations.

The promoters of the colonization of North America offered a variety of incentives and told a multitude of stories to encourage people to leave the relative safety of Europe for the unknown hazards of America. Promoters offered would-be colonists a share of company profits, free or cheap land, low taxes, and political and religious freedom, and they extolled the beauty and fertility of the natural environment, often greatly exaggerating about landscapes the writers had never seen.

Within the genre of 17th-century promotional literature, it is important to distinguish between works written by individuals who had actually been to America and those who had not. Promotional material provided many different types of information: weather and climate, soil types, types of crops expected to grow, opportunities for animal husbandry, location of rivers and streams for mills, types of trees and other flora, animal life, anthropologies of American Indians, opportunities for land ownership, religious and civil rights, taxes, and the type of government functioning in the colony. But how much of this information was fantasy, the product of a writer's imagination versus experience, varied considerably from text to text.

There were also different styles of promotional writing. Many publications written about America were in the form of letters, either actual letters people wrote to others, which were then copied and circulated, or as pamphlets written in the style of a letter. The question-and-answer format, in which information was provided in the form of a series of questions posed and then answered, was also popular among promoters. In addition, sermons, which were often both spoken from the pulpit and published, were frequently used to encourage people to migrate to the colonies and gave promotional literature a religious tone.

The fertility and bountifulness of America was a constant theme in early-17th-century literature, reflecting the general ignorance of the authors. Virginia's swampy coast was described as "fruitful and pleasant," while New England's rocky soil was claimed to be particularly fertile.[3] Everywhere the weather was pleasant, excessive summer heat and winter cold apparently bypassing the North American continent. With flowery, exaggerated praise the norm in colonial promotional writing, it was no wonder that many 17th-century Europeans came to America with incorrect information, bad assumptions, and unrealistic expectations of the challenges of establishing new lives in an unfamiliar environment.

Promotional literature written at the beginning of the colonial period tended to emphasize the diplomatic and economic benefits that would result from England challenging Spain's claim to the New World as well as the supposed spiritual benefits of colonization for America's native peoples. Colonization would both make England great and reflect her natural greatness. Literature written in the late 17th century, particularly to promote Carolina and Pennsylvania, stressed the natural environment, its alleged Edenic beauty in the case of Carolina and its cheap availability in the case of William Penn's Pennsylvania. Both colonies also offered far greater personal freedoms, especially in the area of religion, than either Virginia or Massachusetts. Offers of cheap or free land and greater personal freedom were the two most powerful incentives promoters could offer to persuade Europeans to make the dangerous trip across the Atlantic during the colonial period.[4]

Seventeenth-century Europeans did not simply set out in wooden ships to sail across 3,400 miles of Atlantic Ocean, build homes on the shores of North America, and create new communities. Instead, colonization was a carefully planned expedition, organized and funded by corporations created just for that purpose.

Seventeenth-century English joint stock corporations were monopolies created by special charter granted by the Crown or Parliament for a specific purpose, usually trade or colonization (or both) in a specific region.[5] As such, these companies were a form of patronage of the monarchy or government to certain favored individuals, many of them members of the landed aristocracy or wealthy merchants. Nearly half of the individuals who invested in joint stock corporations promoting colonial investment and settlement also sat as members of Parliament, mainly in the House of Commons.[6] Investors bought shares of stock in a company and received a percentage of the profits based on their percentage of ownership.

The English called their early colonies "plantations," which were economic units, usually dominated by commercial agriculture, raising a crop to be marketed and sold overseas versus for local consumption. Profit from the sale of harvested natural resources was the chief motivator for the first colonies, and the first colonists in Virginia, New Netherland, and even in Plymouth and the Massachusetts Bay colonies were employees or tenants of the colonizing corporations, although some were also shareholders. It was not for several years that civil governing bodies, either representative or appointed, emerged separate from the corporations engaged in colonizing North America.[7]

A major weakness of the early plantation model of colonization was that private property ownership, especially of land, was not initially allowed; the colonization company owned all of the territory and natural resources in its chartered domain. In Virginia, private land ownership was not allowed for the first 10 years, while in the Dutch colony of New Netherland, private land ownership was not possible until 1629 and did not become common until after 1639, fifteen years after initial settlement. In Plymouth, the company's failure to adequately supply the colonists caused Governor William Bradford to allocate plots of land to settlers for their own farming in 1623, just three years after initial settlement, but this was unusual for English colonies.[8] It was not until the 1620s that land ownership in America became possible for early settlers and thus a selling point for promoters.

Unable and unwilling to offer land ownership as an incentive for migration, early colonial promoters emphasized the opportunity for adventure—shares in corporations were called "bills of adventure"—and wealth from selling the many natural resources believed to be littering American shores.[9] The high cost of transporting and getting a colonist established with tools, clothing, and other necessities ranged from £14 to £20 (about the annual wage of the average Englishman), which meant that few Englishmen could afford the trip without assistance, and this assistance became costly for the colonization companies.[10] Indentured servitude became a means by which English colonizing enterprises could transport workers who could not afford their own passage and recoup the transportation costs by selling those laborers to pioneering colonists as indentured servants. This system was in place in Virginia by 1620 and became widespread in other English colonies by midcentury.[11]

The difficulty in profiting off colonization caused all of the early English colonization companies to fail, and the private, corporate ventures were taken over by the State and Crown. As English American communities stabilized by the mid-to-late 17th century, it was easier for promoters to attract new migrants with offers of cheap or free land (often after working a period of indentured servitude), lower taxes, and greater personal freedom, especially in the area of religious worship.

The first major colonization effort of North America undertaken by the English was the Virginia Company and the Virginia colony at Jamestown. The company was organized in 1606 by a royal decree from James I and had approximately 1,600 shareholders.[12]

The company had two branches or divisions: the first was based in London and established a colony near the Chesapeake Bay in Virginia; the second was a group based in Plymouth, and its purpose was to establish a colony in New England. The company was responsible for paying for the cost of establishing each colony and would, in turn, own and control all of the land and resources found in the colonies; the colonists, most of whom were shareholders, would be employees of the company, serving seven-year indentures. The largest investors were the managers of the venture.

The treasurer and chief operating officer was Sir Thomas Smythe, who had been governor of the East India Company for three years. The single largest investor was Thomas West—Lord de la Warre—who then served as governor of the colony between 1610 and 1618. A single share in the Virginia Company cost 12 pounds 10 shillings, which was more than six months' wages for an average English working man.[13]

Arriving in Virginia in late April 1607 after a five-month-long voyage on three ships, 104 colonists, all of them men and teenage boys, established Jamestown at the mouth of the James River. After failing to find gold lying on the beach, the colonists decided to focus on timber and other naval stores as their chief products for export back to England. By about 1612, the colonists had learned to grow tobacco, and the Virginia Company embraced this cash crop as the foundation of the new colony's economy.

Since all of the colonists expected (and, in fact, had been promised) that the Virginia Company would provide them food and supplies, and none of the company's managers intended to do manual labor themselves, one of the primary goals of the company was to find laborers to do the actual work of building shelter and creating products for export back to England. Very soon, the colony also needed workers to grow food and tobacco.[14]

There were several types of promotion efforts for Jamestown and Virginia, directed to different audiences. At the highest literary level and read by a very small elite of government officials, aristocrats, and wealthy merchants engaged in risky international trade, were books about the geography and ecology of the Americas. These works, particularly *Divers Voyages Touching the Discoverie of America* (1582) and *The Principal Navigations, Voiages, Traffiques and Discoueries of the English Nation* (1589–1600, both by Richard Hakluyt the Younger), and *A briefe and true report of the new found land of Virginia* (1588, by Thomas Hariot), described in detail the flora, fauna, peoples, and natural environment of eastern North America and encouraged political elites in Elizabethan and later Jacobean England to pursue conquest and colonization of North America to counter Spain's efforts in the Americas.[15]

These works, and others written by English and other European scientists, debated the purposes and methods of colonization, with the spread of Protestant Christianity and the dissemination of classical civic virtues in a new, improved commonwealth being most popular among intellectuals.[16]

But the hundreds of merchants, nobles, professionals, and guild members who bought "bills of adventure" from the Virginia Company hoped for more than simply a warm feeling of having contributed to England's future national greatness or the triumph of Protestantism over papistry. These appropriately named "adventurers" wanted and expected to profit off their investment.[17]

Unwilling to wait for news of the success or failure of the first voyage, the Virginia Company's directors in London launched an intensive campaign in 1608–1610 to recruit both investors and colonists. This campaign came in the form of sermons, both read from the pulpit and published to be read silently, as well as books and even songs and stage plays.[18] Since literacy in England and Great Britain was approximately 53 percent from 1650 to the early 1800s, far more people heard about Virginia orally than read about it.[19]

Of all the promotional material produced by the Virginia Company in this period, one of the most important was *Nova Britannia, Offering Most Excellent Fruites by Planting in Virginia*, published in February 1609 by Robert Johnson. Johnson was a London merchant, alderman, and son-in-law of Sir Thomas Smythe, the treasurer of the Virginia Company, and so was well connected and respected. Using the metaphor of planting, which itself conjured images of fertility, Johnson argued that the main purposes of the colony were to spread Protestant Christianity, glorify England, and create national wealth. He carefully itemized the many natural resources to be found in Virginia and argued that what Virginia needed most was money and people to make the colony a success.[20]

To try to attract more investors and colonists, Johnson stressed that each colonist would receive his fair share of the wealth and prosperity of Virginia, based on the size of his investment, and later investors would not detract from the value of the share of earlier investors.[21]

As early as 1609, the Virginia Company was advertising for "Artificers, Smiths, Carpenters, Coopers, Shipwrights, Turners, Planters, Vineares, Fowlers, Fishermen, Mettel-men of all sorts, Brick-makers, Brick-layers, Plow-men, Weavers, Shoo-makers, Sawyers, Spinsters, and all other laboring men and women, that are willing to goe to the said plantation to inhabite there."[22] In addition to one share of stock in the company, these people were promised "houses to dwell in, with gardens and orchards, and also foode and clothing at the common charge of the joint stocke, they shall have their Divident also in all goods and Merchandizes, arising thence by their labours, and likewise their Divident in Lands to them and to their heyres for euver."[23]

The use of the phrase "gardens and orchards" gave Virginia a distinctly bucolic English village–like appearance, when in actuality, conditions at Jamestown were very primitive, and the Chesapeake Bay estuary where Jamestown was located is in a humid, subtropical climate.

Between 1607 and 1619, the Virginia Company persuaded 2,000 people to go to Virginia, either as shareholders or as laborers and craftsmen hired by investors. Although many of the first colonists were artisans—carpenters, masons, and bricklayers—others "were an odd assortment of craftsmen, including jewelers, refiners, and goldsmiths—bespeaking the expectations of the company—apothecaries, tailors, blacksmiths, and—mute testimony to the fact that gentlemen must be gentlemen whether in the wilds of Virginia or a London drawing room—a perfumer."[24]

But instead of English gardens and orchards, these adventurers found a hot, humid swamp where their chief task was to dig the graves of their fellow colonists. In the first 10 years, the Jamestown colonists experienced mass starvation, rampant disease, military dictatorship, and Indian attack.[25]

Already by 1610, "vagabond rumor" (as company officials attempted to dismiss them) had reached England that perhaps Virginia was not the Garden of Eden the company claimed it was, and company directors were forced to refute charges of stealing land and food from the Indians, failing to proselytize the Protestant faith, and of "the barrennesse of the countrie," "the unwholesomenesse of the climate," and "the famine amongst our men," among other problems.[26] After first claiming that "for the healthinesse and temperatenesse of the Clymate, agreeing to our constitutions, much neede not be related," the company lamely asserted that "no man ought to judge any Countrie by the fennes and marshes (such as is the place where James towne standeth) except we will condemne all England, for the Wilds and Hundreds of Kent and Essex."[27] Except, as most English people knew, no one expected people to live in the marshlands of England as they were expected to in Virginia.

In 1619, the Virginia Company introduced the head right system, in which 50 acres of land was granted for each person transported to the colony. Although theoretically, a man could receive a head right grant for himself and his family if they paid their way to Virginia, virtually all of the recipients of head right grants were wealthy individuals and land companies, which now had a major incentive to ship indentured servants to Jamestown.[28]

The leading promoter of the head right system was Sir Edwin Sandys, a member of Parliament who replaced Smythe as treasurer of the Virginia Company in 1619. Besides encouraging the establishment of plantations with the use of head right labor, Sandys also recruited artisans and farm laborers. An estimated 4,800 people left England for Virginia between November 1619 and February 1625 in the hopes of receiving free land in the colony after working off their seven years of service.[29]

But even as Sandys was sending shiploads of people to Virginia, the company and its colonists were struggling to stay alive. By 1621, the Virginia Company was heavily in debt and unable to pay dividends; these problems and the news of the 1622 Powhatan massacre made it difficult to find new investors or colonists. In 1624, James I disbanded the Virginia Company and made Virginia a royal colony.[30]

Although the Virginia Company was forced to acknowledge some of the larger problems in the colony (the Powhatan massacre was hard to cover up), promoters continued into the 1640s to disseminate a largely false image of Virginia as a place where the land was "most fruitfull, and produceth with very great increase, whatsoever is committed into the Bowells of it," where skilled labor received high wages and people lived under benevolent English government with spiritual guidance from the Church of England.[31]

What migrants to Jamestown were definitely not told was the fact that they had only a 20 to 50 percent chance of surviving their first year in Virginia. Approximately 80 percent of the first group of colonists at Jamestown died of starvation and disease the first year, and similar death tolls were common for the first several shiploads of colonists. Colonists recruited under Sandys's head right system died at an especially high rate. Edmund S. Morgan has estimated that the Virginia colony had a death rate of approximately 50 percent for the first 40 to 50 years, and it was not until the 1640s that the death rate began to decline and then only gradually. It would be generations before Virginia would achieve natural increase of population.[32]

Scholars have documented many factors that contributed to Virginia's initial problems and its eventual success.[33] The colony's corporate structure and purpose, poor management, the absence of private property in land and labor, the harshness of the indentured servant labor system, and the lack of familiarity with, and preparedness for, Virginia's climate are the main reasons why Virginia struggled in its first decades. The head right system of granting land for people, the indentured servant system, and chattel slavery contributed to the colony's eventual success, but these methods of importing large numbers of laborers to work Virginia's tobacco plantations took several decades to develop, and tens of thousands of people died in the process.

At the same time that Sandys was sending shiploads of colonists to Virginia, 102 religious dissenters sailed from Plymouth to Massachusetts in what would become the most famous ocean voyage in American history.[34] The Plymouth colony and its neighboring Massachusetts Bay colony, established in 1628, were ultimately successful because, almost from the beginning, they offered colonists free land and local control in political and religious affairs, which in 17th-century England was often the same thing.

Of the two New England colonial projects, the Massachusetts Bay Company was larger and attracted more colonists in what would come to be called the Great Migration of English Puritans to America.

The Massachusetts Bay Company was organized in 1628 and granted a royal charter in 1629. Its chief organizer was John White of Dorchester, a Puritan businessman. Of the 122 individuals who invested in the Massachusetts Bay Company, only 25 were gentry, and most were related to each other through marriage, business, and church.[35] John Winthrop, a Puritan and a lawyer from a wealthy merchant family from Suffolk, was chosen by the company to be the colony's governor.

Alone of the first English colonization corporations, the charter of the Massachusetts Bay Company did not require that shareholders meet in London, so the colonist-shareholders were able to control the company's business affairs locally, in Massachusetts.

The first 11 ships (the "Winthrop Fleet"), carrying 1,000 colonists, sailed for Massachusetts in the summer of 1630, and over the next decade, approximately 20,000 English migrated to New England. Most of the people who participated in the Great Migration were from East Anglia (Norfolk, Suffolk, Essex, Kent, and East Sussex), and many were skilled craftsmen and their families struggling to survive in a depressed cloth industry.[36]

English Puritans chose to go to New England versus Virginia for several reasons: the original Virginia Company had sought to establish a colony on or near Massachusetts Bay, separatist communities had already been established nearby at Plymouth and Salem in 1620 and 1623, respectively, and the writings of Virginia Company captain John Smith persuaded them that "New England" was as fertile as Old England.

Smith's propaganda was particularly influential. Between 1616 and 1631, Smith produced detailed maps of New England, and he either compiled or wrote six books about the region. His first and most important work was published in June 1616 and was called *A Description of New England: or the Observations, and Discoveries, of Captain John Smith (Admirall of That Country) in the North of America.* In this and his later works, Smith "sought to counter the common English perception that the North American northeast was a cold, forbidding, and uninhabitable land. Dubbing it 'New England' and recasting it as, in almost every respect, an extension of old England, Smith produced one of the earliest recorded and most successful attempts ever undertaken to create and market a regional identity," as Walter W. Woodward noted.[37] What especially made "New England" better than England was the opportunity for land ownership.

Believing Smith's claims about New England's climate and geography, the leaders of the Massachusetts Bay Company encouraged migration to the colony in two ways: by offering free land and freedom from political harassment in the area of religion, provided, of course, that the individual was a Puritan (other religious minorities, particularly Catholics, Baptists, and Quakers, were not welcome in Massachusetts). The willingness of prominent Puritan and Separatist leaders, such as Edward Winslow, who had sailed on the *Mayflower* in 1620, to go to Massachusetts also persuaded many English Puritans that their leaders were serious about establishing a theocracy in New England.[38]

Unlike in Virginia, private property ownership in land was possible from the beginning of the Massachusetts Bay Colony, and was, in fact, a major incentive for people to migrate to Massachusetts. The amount of land allotted to a proprietor (as investors were called) was generally based on the amount of money he had invested in the stock of the company. Property could only be sold to nonproprietors with the unanimous consent of all of the proprietors in a community.[39]

The Massachusetts Bay Company distributed land rent-free to the original members of the company. Unlike in some other colonies, members of the company also had political rights of the franchise and the right to hold public office. Indentured servants were not allowed to own land or vote, thus ensuring that they remained politically powerless and economically dependent on their masters.[40]

The colonies of Carolina and Pennsylvania were the first English colonies to aggressively promote and recruit colonists from Europe, especially Germany, by offering cheap or free land, religious freedom, and low taxes, beginning in the 1680s. Pennsylvania's promoters stressed the image of economic opportunity and religious liberty while Carolina's advocates painted a picture of an Eden-like natural environment where virtually anything could grow with little effort.[41] But promoters in both colonies relied on a variety of messages to encourage Europeans to immigrate.

After a failed attempt to create a new colony south of Virginia in the late 1620s, Charles II granted a new charter to the Lords Proprietors—eight English noblemen—in 1663 to establish the colony of Carolina. The Province of Carolina was controlled from 1663 to 1729 by these aristocrats and their heirs, which was informally led by Anthony Ashley-Cooper, the first Earl of Shaftesbury.

As a royal colony versus a commercial project, Carolina was managed differently from the start. Unlike in the commercial colonies, such as Virginia and New Netherland, Carolina's colonial government was comprised of a governor; a strong council, which were members appointed by the Lords Proprietors; and a weak, democratically elected assembly. Even though the Proprietors had sent 150 colonists to found what is now Charleston, South Carolina, in 1670, finding settlers was still a challenge.

In order to attract new colonists, two of the Proprietors—the Earl of Craven and John Archdale, a wealthy Quaker who bought Lord John Berkeley's share in 1678—revised the colony's legal and governmental systems, writing a new Fundamentals of Constitutions of Carolina in August 1682. This new Constitutions said that non-Anglicans could not be taxed to support the Church of England in America and that each congregation had a right to tax its own members. This immediately made the colony attractive to minority religious sects, especially those from the German states, where both state churches and governments assessed onerous taxes of many kinds.[42]

Carolina's land policy also encouraged immigration. Initially, the Proprietors charged the first settlers quit rents, rent paid in lieu of services, usually labor, but also military service or in-kind payment. But within a few decades, the Proprietors realized that the ability to buy land was an attractive reason for many Europeans to immigrate, and so they began to sell land to newcomers. By 1695, most colonists in Carolina had ceased paying quit rent and had bought their land directly from the Proprietors.[43]

Between 1696 and 1741, the Carolinas (the colony split into north and south in 1712) enacted laws designed to attract immigrants, including one that naturalized the deceased and then conferred property titles to those living individuals born in a foreign country.[44]

A major claim of Carolina promoters was that the weather was especially mild and that the land was particularly fertile. Sir Walter Raleigh had claimed in his 1650 book *The Marrow of Historie* that Paradise was located at latitude 35°, and Carolina promoters eagerly latched on to this, asserting that Carolina was located between 29° and 36°, and thus the colony had the potential to produce a wide variety of marketable exotic crops with very little labor. A typical example of this type of promotional material written about Carolina was *In Account of the Province of Carolina*, written by Samuel Wilson and published in 1682. Wilson claimed, "In short, This Country being of the same Clymate and Temperature of Aleppo, Smyrna, Antioch, Judea, and the Province of Nanking, the richest in China, will (I conceive) produce anything which those Countrys do, were the Seeds brought into it."[45]

Another Carolina promotional writer, Thomas Amy, who had journeyed to Carolina in 1680 as a clerk on board the ship *Richmond*, claimed that the air was so healthful that "the Indian Natives prolong their days to the Extremity of Old Age" and that "the Seasons are regularly disposed according to Natures Laws; the Summer not so torrid, hot and burning as that of their Southern, nor the Winter so rigorously sharp and cold, as that of their Northern Neighbours."[46]

Pamphlet writer Joel Gascoin also depicted Carolina as a type of paradise ("The Heavens shine upon this famous Country the sovereign Ray of health; and has blest it with a serene Air, and a lofty Skie, that defends it from noxious Infection; nor is there any known distemper incident to the Inhabitant whereby to terrify and affright him; who for the most part, lives by the Law of Plenty, extended to the utmost limits of Sanity") and reminded his readers that the colony was parallel to Jerusalem, a reference that conjured up both Mediterranean wealth and religious rectitude.[47]

Unfortunately for the readers of Carolina promotional literature, 17th-century English colonization promoters operated under a flawed understanding of climate and latitude. As Carville Earle explains: "Relying upon a Greek model of global climate, they believed that latitude was the prime determinant of a region's climate and, ergo, its economic potentiality. They reasoned by analogy that the optimal lands on the Atlantic Seaboard of North America would occupy Mediterranean latitudes and would produce valued commodities such as citrus, sugar, grapes for wine, and mulberries for silkworms and silk; and that the poorest lands would be located in the latitudes of England and would produce redundant commodities of little use to the nation [hence the epithet 'New England']."[48] Colonists actually on the ground were quick to reject these ideas and began planting crops that actually grew well in their respective environments.

Carolina promoters increasingly emphasized the mildness of winter versus the warmth of summer as Europeans became more and more aware of the heat and humidity of the southern regions of North America. Europeans believed that the body existed in harmony with its physical environment, that health was affected in particular by climate, air, and diet, and that that individual personality and culture were shaped by climate. Therefore, people born and raised in cooler climates were thought to suffer from heat-related illnesses in warmer climes, and climate explained why English were "moderate," while Spaniards were "hot blooded" and unpredictable, and Scandinavians stolid and slow.[49] The initially high death rates of Englishmen in Virginia in the first decades of settlement in the 1610s to 1650s reinforced this belief in the importance of matching ethnicity and nationality to regional climate. Unable to do this in the cases of Virginia and Carolina, English colonization promoters simply threw more bodies at the problem in the hopes that some lucky ones would survive.

Despite their emphasis on Carolina's supposed paradise-like climate, the Proprietors were more successful in attracting immigrants by advertising cheap land and religious liberties. The Proprietors commissioned several promotional pamphlets between 1682 and 1685, two written in French to appeal specifically to French Huguenots and published in Holland just a few months after Louis XIV revoked the Edict of Nantes's protection for religious minorities in 1685. Other pamphlets were written for English and Irish dissenters who continued to chafe under Charles II's rule.[50] Even more unusually, the Carolina Proprietors allowed Jews to settle in their colony.[51]

This promotional campaign had great success. Approximately 500 English Baptists and Presbyterians migrated to the Carolinas between 1682 and 1685, while more than 600 Huguenots journeyed to Carolina between 1685 and 1690. A group of Scottish Presbyterians, under the leadership of Henry Erskine, third Baron Cardross, also established a community at Port Royal in 1684.[52]

Promotion of migration to Carolina took a strange turn in the early 1700s, when a book extolling the beauties and virtues of the colony was published in the Palatinate region of southwest Germany with the promise of free passage to America to anyone who could get to England. This book, Joshua Kocherthal's "Golden Book" of 1710, sparked the first mass migration and refugee crisis of the modern era.

The Palatinate and the larger Rhineland region had been devastated by repeated invasion in the Thirty Years' War (1618–1648) and then was again invaded and occupied by France several times between 1701 and 1714, during the War of Spanish Succession. A brutal winter in 1708–1709 destroyed crops and further impoverished the population.

In 1704, a Lutheran minister, Joshua Kocherthal of Heidelberg, visited London and met investors in the Carolina colony. It is possible that he also met John Archdale, a wealthy Quaker who had served as colonial governor in 1695 and was one of the Proprietors of Carolina.

Archdale had been promoting settlement of Carolina since his time as governor. In 1705, he entered into negotiations with a group in Thuringia, the High German Company of Thuringia, to transport Germans to Carolina at his expense, with the colonists eventually repaying the cost of passage. In 1707, Archdale published the pamphlet *A New Description of the Fertile and Pleasant Province of Carolina, with a Brief Account of Its Discovery, Settling, and Government up to This Time, with Several Remarkable Passages during My Time.*[53]

Inspired by his meetings with the Carolina Proprietors, Kocherthal wrote the book *Ausführlich und Umständlicher Bericht von der berühmten*

Landschafft Carolina in dem Engelländischen America gelegen ("A Complete
and Detailed Report of the Renowned District of Carolina Located in English America") in 1706 to encourage immigration from the Palatinate to
the English American colonies.

Kocherthal's main selling points were that Carolina had fertile soil,
low taxes, and religious freedom, all attractive elements to Germans
suffering from overworked land, high taxes, religious and political persecution and harassment, and war. Yet the book was not a great success, and it did not initially encourage large-scale (or even small-scale)
immigration.[54]

In 1708, Kocherthal and 50 Germans sailed to England, where Kocherthal was able to persuade Queen Anne to financially and materially
support the Germans in their efforts to reach America because they were
Protestant refugees fleeing war and religious persecution by England's
enemy, France. Anne paid for Kocherthal's and the families' passage to
New York, not Carolina, and gave them starter funds. Although the families had immigrated with the intention of going to Carolina, the fact that
their passage to America was paid for by the queen meant that they could
not be choosy about where they were sent. The first group of 50 Germans
arrived in the Hudson River Valley and founded the town of Newburgh.
Kocherthal then returned to Heidelberg and reissued three new editions
of his book, each one more detailed, describing conditions in New York
and including the strongly worded suggestion that any German who
could make it to England would be granted free passage and land in the
English colonies by the British Crown.[55]

These new editions of what came to be called Kocherthal's "Golden
Book" (because of its gold-embossed cover) spurred a mass exodus from
the Palatinate. By March 1709, a steady stream of would-be immigrants
were traveling to Rotterdam, in the Dutch Republic, to seek permission to
travel to England.[56] By the summer of 1709, 10,000 Germans were
camped out in the streets of London, waiting for permission to sail to the
New World.

Finally, in January 1710, ten ships carrying 2,800 Germans sailed for
America. It was a long and difficult journey, with storms, inadequate pro-
visions, and ship-board illness; 470 people died during the five-month
voyage, one ship wrecked on the American coast, and then another 250
people died in quarantine on Nutten (Governor's) Island in New York
Harbor. The British government thought to use the Germans as a type of
defensive barrier between English and French North America and put
them to work harvesting naval stores, primarily timber, and making pitch
for the Royal Navy.[57]

Most of the survivors settled in the Hudson River Valley but also in New York City and in northeastern New Jersey. Wealthy Scottish fur trader Robert Livingston, who had just received a grant of 160,000 acres (650 sq km x 250 sq mi) from the British Crown, offered his land to be used as work camps for the Palatinate refugees until they could be settled elsewhere, and he made a substantial profit from selling the Germans supplies and receiving rent from the British government. In 1718, there were more than 1,020 Germans living along the Hudson, while another 580 people lived in Schoharie County to the west of the Hudson River.[58] Most of these Germans were dairy farmers and vintners, but there were also carpenters, tailors, linen weavers, masons, coopers, and brewers among them, all useful trades in America.[59]

Germans from the Palatinate also settled in the Mohawk River Valley, ultimately on both sides of the river, buying land from the natives, while other Germans from this group settled in North Carolina, founding the community of New Berne at the junction of the Trent and Neuse rivers.[60] Kocherthal was among this mass migration, having migrated with his wife and family in 1709.

The message of religious liberty and fertile, available land continued to be used to promote Carolina in Europe into the early 18th century. In the 1720s, promotional writer Jean Pierre Purry began aggressively promoting Carolina in Switzerland, which at the time was suffering from religious conflicts between Protestants and Catholics. Between 1729 and 1731, Purry was able to establish the Swiss village of Purrysburgh in South Carolina with the assistance and blessings of the Duke of Newcastle and South Carolina governor Robert Johnson.[61] One reason why Purry was able to gain so much political support for his colonization plan was that already by the 1730s, political authorities were growing concerned about the size of the black slave population in South Carolina and sought to distribute white settlers throughout the colony.[62]

At the same time that Carolina was rewriting its Constitutions to make settlement more attractive to religious dissenters, one of the most active English promoters, William Penn, was laying the political and institutional groundwork for his own proprietary colony. Penn had become the largest private landowner in America in 1681 when Charles II gave him more than 45,000 square miles (120,000 km) in America as payment for a debt the king owed Penn's father, an English admiral. Penn, a convert to the Society of Friends (Quaker), had already traveled to the Netherlands and several Rhineland German states between 1671 and 1677 to proselytize his new faith.[63] He had also been involved in purchasing real estate in what is now New Jersey in 1677 and 1682 to create refuges for Quakers being persecuted in England and Europe.[64]

With the receipt of what he called Pennsylvania, Penn now began actively promoting Quaker and other religious dissenter settlement of his property in England, the Netherlands, and the German states. In 1681, even before he had been to Pennsylvania, he published the book *Some account of the Province of Pennsylvania in America*, which was quickly translated into Dutch and German and distributed widely in the Rhineland. In his book, Penn departed from traditional corporate colonization practice and offered to sell or rent land to would-be colonists at cheap prices and low rents. As further incentive to wealthy individuals to bring servants and other tradesmen, Penn offered colonists 50 acres of land for each servant transported. Servants were promised land after they had served their indenture. Between 1681 and 1686, Penn published twenty editions of seven pamphlets in English, five editions of four pamphlets in Dutch, four editions of three pamphlets in German, and a compilation of several pamphlets in French, all promoting Pennsylvania.[65]

Penn also established Pennsylvania's system of government, in the Frame of Government of 1682, revised in 1683, in which freedom of worship (even for Catholics) was protected, and equally important, no state church supported by taxation was allowed. All religious denominations were deemed legally equal and had property rights. Although foreign-born Catholics could not own property or naturalize, they could worship openly, unlike in other English colonies, and English laws against Catholics owning property were not enforced in Pennsylvania.[66]

In 1683, as Penn was trying to establish the legal foundations of his colony, he met with a German Pietist lawyer, Francis Daniel Pastorius, who represented a group of German Pietists calling themselves the Frankfort Company. Penn had met several of these people during his travels in the Rhineland in 1677.[67] Pastorius bought 25,000 acres of land in Pennsylvania on behalf of the Frankfort Company and was granted power of attorney with the authority to manage the company's property in the New World.[68] Like other European colonization corporations, the investors in the Frankfort Company did not plan on living on their property but instead intended to lease the land to others. One of Pastorius's jobs, besides handling legal and tax issues for the company, was to recruit settlers. He found a group of 13 Quaker and Mennonite families from Krefeld, near Düsseldorf, in the lower Rhineland, who were interested in emigrating, and these families became the founders of what would become Germantown, the first German settlement in America.[69]

In June 1683, Penn conveyed 6,000 acres to six members of the Krefeld group, and that same month Pastorius sailed from England to Pennsylvania on the ship *America*, arriving in Philadelphia in late August.[70] The Krefeld families, a total of 33 people, nearly all interrelated, arrived on October 6, 1683, and established their community six miles north of Philadelphia. Within two years, more people from Krefeld and Mülheim an der Ruhr, and then Swiss Mennonites from Kriegsheim, another town visited by Penn in 1677, arrived in Germantown. Many of these early settlers were weavers, and they brought this trade to America.[71]

A group of 17 Welsh families had also arrived in Pennsylvania in the fall of 1682. Between August and November 1682, 134 individuals and an unknown number of family members and servants arrived and quickly built homes, farms, and businesses.[72] By 1700, Pennsylvania had 21,000 residents, nearly all of them immigrants.

Several things distinguished Pennsylvania from other 17th-century colonization efforts. Penn's willingness to sell land; the encouragement of private, family enterprises such as farms, grist mills, and weaving versus the growing of commercial crops such as tobacco or rice, and Penn's and Pastorius's willingness to put their proverbial mouths where their money was and settle in Pennsylvania themselves made settlement of the colony different from the Virginia or Carolina colonies. The legal protection of religious freedoms in the Frame of Government also made Pennsylvania distinctive.

Penn's and Pastorius's writings also had a more authoritative tone, since both men had actually been to the colony and, in fact, lived there. Besides his first book about Pennsylvania, Penn authored other publicizing tracts that were disseminated in German-speaking territories in 1700, 1702, and 1704.[73]

Penn's *Letter to the Free Society of Traders* was published in 1683 and is considered to be his most successful promotional tract. In it he described the natural environment, particularly native flora and fauna, as well as which crops were being cultivated in the region. Penn also described the native people and some of their customs and explained how the Dutch and then Swedes had initially settled in the southern part of the colony (what is now Delaware).[74]

In 1700, Pastorius wrote the book *A Detailed Geographical Description of Pennsylvania*. Two years later, in 1702, another German Pietist, Daniel Falckner, published the book *Curieuse Nachricht von Pennsylvania* ("Interesting News from Pennsylvania") about his experiences in 1694, when he had accompanied a group of Pietist settlers to the new colony. Falckner's book was written in the form of a list of 73 questions and answers, the questions having been posed by the Pietist minister August Hermann Franke of Halle, who was interested in Pennsylvania as a possible place for Pietists to settle. Falckner's questions, which were supplemented with another 22 questions, focused on travel to the New World as well as the physical environment and climate; the native peoples and their customs; types of crops that could be grown; suggestions about how to be economically successful; and ideas about how to proselytize among the Indians and other Europeans in the colony.[75] In 1704, Falckner and Pastorius's writings about Pennsylvania were published as one volume.[76]

By the early 18th century, the English had become experienced at establishing colonies in North America and recruiting people to populate them. Except for New England, which was able to achieve natural increase in population by 1640, most of the English colonies depended on immigration, and increasingly, the importation of African slaves, for their labor forces. The promotion of Pennsylvania and Carolina, as well as the Palatine refugee crisis of 1710, created chains of migration from German states to North America that brought more than 108,000 Germans to North America by the time the Revolution began, many arriving as indentured servants. Pennsylvania and the Carolinas also attracted 140,000 Scots-Irish Presbyterians from Ulster, Ireland, in the late 18th century with promises of cheap land, no landlords, and religious freedom. The new United Kingdom also used its American colonies as a place to deport thousands of unruly Scots, who rebelled against English rule in 1715 and 1745. Another 25,000 Scots came to America between 1760 and 1775.[77] As these migration chains were being forged, 348,000 Africans were brought as slaves to British North America—the majority of them arriving in Virginia and the Carolinas.[78]

Whether migrants came because of promotion and recruitment, family connections, or enslavement, the tight connection between migration and labor in the American economy was, by the end of the 18th century, well established. Promoters used various schemes to attract colonists and workers to America and found that offers of free or cheap land and greater personal freedom attracted many Europeans. Exaggeration, especially about the physical environment, would also prove to be an effective formula, and misinformation and outright lies would continue to be found in promotional literature throughout America, especially in the 19th century, the period of the most active promotional campaigns.

CHAPTER TWO

Antebellum Immigration Promotion by States, 1845–1860

A new phase of promotion of immigration to the United States began in the mid-1840s in the Midwest, as territories and states sought to attract new residents to transform Indian lands into settled states. The pioneers in state-based immigration promotion were Michigan, Wisconsin, and Minnesota, which developed programs between 1845 and 1860 and then continued these efforts in various forms after the Civil War.[1] These states and territories—Michigan and Wisconsin were states and Minnesota was a territory when they began their promotion policies—sought permanent settlers to build farms and businesses and establish the sociocultural institutions of communities—schools, churches, social organizations. In turning to Northern Europeans—particularly Germans, Dutch, and Scandinavians—and English Canadians, state promoters indicated that they believed these immigrants would make desirable citizens.

With the United States deep in the middle of an intense, soon-to-become violent debate about slavery and the nature of American citizenship, these Midwestern states and territories, which already prohibited slavery within their borders, did not desire free blacks as residents and rejected arguments that foreigners were dangerous and unable to assimilate into American culture and society. But Michigan, Wisconsin, and Minnesota also recruited immigrants from primarily Protestant Northern European countries, thus reinforcing (or, at least, not challenging) the widespread belief that Roman Catholics could not make good citizens in a democratic republic.

The states and territories that pioneered immigration promotion had several things in common. They were all located in the northern Midwest, had a mix of prairie and woodland in environment, and were primarily agricultural in economy. They entered the Union between 1837 and 1858 as free states. Elections were highly competitive in these states, although the Democratic Party more often controlled their state houses than did the Whig Party. After 1855 in Michigan, 1856 in Wisconsin, and 1860 in Minnesota, the new Republican Party—with its opposition to slavery and its support for federal subsidy of transportation networks, especially railroads, canals, and roads—dominated these states' governments.

These states were also recently carved out of Indian Territory. According to the Indian Intercourse Act of 1834, all of the land west of the Mississippi River and not within Michigan Territory, the states of Missouri and Louisiana, or Arkansas Territory, was defined as "Indian Territory," in which white settlement was not allowed. This territory included all of the states of Wisconsin, Minnesota, Iowa, North Dakota, South Dakota, Montana, Wyoming, Colorado, Kansas, Nebraska, and Oklahoma. But within two years of the act's signing, this Indian Territory began to be broken up into territories for white settlement and state development with the establishment of the Wisconsin Territory in 1836.

This practice of confiscating Indian land and redistributing it to white Americans and European immigrants had begun with the organization of the Northwest Territory in 1787. This territory, which encompassed the states of Ohio, Indiana, Michigan, Wisconsin, and the northeastern part of Minnesota, was populated by 45,000 American Indians, of the Wyandot, Chippewa, Ottawa, Potawatomi, Wea, Piankashaw, Illinois, Menominee, Shawnee, Lenape, Miami, Kickapoo, and Kaskaskia nations. In a series of wars ending in the American victory at the Battle of Fallen Timbers in 1794, the United States forced these people to move out of the Ohio River Valley and closer to the Mississippi River, and by 1850, the Old Northwest had been transformed into five states containing 4.5 million people, one quarter of the nation's white population.[2]

Michigan, Wisconsin, and Minnesota used a variety of methods to promote immigration: advertising in European newspapers; sending agents to European countries; bringing immigrants over in colony groups; distributing information to newly arriving immigrants at the Port of New York; and advertising in the foreign-language press in the United States to reach immigrants already in the country. Their goals were to make Europeans aware of their presence and their desire for immigrants. Their ideal immigrant was a farmer from Canada, Germany, or Sweden, someone accustomed to hard physical labor and cold climates who would bring his family with him and stay permanently as a settler and a citizen. The image all of these states portrayed of themselves and of the United States was of a prosperous, expanding, vigorous country, full of opportunities for people willing to work hard and take risks.[3]

Michigan was the first new state to develop an immigration promotion policy. Although the Michigan Territory was organized in 1805, the population was primarily American Indian; the Potawatomi, Ottawa, and Chippewa tribes were the largest groups, but the peninsula was also home to Sauk, Fox, Kickapoo, Miami, and Mascouten bands, as well as Iroquois who had moved west after whites had occupied western New York and Pennsylvania in the 18th century.[4] In a series of treaties negotiated between 1795 and 1837, Michigan's native populations ceded their lands to the U.S. government and agreed to move west of the Mississippi River; the government then opened Michigan to white settlement.[5]

But Michigan's white population grew slowly until the opening of the Erie Canal in 1825 made it easier for Americans to access the region. Michigan became the 26th state in 1837, joining as a free state. Although Michigan had approximately 200,000 residents in 1837 and 212,267 residents in 1840, the new state legislature equated population with prosperity and so desired rapid growth.

Michigan's state government in the 1840s and 1850s was dominated by the Democratic Party, except for a brief two-year period between 1840 and 1842, when the Whigs held the governorship.

In March 1845, the Michigan state legislature created the Office of Foreign Immigration, and the following month Democratic governor John Barry appointed 40-year-old John Almy, a civil engineer from Grand Rapids, to be Michigan's "emigration agent" in New York. Almy was a good choice: an experienced promoter, he was the land agent for Lucius Lyon, a land surveyor and the developer of Grand Rapids and other towns who had served as Michigan's territorial representative prior to statehood.[6] Almy was also originally from New York and so was familiar with the city.[7]

Almy's job was to attract settlers to Ottawa and Kent counties, sparsely populated areas on Lake Michigan. He was paid 60 dollars for two months of work and another 30 dollars for the production of a six-page pamphlet, "State of Michigan—1845—To Emigrants."[8] Almy's home of Grand Rapids was in Kent County and was next door to Ottawa County, so he knew the area well. Almy distributed 5,000 copies of the pamphlet, which described the state's natural environment, economy, social and cultural institutions, and political system, plus a map, to new arrivals disembarking from ships at the Port of New York.

When Almy arrived in New York in 1845, the city's population had grown to 371,223 residents, thanks to the hundreds of Irish, German, and British immigrants arriving at the port every week. Germans were creating the United States' first ethnic enclave, Klein Deutschland (Little Germany) on the Lower East Side, while Irish immigrants clustered in the Five Points, West Greenwich Village, and Chelsea neighborhoods. New York was also a hotbed of anti-immigrant politics: the Native American Party and the American Republican Party were based in New York, and the new mayor, publisher James Harper, was fulfilling his pledge to kick immigrant workers out of city jobs. The city's 96,581 Irish Catholics were still angry about Protestant reformers' capture of the city's school board in 1842 and their imposition of a tax to fund public schools, schools that required daily reading of the Protestant King James Bible.[9]

Almy apparently did not enjoy living and working in this contentious environment, because when Barry sought to extend his contract by another 60 days, he declined and resigned as emigrant agent. In 1849, Democratic governor Epaphroditus Ransom revived the Office of Foreign Immigration and hired Edward Hughes Thomson, a former state senator from Flint and immigrant from England, to be the state's agent in New York. Like Almy, Thomson also prepared a pamphlet to distribute to potential immigrants, the 47-page "The Emigrant's Guide to the State of Michigan," which was written in both English and German and provided extensive detail about Michigan's climate, agricultural and commercial opportunities, railroads, and educational and social institutions. Thomson distributed 14,000 copies of this pamphlet in the second half of 1849.[10] He also traveled to Stuttgart to promote immigration to Michigan, and a 1916 history of the state claimed that due to "his indefatigable efforts he was directly responsible for the removal of over twenty thousand hard-working Germans to the state."[11]

The message of Thomson's "The Emigrants Guide" was that Michigan was a good place for German farmers and craftsmen seeking economic independence and political freedom. Published at a time of great political and economic turmoil in the German states, German immigration to the United States was increasing in this period, and Thomson sought to direct as many of those immigrants to Michigan as he could.[12]

Although Governor Barry had supported the state's promotional program, he chose not to extend Thomson's contract when he was reelected governor in 1850.[13] This was mainly because while Michigan had nearly doubled its population since statehood, only 15 percent of Michigan's 397,654 residents were foreign born.[14]

But Thomson was convinced of the validity of the promotion program. As an immigrant himself, Thomson believed himself proof of the opportunities available to immigrants in Michigan and in the United States generally. Born in 1810 in Kendal, Westmorland, England, he had immigrated to the United States in 1820 as a child with his widowed father.[15] He grew up in Boston and then studied law in New York, where he practiced out of future president Millard Fillmore's law office in Buffalo. He lived briefly in Cleveland, Ohio, before moving to the Flint area in 1837, at the beginning of Michigan's statehood. By the mid-1840s, he had become active in local and state politics, being elected first to the state Senate in 1845.[16]

Thomson was reelected to the state legislature in 1859, and that year he proposed that the state appropriate $2,500 to pay for a new emigrant agent. Republican governor Moses Wisner agreed, and two Prussians, Rudolph Diepenbeck and George Veenfliet, were hired to staff offices in New York and Detroit, respectively. Veenfliet had been a professor of mathematics and physical sciences at the University of Bonn until he had to flee after the failed revolution of 1848. He moved to Michigan upon arriving in the United States in 1849 and had served as postmaster in Blumfield (Saginaw County), the township he had helped found in 1850. Little is known of Diepenbeck except that he had been born in Prussia in 1820.[17] Diepenbeck and Veenfliet updated Thomson's old promotional pamphlet from 1849 and distributed 5,000 copies. Although few Germans overall settled in Michigan, they were, nonetheless, the largest immigrant group in the state, in part due to the state's promotional efforts.[18]

Yet despite its immigration promotion campaigns, most residents of Michigan were Americans born in other states. The immigrant population was never more than 22 percent of the state's overall population, although by the end of the 19th century, more than 40 percent of Michigan residents had foreign-born parents.

Wisconsin was more successful in attracting immigrants. Wisconsin entered the Union as a free state in 1848, after the creation of the Wisconsin Territory out of the larger Michigan Territory in 1836. The original possessors of Wisconsin had been the Chippewa, Menominee, Potawatomi, and Winnebago peoples, along with Illinois, Mascouten, Miami, Sauk, and Fox bands.[19] Between 1804 and 1836, these people were forced by the federal government to cede their land to the United States in order that it could be organized into the Wisconsin Territory and then opened to white settlement.[20]

This diplomatic pressure was exerted after successful military force had been used. The southern part of Wisconsin by Lake Michigan had been the site of several battles in the Black Hawk War of 1832, which broke out when the United States began pressuring the Sauks to vacate territory ceded in the controversial Treaty of St. Louis of 1804.[21] The United States' victory in the Black Hawk War was the last major military conflict between American Indians and the United States in the Old Northwest and marked the beginning of a new policy of the United States to push Indians west of the Mississippi River, mainly through treaty negotiations but also force when necessary.

Wisconsin experienced dramatic population growth in the 1840s and had 305,391 residents in 1850, an increase of 891 percent from its 1840 population of 30,945.[22] Of the white population (Wisconsin had only 635 black residents in 1850), 110,471 (36 percent) were foreign born, with Germans, English, Scottish, and Welsh being the largest immigrant groups.[23]

In May 1852, the newly elected Whig governor, Leonard J. Farwell, appointed Gysbert van Steenwyk to be commissioner of emigration. Van Steenwyk had been born and raised in Utrecht, the Netherlands, in 1814, the son of a prosperous farmer. He studied philosophy and classical literature at the University of Utrecht and then served in the Dutch army and national guards before immigrating in 1849. He settled first in Milwaukee and then Newport, Sauk County. The same year he arrived in Wisconsin he was appointed consul for the Netherlands to Wisconsin and additionally for Michigan and Minnesota in 1850. Besides being classically educated, van Steenwyk was fluent in Dutch, French, German, and English.[24]

Thus, in this dual function as consul for the Dutch government and emigrant agent for the state of Wisconsin, van Steenwyk traveled to New York City, opened an office at 110 Greenwich Street, and began meeting with ethnic societies, consuls, and shipping companies to promote Wisconsin. The state legislature appropriated $1,250 for publications, and Van Steenwyk had nearly 30,000 pamphlets printed in total: 20,000 in German, 5,000 in Norwegian, and 4,000 in Dutch. He distributed these pamphlets to immigrants disembarking from ships and left them in taverns and hotels near the New York waterfront. He also mailed 5,000 pamphlets to Europe, placed advertisements in English, German, and Dutch newspapers published in New York, as well as in the *Dorfzeitung*, the *Schwäbische Merkur*, the *Bremer Auswanderungzeitung*, the *Köllnische Zeitung*, the *Manheimer Journal*, and the *Amsterdam Handelsblad*. To help him with his work, van Steenwyk employed a Norwegian and then two Germans and an Englishman as assistants.[25]

Wisconsin continued this promotional campaign into 1853, but a change in state politics from Whig to Democratic control in 1854 resulted in van Steenwyk being replaced by Herman Haertel, a German land agent and coal dealer from Milwaukee. Haertel had been born in Schwieberg, Saxony, in 1817, and had immigrated to Wisconsin in 1842.[26]

Haertel opened an office at 89 Greenwich Street in New York, from which he continued van Steenwyk's work of advertising in New York and foreign newspapers, but he expanded the number and the scope, placing notices in the *London Times*, the *Tipperary Free Press*, the *Baseler Zeitung*, and *Leipziger Allgemeine Zeitung*. Haertel also wrote a series of articles to the *New York Tribune* encouraging migration to Wisconsin. He distributed 30,000 pamphlets in 1853, sending half of them to Europe. Haertel also took advantage of the fact that the U.S. consul in Bremen, Dr. William Hildebrandt, was from Mineral Point, Wisconsin, and was willing to help distribute information about Wisconsin around Bremen, which was becoming one of the main ports for German emigration in the 1850s. Haertel also responded to letters of inquiry sent to the Wisconsin emigration commissioner's office; more than 300 letters were received, and 3,000 people, 2,000 of them newly arrived immigrants, came to the office seeking information. Two-thirds of these people were Germans; the rest were Norwegians, Swedes, Irish, English, Scottish, and Dutch. Another service Haertel offered was to pass along funds from immigrants already in Wisconsin to relatives and friends newly arriving in New York to help them with their journeys to the Midwest.[27]

To give his promotional literature a scientific, and thus more accurate, appearance, Haertel also recruited a natural scientist, Allen Lapham, to write the descriptions of Wisconsin's natural environment.[28]

Haertel was replaced by Frederick W. Horn of Ozaukee County in 1854. Horn was a 40-year-old lawyer who had emigrated from Prussia in 1837 and had settled in Cedarburg.[29] While Horn worked in New York, he opened a branch office in Quebec and hired Elias Stangeland to work there for six months, beginning May 1, 1854.[30] Stangeland was a 27-year-old bookseller from Norway who had immigrated in 1849 and had settled in Madison, where the state had just founded the University of Wisconsin.[31]

Although most of the immigrants arriving in Wisconsin from Quebec were English and Irish, 2,000 Norwegians settled in the state, possibly directed by Stangeland. Horn claimed that 16,000 Germans arriving in New York in the spring and summer of 1854 were destined for Wisconsin thanks to his advertising efforts.[32]

Between 1845 and 1860, Wisconsin multiplied its population 25 times.[33] Most immigrants to Wisconsin came from German states (mainly

Prussia, Bavaria, Hesse, and Baden, as well as Austria), Ireland, Great Britain, Norway, and Canada.[34]

What probably attracted these immigrants to Wisconsin was the state's message that Wisconsin was a good place to farm. Wisconsin's agents emphasized the fertility of the soil, the cheapness and availability of good farmland for crop and stock raising, high wages for skilled labor, and the state's liberal constitution in terms of residency and citizenship. The fact that Wisconsin was advertising for immigrants in both New York and in Europe also meant that nativists had no political clout in the state's politics.[35] During the 1850s, political control of Wisconsin was mainly in the hands of the Democratic Party, except for Whig governor Farwell's term between 1852 and 1854, until the new Republican Party gained control in 1856.

Despite its apparent success, Wisconsin ended its immigration promotion program in 1855 and did not reactivate it until 1867. Wisconsin's Republican governors were more focused on promoting railroad development and then on the state's military contribution to the Civil War. In addition, overall immigration to the United States declined in 1855, particularly from German states, and did not begin to increase until the mid-1860s, so the state legislature was unwilling to devote resources to a policy that was seen as achieving diminishing returns.[36]

Unlike Michigan and Wisconsin, which began their promotional policies after achieving statehood, Minnesota, which was organized as a territory in 1849, initiated its program specifically to gain enough white population to petition for statehood, although there was no specific population requirement for a statehood petition.[37] Prior to the creation of the Minnesota Territory, Minnesota had belonged to the Dakota Sioux and Chippewa nations. In 1851, the United States negotiated the Treaty of Traverse des Sioux and the Treaty of Mendota with the Mdewakanton and Wahpekute bands of the Sioux Nation, which ceded nearly 24,000,000 acres (97,000 sq km) of land in southern Minnesota, northern Iowa, and eastern South Dakota for $3 million in return for relocating to two reservations along the Minnesota River.[38]

In 1855, the same year Wisconsin decided it was no longer worth promoting immigration, Minnesota's territorial legislature authorized the employment of an agent in New York to advertise the territory to newly arriving immigrants. Democratic governor Willis A. Gorman appointed Eugene Burnand to be commissioner of emigration.[39]

Burnand was an immigrant from Geneva, Switzerland, and fluent in French, German, and English. Classically educated at the University of Heidelberg, he had come to the United States in 1844 at the age of 40 and quickly embraced the United States' entrepreneurial spirit.[40] Soon after immigrating, he had attempted to create a Swiss colony on lands he had bought in Lewis and Jefferson counties, New York. The venture failed because, according to an 1855 newspaper editorial on Burnand's appointment as commissioner of emigration, "when its members arrived in this country and found that their promised location was upon lands covered with heavy forests of timber, and that 'out West' there were millions of acres delivered over by the hand of nature ready for the plow, they started for the Illinois prairies, much to the disappointment and pecuniary disadvantage of Mons. Bernand [sic]." Burnand moved to St. Paul in 1854, and by 1855 he had gained the attention of the governor and other political leaders.[41]

After an initial struggle with the legislature to get funds for the trip, Burnand arrived in New York in June 1855 and set up shop on the Battery. He advertised Minnesota to mainly Germans and Belgians, but also to Swiss and French immigrants, by distributing pamphlets and answering inquiries through the mail and in person. He also advertised extensively in German and Swiss newspapers and in German-language newspapers in New York and cultivated relationships with the editors of European newspapers specializing in immigration.[42]

Burnand focused mainly on German- and French-speaking immigrants, reflecting his fluency and cultural comfort with speakers of those languages. Although a common assumption was that immigrants were attracted to environments similar to those they had left in Europe (the so-called isothermal theory of migration), Burnand devoted little to no attention to attracting Scandinavians, who were beginning to immigrate in large numbers. Despite this neglect, the number of Norwegians and Swedes in Minnesota increased from 12 to nearly 12,000 between 1850 and 1860.[43]

Regardless of how or why they came, these Northern Europeans were seen as having the right character needed to survive and thrive in Minnesota. An early Minnesota booster, William G. Le Duc, commented in 1853: "The greater part of the Germans, Norwegians, and Swedes who now emigrate, bring with them not only the means of reaching their respective destinations, and establishing themselves in some honest, if humble occupation, in our cities, towns, and inland counties, but they also bring what is incomparatively [sic] more valuable, honesty, sobriety, persevering industry, and mental cultivation sufficient to bring them, after a short residence among us within the benign influence of a Free Press."[44] Burnand commented of the Belgians: "Belgians who come here, have generally large means, make good citizens and although Roman Catholic, are not Priest-ridden."[45]

The image of Minnesota Burnand and other promoters disseminated was of a flat, fertile land of endless prairies waiting to be plowed, 10,000 lakes waiting to be fished, a not-at-all cold place that only needed sober, hardworking people to make it a northern paradise.[46]

Of major concern to Burnand and Minnesota state officials was the widespread belief that Minnesota's northern latitude meant a hostile climate, one where snow and ice were on the ground 12 months of the year and where most crops could not grow. Burnand wrote to the governor in St. Paul: "Our high northern latitude particularly, has, in many instances, been made a bug bear to the emigrant and frightened him from risking his life among the alleged mountains of ice in this Territory."[47] Much of Burnand's work focused on convincing Europeans that Minnesota's prairie land was conducive to farming grains and raising stock and that the climate was similar to that of Northwestern Europe.

Immigration to the United States between 1855 and 1857, when Burnand was in New York, was about 200,000 entries per year, half of what it had been in 1854, the high point of the Irish famine, when 427,833 people had immigrated. The Panic of 1857 caused immigration in 1858 to drop significantly, down to only 123,126 entries, and immigration numbers did not achieve such levels again until 1873.[48]

Burnand remained in New York until early 1857, when he returned to St. Paul, discouraged about the lack of financial support for immigration promotion from the legislature. The office of emigration commissioner was discontinued, and a year later, in 1858, Minnesota entered the Union as a free state, and the need for immigration promotion appeared to be at an end.[49]

At the same time that Michigan, Wisconsin, and Minnesota were promoting immigration, other, eastern states were experimenting with regulating immigration. In 1847, New York State had established the New York State Board of Commissioners of Emigration to regulate conditions at the Port of New York and to provide temporary housing and financial assistance, medical care, and burial services for immigrants who entered the country impoverished, sick, or dying.[50] But despite access to funds from a head tax of $1.50 per passenger and a hospital tax to pay for medical care for sick immigrants, the commissioners quickly began to feel overwhelmed with meeting the needs of so many new arrivals.

A few months after Burnand arrived in New York to promote Minnesota, on August 1, 1855, the Board of Commissioners of Emigration opened an emigrant depot at the former concert hall, Castle Garden, in Battery Park, to provide a single landing place where immigrants could collect their luggage, bathe and change clothes, exchange money, buy train tickets and food, and get information about travel routes west or jobs and housing in New York.[51] Being able to distribute information at Castle Garden versus going from pier to pier or hoping for new arrivals to come to the Battery to ask for information made Burnand's job of promoting Minnesota much easier.

Burnand probably also witnessed the angry protests from New York residents of the city's First Ward, who objected to the construction of a public facility for "paupers" in their neighborhood. The loudest protesters against Castle Garden, however, were the men who worked the piers, assisting immigrants in transferring themselves and their luggage to western-bound trains and/or hotels; changing money; selling food and beverages; and recruiting for jobs at the docks. On August 3, 1855, the first day Castle Garden received a shipload of passengers, city guides, or runners, angry at the new tall fence that kept them out of the facility, threw rocks at commission president and German Society representative Rudolph Garrigue and other commission employees. The violence prompted Irish commissioner John A. Kennedy to brandish a revolver in defense.

Runners and residents of the First Ward organized two mass "indignation meetings," the first attended by 3,000 people and the second by several hundred, in the first week of August to protest what they alleged was the corruption of the emigration commissioners and their conspiracy to profit off immigrants themselves. Articulating the rhetoric and values of Jacksonian America, the runners argued that competition was a core value of American society and that the emigration depot represented a

"Arrival at Castle Garden," Frank Leslie's illustrated newspaper, vol. 21, January 20, 1866, p. 280. (Library of Congress)

monopoly (as well as a loss of business to themselves). Other arguments against the depot were that a public space should not be privatized (although the Emigration Commission was a joint state–municipal entity) and that immigrants should be received first on an island in the harbor, not in the city, for public health reasons.[52]

Native-born New Yorkers were also increasingly unhappy that by 1855, Irish men were the largest group of cartmen in New York City, an unskilled job that nonetheless required a city license, and in turn "pull" with City Hall, or that Irish men accounted for 27 percent of the city's new police force, with about 300 Irish-born policemen patrolling the streets of their neighborhoods. So while Minnesota was paying Burnand to promote immigration, New Yorkers were protesting what they considered to be special and unfair treatment of immigrants.

The promotional work of Michigan, Wisconsin, and Minnesota occurred within the context of a vigorous and increasingly violent debate about nature and exercise of American citizenship. Immigration, slavery, market capitalism, wage labor, and westward expansion were all linked to questions about who could be an American citizen, what that citizenship meant in both political and economic terms, and how the United States could claim to be a country of liberty and opportunity while at the same time sanctioning chattel slavery.

Michigan launched its promotional campaign in the midst of a large, increasingly powerful anti-immigrant political movement called nativism. Hostility toward immigrants merged with an older loathing of Roman Catholics that had existed in America since early colonial times. The reason for this conflation was the surge in immigration from Ireland in the 1830s, which only increased with the Irish Potato Famine of 1845–1852. Economic displacement by industrialism also sent increasing numbers of Northern Europeans, especially Germans, to the United States in this period.

Nativist Americans claimed that white Protestants made the best citizens in a democratic republic, which required independent-minded, educated voters in order to function properly. Foreigners, by contrast, had not been raised in American republican political culture with American political (Protestant) values and brought with them older loyalties to autocratic monarchies, or even worse, to the Roman Catholic Church, an antirepublican, antidemocratic authoritarian institution that interfered in European politics to promote its conservative interests. Nativists argued that Roman Catholics would vote as their priests told them to and so could not be independent-minded voters and citizens. If allowed to naturalize, Roman Catholic immigrants would be the means by which the papacy would undermine the American Republic.

Thomas Nast, "Religious liberty is guaranteed: but can we allow foreign reptiles to crawl all over us?" (Library of Congress)

To confront the threat of immigration and immigrants, nativists proposed extending the naturalization period (the number of years before a native-born citizen could vote) from five years to twenty-one years and barring Roman Catholics from holding public office or holding occupational licenses such as carting, trash collecting, or butchering, jobs Irish immigrants were moving into in large Eastern cities such as New York. Many nativists also advocated requiring Protestant Bible reading in public schools and compulsory public education to try to educate and assimilate immigrant children into an English-speaking Protestant culture.

So, the 4.9 million immigrants who arrived from Europe between 1830 and 1860 confronted a strong anti-immigrant, anti-Catholic social and political movement that sought to exclude them on the basis of first, religion, in the case of Catholics, and then language, ethnicity, and culture.

Ironically, the one option nativists did not propose was to restrict immigration, mainly because the question of which level of government, federal or state, was responsible for immigration was constitutionally unclear, and Americans were not willing to devote the money to develop a bureaucracy large and powerful enough to limit immigration for reasons other than medical quarantine and for an extended period of time.

Nativism had other contradictions and inconsistencies. Although nominally upset about immigration, nativists were at their most hysterical when talking about Roman Catholicism and Catholics, and their conflation of "immigrant" and "Catholic" centered primarily on Irish immigrants. Nativists disparaged Germans' pride of language and their creation of "Klein Deutschlands," especially in New York City, but they could not deny that Germany had produced many great writers, artists, and musicians, unlike America. And German immigrants had among them a small but influential minority of intellectuals, the Forty-Eighters, who had fled political persecution in the failed revolutions of 1848 and who were able to vigorously defend the liberty of German immigrants to integrate into American society on their own terms.[53]

Nativism cut across class lines but received significant support from native-born Protestant artisans in Northeastern cities who felt economically threatened by immigrant workers.[54] Nativist political parties were organized at the local city, state, and then ultimately national level with the American or Know-Nothing Party, which attracted many former Whigs and convinced former president Millard Fillmore to be its presidential candidate in 1856. The American Party was a national party but was electorally strong in New York, Massachusetts, Connecticut, Pennsylvania, and Ohio, where nativists made a point of stressing anti-Catholicism versus anti-immigrant in an effort to attract German Protestant voters.[55]

Yet nativism had little to no sway in the new Midwestern states. Exuding confidence that the American environment would assimilate immigrants and that the process of developing a state would teach foreigners American political values, Michigan, Wisconsin, and Minnesota rejected nativist arguments about the dangers of immigration.

An important factor in these states' rejection of nativism was the dominance of the Democratic Party in these states' politics in the 1840s and 1850s. The Democratic Party positioned itself as the party of farmers, small government, and states' rights and was especially strong in rural and frontier areas, such as the new states of Michigan and Wisconsin. Northern Democrats were also strong supporters of homestead bills that limited the size of claims on public land to only 160 acres per family in order to further the development of small farms. The homestead movement was closely tied to the "Free Soil" branch of the antislavery movement and was strongly opposed by Southern politicians and other defenders of slavery.[56]

The Democrats also welcomed immigrant voters and fought back Whig and later Republican efforts to legislate Protestant morality through blue laws against drinking and other forms of recreation on Sundays that many immigrants saw as an attack on their cultural traditions. The fact that the Republican Party was filled with conservative Whigs desperate to unify Americans against foreigners instead of dividing sectionally over slavery did not endear the Republicans to immigrant voters in many states, especially in the new Middle West. It was not until the Republican Party denounced nativism (on pressure from German American voters) in the late 1850s that the Republicans were able to attract immigrant voters.[57]

But despite being controlled by antinativist Democrats, both Michigan and Wisconsin focused most of their promotional efforts on predominantly Protestant countries: Norway, Sweden, the Netherlands, Great Britain, and the Protestant German states. Ireland was the only predominantly Catholic country that sent significant numbers of immigrants to Michigan and Wisconsin, and that had more to do with the fact that Ireland sent more than 1.6 million people to the United States between 1840 and 1859 than any deliberate promotional efforts by state immigration agents.

Minnesota attempted (largely unsuccessfully) to recruit immigrants from France and Belgium in the 1850s, but these were the only Catholic countries where such efforts were attempted, and in the case of Belgium, Burnand focused on Flanders, the Protestant part of Belgium, and France had a strong anticlerical tradition since its revolution. No effort was made to recruit immigrants from Spain, Portugal, or Italy, countries that were seen by Americans as too poor, too Catholic, and not on the trans-Atlantic shipping routes between the United States and Europe.

States promoting immigration in the 1840s and 1850s did so selectively also because the length and duration of the journey from Europe (about 10 weeks) made immigration a permanent move for most people in this period. Although the passenger shipping industry began to embrace steam in a big way in the mid-1850s, many people still immigrated on slow-moving sailing ships into the 1860s because it was cheaper.[58]

Raymond L. Cohn has argued convincingly that the nativist movement of the 1840s and 1850s did affect immigration rates, causing a sharp decline in immigration in 1855 after reaching a high point of 427,833 entries in 1854 and not reaching antebellum levels again until after the Civil War.[59]

A rise in anti-immigrant violence after the Know-Nothing Party's successes in the election of 1854 prompted immigrants to write home of the troubles in the United States, and foreign newspapers reported widely on the anti-immigrant riots that occurred in many American cities.[60] The immigrants who did arrive between 1855 and 1860 went to parts of the Midwest, particularly Illinois, Wisconsin, and Iowa, where nativism and the Know-Nothing Party were weak.[61]

Immigration promoters, especially in the Midwest, viewed nativism and the Know-Nothing movement as a deterrent to Europeans deciding whether to immigrate to the United States versus other countries.[62]

Acknowledging the effects of the Crimean War of 1853–1856 on trans-Atlantic shipping, a Minnesota booster nonetheless argued that "these causes are subordinate to the effects produced upon the people of Germany and Ireland, and in fact upon all the emigrating countries of Europe, by the Know-Nothing movement and the aversion and prejudice manifested towards those of foreign birth in the United States and to the indignities and violence to which they have been subject," adding that Know-Nothing violence against immigrants had been widely published in German newspapers in particular and that German state officials were using nativism as an argument for why Germans should not immigrate to the United States.[63]

Americans heatedly and sometimes violently debated immigration and immigrant assimilation, but one thing Americans did not disagree on was the need for the federal government to remove American Indians farther west to allow white settlement. Between 1830 and 1860, the Chickasaw, Choctaw, Muskogee, Creek, Seminole, and Cherokee peoples were forcibly removed from their lands in the Southeast to Indian Territory (what is now Oklahoma and Kansas), while the Potawatomi, Chippewa, Winnebago, Sauk, Fox, and Wyandot were forced to move west of the Mississippi River. When Indians resisted, as the Sauks did in the Black Hawk War of 1832, the United States did not hesitate to send in the army.[64] In 1832, U.S. military expenditures on Indian affairs reached more than $1 million for the first time, and the United States would spend between $1 million and $5 million per year between 1832 and 1842 on conflicts with American Indians.[65]

The American state was also increasingly willing to spend money on developing internal transportation systems. Michigan and Wisconsin's immigration promotion policies were part of a larger program to develop roads, canals, and railroads to connect these new Midwestern states to Eastern and European markets. Although the Democratic and Whig parties argued about who should pay for such internal improvements—the federal government, the states, or private corporations—by the 1850s, both parties actively supported the construction of these transportation networks that were essential to the movement of goods and people around an expanding country.

The Democrats were great proponents of westward expansion and the organization of the Old Northwest Territory and Louisiana Purchase into new states, while the Whigs and the Republicans vigorously advocated for the roads, canals, and, most importantly, railroads that would allow Americans to easily access these territories. Between 1803 and 1858, Ohio, Indiana, Illinois, Michigan, Wisconsin, and Minnesota were organized as states. These, and the other new Western states, Iowa and Missouri, experienced explosive growth in the antebellum period, as millions of white Americans and Europeans moved west. For instance, Minnesota went from having a population of 6,077 people in 1850 to 172,023 people in 1860, a growth rate of nearly 1,000 percent.[66]

The westward movement of people and the creation of new states, of course, became intimately intertwined with political leaders' efforts to maintain a balance between free states and slave states in the Senate. Between 1821—when the Missouri Compromise, which prohibited slavery north of latitude 36°30′ was negotiated—and 1860, Michigan, Wisconsin, Minnesota, and Iowa were admitted to the Union as free states, while Missouri, Arkansas, Florida, and Texas were admitted as slave states.

But population growth in Western states that prohibited slavery was greater than in the new Southwestern states that did allow slavery, and the promotion of immigration by northern Midwestern states worried Southern political leaders who saw thousands of Europeans migrating to Northern and Western states and avoiding the South specifically because of its slave labor system.[67]

The combination of westward movement and settlement, economic opportunity, and political freedom was a major selling point of promoters around the United States and was articulated in the political slogan "Free Soil, Free Labor." This ideology, promoted most aggressively by Jacksonian Democrats, argued that wage labor was a form of slavery for white men and that access to land, and the economic freedom and independence it promised, was essential to American democracy. While Democrats would come to argue in the 1850s that the decision of whether to tolerate black slavery in the new western territories should be a local one, based on the "popular sovereignty" doctrine, opponents of slavery used the "free soil" argument to argue against the expansion of slavery into the West. And northern Democrats recognized that the prohibition of slavery in northern Midwestern states and territories made that region more attractive to Europeans, especially farmers who had no experience with, or interest in, slavery.[68]

Immigration numbers fluctuated in the 1850s due to both events in Europe and the Panic of 1857, which began in August of that year. The outbreak of the Civil War in the spring of 1861 further discouraged immigration, and immigration numbers did not begin to increase until 1863, as word of the federal government's new policy to give away millions of acres of land reached Europe.[69] States and railroads would soon begin new campaigns of immigration promotion after the Civil War.

CHAPTER THREE

Corporate Immigration Promotion and Labor Recruitment in the 19th Century

The railroads were the most aggressive promoters of America in the 19th century. Given millions of acres of land by the federal and state governments to help fund the construction of their lines, railroad corporations had a vested economic interest in recruiting settlers to buy and develop their property.

But unlike newly organized states and territories, which promoted immigration in order to gain residents and future citizens, the railroads were in the business of making money. Transportation companies that found themselves in the real estate business, railroad corporations sought to quickly divest their property holdings to people who had the resources to found towns, start businesses, and make the railroads an essential component of their communities' local economies.

Yet both state and corporate immigration promoters targeted the same groups of Northern Europeans: Germans, Scandinavians, and British and British Canadians, as well as white Americans, in the belief that these groups made the best settlers of new lands. Propertyless peasants from Southern or Eastern Europe were not seen by the railroads as desirable customers. Some railroads promoted immigration in Ireland as part of their campaigns in the United Kingdom, but more often, railroads hired

Irish immigrants already in the United States to be construction workers, not settlers. Black Americans, whether free or freed slave, were definitely not wanted because white Americans did not want to live with blacks. The railroads aggressively recruited Chinese immigrants to be guest construction workers but not immigrant settlers.[1] So although the railroads had their own motivations and reasons for promoting immigration from certain countries and not others, the racial and cultural assumptions railroad promoters made about Northern Europeans' supposed superiority as settlers were the same as those of state promoters.

Railroads constructed many different images of America in their efforts to sell their property, but the most important and prominent were the dual ideas of fertility and opportunity. Whether it was the land personified as a young woman, images of bucolic farms bursting with juicy fruits and vegetables, golden stalks of wheat and corn, or maps that showed tracks civilizing an infinite landscape, the United States (as depicted by the railroads) was a place where most crops could be grown with relatively little effort, and the opportunity to become independent and prosperous, even rich through property ownership, was open to (virtually) anyone at low cost and low risk. If one was willing to work hard to develop a farm, a business, a town, then he would find lasting success, opportunity, and upward mobility in America.

The construction of this image of fertility and opportunity, however, was constrained by the physical environment. The predominance of prairie land in the Midwest meant that railroads such as the Atchison, Topeka & Santa Fe and the Northern Pacific emphasized cattle raising and grain. The more arid environments of California, the Southwest, and Texas caused some railroads, such as the Southern Pacific, to create an exotic and romantic image of sun, health, and relaxed prosperity. Railroad promoters largely ignored the fact that territory west of the hundredth meridian was considerably drier than that to the east and so was not suited to the same kinds of agriculture, or else they celebrated irrigation as a sign of advanced civilization.[2]

Promoters also either ignored or significantly downplayed the fact that most of the property being sold by the railroads had very recently belonged to American Indians, who were violently resisting federal and state government's efforts to remove them from their lands in the 1860s–1880s.[3]

This chapter focuses on the promotional efforts of the Atchison, Topeka & Santa Fe, the Northern Pacific, and the Southern Pacific railroads because of the size and geographical locations of their land grants, but the policies of these railroads did not differ significantly from those of other land grant roads in the 19th century.

F.F. Palmer, "Across the continent, Westward the course of empire takes its way," Currier & Ives, 1866. (Library of Congress)

Railroad corporations received significant subsidies from the American state, at both the state and federal level, from the construction of the first lines in the 1820s. These subsidies included tax breaks, low-interest or no-interest loans, and the use of eminent domain, but the most common form of subsidy was the land grant. Possessing millions of acres of land acquired through treaty and the military conquest of Indian nations, the federal government gave land directly to railroad corporations and to states, which, in turn, granted land to railroads operating within their jurisdictions.[4] Depending on what types of grants are counted, railroads received up to 223 million acres of American territory—a little more than 131 million of these acres from the federal government. Historians have hotly debated the value of this property, but it was clearly in the hundreds of millions of dollars.[5]

There were 73 federal land grants to railroad corporations in the 19th century; the largest recipients were the Northern Pacific (41 million acres), the Union Pacific (19 million acres), and the Chicago and Northwestern (7.4 million acres). These three companies account for more than half of the total acreage granted (130 million acres).[6]

The purpose of these land grants was to allow railroads to fund their construction through the sale of land, as well as giving the companies property to serve as collateral for loans and preventing them from having to purchase the land on which their roads were constructed. In many cases, land sales proceeded apace with construction, and railroads were eager to divest themselves of their real estate holdings so they could concentrate on the transportation part of their business.

The federal government also subsidized the railroads by requiring Indian nations to allow railroads to traverse reservations and often provided military protection during road construction.[7]

In marketing their land grants to Northern Europeans, American railroad corporations were selling two things: immigration to a new country and settlement in a specific place. The land-grant roads owned property across multiple states and territories, so their managers tended to think in terms of regions versus states, but the companies' land and immigration departments knew enough about their grants to recognize that there were differences between Minnesota and Montana, or Colorado and New Mexico. These two themes of America versus a specific place ran in tandem through the railroads' promotional campaigns.[8]

Another idea that was ubiquitous in railroad promotional work was that of the frontier. Europeans were well acquainted with the image of America as a savage, lawless place, populated by wild Indians and desperate outlaws, through their voracious consumption of both American and European pulp fiction.[9] The railroads faced the challenge of portraying the western United States as being empty of native peoples and tamed by white civilization at a time when the West was actually populated by hundreds of thousands of people: 85,000 Mexicans who had stayed in their homes after the Mexican-American War of 1846–1848; approximately 90,000 Chinese immigrants who had come to construct the transcontinental railroad, and 360,000 American Indians divided into dozens of tribes and all vigorously resisting American efforts to take their lands and remove them to reservations.[10]

The railroads crafted this image of an empty, safe space full of opportunity through reassurances and vague language. In an 1876 advertisement for land in Kansas that had previously belonged to the Potawatomi Nation but was now owned by the Atchison, Topeka & Santa Fe, the railroad assured prospective settlers that "the Indians have, for the last four or five years, been 'passing away,' 'down South,' into the Indian country, where they have selected their new homes, and now all have gone, except a few quiet half breeds."[11]

The Santa Fe did not discuss the Meeker Massacre of September 29, 1879, by the Ute Indians in western Colorado or other incidents that occurred in the 1870s and 1880s within the Santa Fe's land grant in which American Indians violently resisted their segregation on reservations.[12]

The Santa Fe's depiction of Arizona in 1882 offered Northern Europeans both reassurance and titillation with its descriptions of the violent struggle between the Apache Nation and the U.S. Army for control of the Arizona and New Mexico territories in the 1860s and 1870s, before declaring, "It is no idle statement that life and property are secure in Arizona."[13]

In case the message that savage Indians had been replaced with civilized whites was not clear enough, the Santa Fe insisted, "Where thousands of Aztecs have lived and prospered there must be room for thousands of Americans," ignoring the fact that the Aztecs had never lived in the Southwest.[14]

While the Santa Fe railroad's promoters were no doubt thinking that the army had finally subdued the Apache at the Battle of Big Dry Wash (or Chevelon's Fork) on July 17, 1882, the fact was that Apache escapees from the San Carlos Reservation in southeastern Arizona continued to raid ranches and communities along the Gila River into the mid-1880s. The most dramatic of these attacks were the raids of Geronimo in May 1885 and of Josanie in December 1885, in which he and several followers rode 2,500 miles, killed 38 people, and stole 250 horses before escaping over the Mexican border.[15] Clearly, despite railroad claims, life and property were not secure in Arizona.

The northern Midwest and Pacific Northwest were also wracked with violence between American Indians and whites, something the Northern Pacific Railroad either downplayed or ignored in its promotional literature to Northern Europeans.[16]

When the Northern Pacific began laying track through Sioux lands in Montana in the summer and fall of 1872, complete with army escort and protection, the Sioux attacked the construction crews. Although the army successfully defended the railroad's workers and property, the Sioux continued to attack the railroad as it was being built across their lands.[17] Cheyenne and Arapaho warriors also attempted to stop the Union Pacific's laying of track across Kansas in 1868 but failed.[18]

In the summer of 1877, one of the great Indian-American wars of the 19th century occurred in Montana and Idaho, when nearly 3,000 Nez Perce resisted removal to the Lapwai Reservation in Idaho. In 1877, between the Battle of White Bird Canyon, Idaho, on June 17 and the Battle of Bear Paw Mountain, Montana, on September 30, the Nez Perce fought five battles against the United States during their attempt to escape to Canada.[19] The "Sheepeater War" fought by Shoshoni and Bannock Indians against the United States in the Salmon River region of Idaho in summer and fall of 1879 also threatened the Northern Pacific Railroad's settlement of Europeans and American whites in that area.[20] But there was no acknowledgment by the railroad that life in its land grant was violent, dangerous, or otherwise disturbed.

This idea of a safe frontier, of having the best of both worlds—fresh, undeveloped wilderness and Western civilization—was clearly articulated in Southern Pacific promoter Charles Nordhoff's 1874 claim that Southern California "is the first tropical land which our race has thoroughly mastered and made itself at home in. There, and there only, on this planet, the traveler and resident may enjoy the delights of the tropics, without their penalties; a mild climate, not enervating, but healthful and health-restoring; a wonderfully and variously productive soil, without tropical malaria; the grandest scenery, with perfect security and comfort in travel arrangements; strange customs, but neither lawlessness nor semi-barbarism."[21]

The Atchison, Topeka & Santa Fe Railroad fully embraced the idea of a safe frontier in its promotional material. The company's advertising department, which was created in 1895, adopted the Pueblo Indian sun symbol, Zia, to be the Santa Fe's corporate logo, thus firmly linking the railroad to white Americans' and Europeans' perception of the Southwest as a place of ancient and mysterious exoticism. The Santa Fe advertising department also used the image of an American Indian with a Plains Indian feathered headdress to represent both its Southwestern and Kansas lines, blurring and conflating two radically different native cultures.[22]

The railroads sold Europeans and white Americans the idea of the West as a place of infinite space by offering larger farms than were available through the federal Homestead Act of 1862, which offered 160 acres of land for free after five years of settlement and development. The Northern Pacific encouraged industrial-scale wheat farming in its Red River Valley region on the border of Minnesota and the Dakotas, while the Atchison, Topeka & Santa Fe hyped the availability of 1,000-acre farms in Kansas for only $6,000, to be paid over the course of 11 years.[23] For Europeans accustomed to surviving on plots of less than 20 acres, 1,000 acres was massive. And for those who had difficulty imagining the vastness of the Northern Pacific's grant and the size of the farms available, the railroad helpfully noted that its land grant was seven times the size of Belgium and 3.5 times the size of the Netherlands.[24]

Yet the railroads' sale of their western lands involved a chicken-egg proposition. The railroads needed people to settle and develop their property into communities in order that the railroads might profit off of their land grants and have goods and people being transported on their lines. Yet for Europeans used to living in small villages, even the temptation of 1,000 acres could not overcome the unattractiveness of being isolated on the prairie with one's nearest neighbor miles away. Free or cheap land was the primary draw for Europeans interested in immigrating to

America, but would-be settlers also wanted evidence of civilization: schools, churches, businesses, and social institutions, as well as law and order.

Selling the "civilized frontier" idea, the Atchison, Topeka & Santa Fe assured prospective settlers in Kansas that its lands were being settled by "intelligent, enterprising, industrious, moral citizens who not only have the advantages of the wealth of rich soil, healthy air, pure water, and lasting fuel, that Nature has lavished upon the Reserve, but they have also the advantages of the railroads, the schools, the churches, and the society that have been brought into and about the Reserve by the enterprise and energies of the people who have been for twenty years settling and accumulating around it. Thus, while the settler on the Reserve is emphatically in A NEW COUNTRY, he is decidedly WITHIN the fully developed civilization of AN OLD COUNTRY."[25]

Another danger of life in the West, and one that could not be defeated by military force, was the weather and climate. The territory between the Cascade Range and the hundredth meridian that the Northern Pacific, the Atchison, Topeka & Santa Fe, Southern Pacific, and other western railroads were marketing to Americans and Northern Europeans in the 1870s–1890s had been called "the Great American Desert" for most of the 19th century for a reason.[26] This territory could not sustain agriculture without irrigation, and most of this land was only suited for stock raising at best.

When forced to, the railroads acknowledged the difference in rainfall west of the hundredth meridian, but they always managed to find a positive aspect to the aridness of the environment. For instance, the president of the Kansas State Agricultural College, J. A. Anderson, noted the dryness of western Kansas as compared to the eastern part of the state but called the area a "promising desert" and argued that the lack of rainfall meant that the region was well suited to stock raising, particularly of cattle.[27] But most of the Northern Europeans the railroad was trying to attract had little experience with cattle raising outside of dairying.

When on the heels of the Panic of 1873 Kansas was plagued by drought, a grasshopper infestation, and a harsh winter in 1874–1875, Santa Fe Railroad land department head A. S. Johnson organized a huge tour of the railroad's property for 225 journalists who were persuaded to adopt the Santa Fe's description of Kansas as the "Garden of the West."[28]

The railroads worked hard to spin arid and desert climates as something positive. In the Southwest, the desert was praised as being beneficial for people suffering from respiratory ailments and allergies, and the town of Santa Fe was marketed as a health resort. "The climate is remarkably equable, summer and winter, cool in summer and sunshiny in winter," the Santa Fe Railroad said of New Mexico.[29]

The Northern Pacific Railroad made the same claim about Minnesota. "The fact of this mildness of climate is abundantly established," the company declared in 1872, while insisting a few months later that the brutally cold and snowy winter of 1872–1873 was "unprecedented."[30]

The Northern Pacific further proclaimed that "the air of Minnesota is very clear, pure and bracing. There are many people living in the State who formerly were threatened with consumption, but who in their new homes enjoy perfect health."[31] As proof, the railroad's newspaper, *Land and Emigration*, published testimonials in the form of letters supposedly from Minnesota residents attesting to the healthfulness of the climate. "I arrived here, at Detroit, in September, 1871, in feeble health, and not able to do a few days' work," wrote C. H. Rand. "In three months I felt like a new person. The clear, bracing air of this portion of Minnesota has an exhilarating effect, and renews the strength at once."[32]

The Northern Pacific also asserted that the climate of its land grant was particularly well suited to the vigorous and hardy Northern Europeans it was working to attract. "The belt of country tributary to the Northern Pacific Road is within the parallels of latitude which in Europe, Asia, and America, embrace the most enlightened, creative, conquering, and progressive populations."[33]

The main European groups the railroads targeted with this message of opportunity on a civilized frontier were Germans, Scandinavians, and British. Occasionally, groups such as the Dutch or French were encouraged to buy railroad land, Spaniards rarely, and Italians, Greeks, and Eastern Europeans never. Germans in Russia were the only people in Eastern Europe whom the railroads targeted for immigration promotion. "The intelligence, the energy, the thrift, the money, and the progress, all come from Northern Europe," according to Minnesota congressman William Windom.[34]

Germans and German speakers in Russia were aggressively courted by the railroads. The Atchison, Topeka & Santa Fe Railroad hired Carl Bernhard Schmidt, an immigrant from Saxony, to be its European agent in 1873. Schmidt focused first on German immigrants already living in the United States. To encourage them to move to Kansas, he mailed German-language brochures describing Kansas and the availability of the railroad's lands to every known German community in the United States.[35]

Schmidt then traveled to Prussia, which was beginning to send large numbers of immigrants to the United States in reaction to Chancellor Otto von Bismarck's crackdown on the Roman Catholic Church, and then to the lower Volga River Valley to encourage the immigration of Germans living in the Russian Empire. These Germans had migrated east to Russia on the invitation of Empress Catherine the Great in the 18th century and had been granted numerous privileges in terms of exemption from military service, free land, and freedom of religion, language, and self-government. But in the early 1870s, the Russian government began to revoke these privileges that Germans in Russia enjoyed, and so community leaders visited the American Midwest in 1873 looking for a new home. Because of the Santa Fe Railroad's salesmanship and Schmidt's 1874–1875 trip to Prussia and Russia, an estimated 15,000 Germans from Russia immigrated to Kansas between 1873 and 1885, a period that saw drought, grasshopper infestation, and economic depression.[36]

Knowing of the Germans' reputation as successful farmers, the Santa Fe was so eager to encourage this immigration that it successfully lobbied the Kansas state legislature to amend the state's militia law to exempt religious pacifists, since many Germans from Russia were Mennonites who had religious objections to military service and oath taking.[37] By 1882, the Santa Fe was highlighting the presence of these Germans from Russia in its promotional literature, saying that they "make excellent citizens, pay their taxes promptly, and were never known to have a law suit."[38]

The Northern Pacific Railroad also eagerly encouraged the immigration of Germans from Russia to its lands in the Dakota Territory.[39] An estimated 100,000 Germans from Russia settled in the United States, primarily in Kansas, Nebraska, and the Dakotas, and they are credited with introducing hard Turkey wheat to the American Midwest.

Scandinavians were also desired as customers by the railroads. Northern Pacific Railroad promoters believed that people from Norway, Sweden, and Denmark were physically and temperamentally suited to the northern Midwest's cold climate and were the most likely to succeed in farming the prairie territory between Minnesota and Washington. Dutch farmers were also seen as practical, hardworking, and good at dairying, an industry the Northern Pacific was trying to establish in the Pacific Northwest. These Northern Europeans were the "industrious, intelligent, and enterprising population" the railroad wanted to attract to its land grant.[40]

As the Northern Pacific's European agent, George Sheppard wrote to Northern Pacific president Frederick Billings: "Common sense dictates the expediency of taking climatic influences into account when judging the probable destination of various peoples. We must seek our emigrants among the Northern peoples of Europe."[41]

This belief that French and Southern Europeans were not well suited for the upper Midwest was widespread among Northern Pacific management.

Seeing French-speaking Alsatians as potential recruits to the still-difficult-to-access Washington Territory after Alsace Lorraine's annexation to Germany after the Franco-Prussian War, A. B. Nettleton, Jay Cooke & Co.'s trustee agent for the Northern Pacific, lamented: "Minnesota and Dakota are too cold for these Alsatians, and I only wish that they could be held for a year or so until we are in a condition to plant them on the Pacific coast where the seasons will be more congenial."[42]

This "isothermal theory of migration," the idea that people were biologically attracted to regions similar in climate and environment to the ones they had left was a variant of the "isothermal theory of slavery" that explained the concentration of slave labor in the South in racial versus economic terms (i.e., that black people were not genetically suited to working in northern climates). Both of these theories were part of the larger intellectual movement of scientific racism that underpinned many immigration promoters' belief that Northern Europeans made the best Americans.[43]

Other immigrant groups were recruited for cultural reasons. British immigrants were desired as settlers because they were English speaking, Protestant, and believed to adapt easily to white American culture. The first settlers on the Northern Pacific's Minnesota lands were English, and the Southern Pacific sent promoters to England and Wales in 1884 to tour agriculturally depressed areas to encourage immigration to Southern California.[44]

But Northern Pacific managers soured on English immigrants after the first colonization efforts and only maintained the offices in London and Liverpool because they were the best places from which to direct networks of European agents. Most of the railroad's efforts in the United Kingdom focused on Ireland, Scotland, and Wales, of which railroad managers had no complaints.[45]

Another reason why the Northern Pacific and other railroads focused on Germans, Scandinavians, and other Northern Europeans was that they were primarily interested in selling land to experienced farmers. Railroad agents targeted agricultural areas in Europe where farmers struggled to own or keep their land or where crop prices were often depressed.[46]

Offering generous credit terms and low prices, the Northern Pacific invited the "millions of intelligent and thrifty people in Europe, who must leave their impoverished land, and who love America as the richest gift of God to mankind" to come to its part of the United States.[47]

America was God's gift to the world because only in the United States was work justly rewarded. Speaking of Great Britain, the Northern Pacific claimed:

Here, men work patiently all their lives for a mere living; they are no better off at the end of twenty years' drudgery than at the beginning; they see their families condemned to the same dull round, year in and year out, with few chances of rising to a higher level.... In the North-West of the American continent life and toil wear an aspect wholly different from this. The bondage of caste is unknown; the pain of unrequited labor is unfelt. The English tenant farmer, with a sum not exceeding that which he has paid yearly as rental, becomes the owner there of the broad acres he undertakes to till. The mechanic and laborer are cheered by the experience of others all around them, proving that the employed of this year may be the employers of the next—that, with industry and thrift, sobriety and intelligence, there is nothing that can keep them down.[48]

Although railroads primarily focused their promotional efforts on Europeans in Europe, some companies preferred to target immigrants already in the United States or as they were just arriving at port cities. The Southern Pacific had an agent in New Orleans who spoke English, French, German, and some Italian and who was responsible for meeting arriving steamships, answering questions, and helping immigrants catch trains to California.[49] In 1883, the year the Southern Pacific's sunset route between New Orleans and Los Angeles opened, the railroad hired German immigrant and *New York Herald* journalist Charles Nordhoff to write the pamphlet "A Guide to California the Golden State," which was distributed at the Port of New Orleans to try to convince immigrants to continue west to Southern California.[50]

The Southern Pacific also had an agent, Edwin Hawley, based in New York City, at 339 Broadway and at 6 Bowling Green, near Castle Garden, where he could be close to immigrants arriving on steamships from Europe.[51] The Northern Pacific Railroad opened offices in New York City, Boston, Philadelphia, and Chicago in the 1880s to distribute railroad literature within the United States while still promoting immigration in Europe.[52] And the Northern Pacific distributed maps of its territories to 2,000 banks to hang on their walls for people seeking loans and mortgages to peruse.[53]

The railroads also had active labor recruitment programs to get the thousands of workers necessary to build their lines. After failing to hire enough white American and European immigrant workers in California in 1865, the Southern Pacific turned to Chinese labor contractors who recruited workers from Guangdong (Canton), especially Sze Yap or the four counties of Taishan, Kaiping, Xinhui, and Enping.[54] The Central Pacific and other railroads recruited workers in eastern American cities, particularly Irish immigrants.

But the Southern Pacific did not expect its Chinese workers to remain in the United States after construction was completed in 1869, and it did nothing to encourage Chinese immigrants to stay, such as providing mechanisms by which they could buy railroad land, as the Northern Pacific did in 1872 with German and Scandinavian immigrants it recruited to work on its Yellowstone, Wyoming section of the line.[55] The railroads had separate administrative departments for labor recruitment and immigration promotion, and which groups were targeted by which division depended on whether railroad managers intended those immigrants to settle and stay or work and then return home.

The railroads used several methods to promote immigration from Europe. These included advertising their property in European newspapers and foreign-language newspapers in the United States; distributing promotional literature in Europe through European railroads, steamship lines, and U.S. consul offices; organizing groups to travel and settle as colonies; and providing temporary housing for immigrants once they arrived in the United States.

Immigration promotion by the railroads was first and foremost about publishing and distributing information, reams of it, in the form of posters, flyers, maps, pamphlets, and books. Publications ranged from one-page circulars and posters to books of 50 pages or more of "scientific" data about climate, soil, water, and other factors that determine agricultural possibility and productivity. Between 1871 and 1873, the Northern Pacific published a four-page tabloid newspaper out of its London office entitled *Land and Emigration* and later produced the promotional magazine *Northwest*. As an example of the volume of material it distributed, the Northern Pacific's Land Department claimed in 1883 that it had mailed 2.5 million pieces of literature in response to 60,000 letters of inquiry about the railroad's lands in Minnesota and the Dakotas.[56]

The most successful and influential piece of railroad propaganda was *Sunset Magazine*, established by the Southern Pacific in 1899 to promote California. Published as a monthly, *Sunset* featured articles that celebrated California's diverse natural beauty and Mediterranean climate, and within its first year it had a circulation of 15,000. Through its articles about California history, *Sunset* helped popularize the Spanish colonial revival architectural and decorative arts movements of the 1910s and 1920s and taught Americans and Europeans alike about such exotic products as avocados and artichokes. By 1911, the magazine averaged more than 100,000 copies and 500,000 readers per month.[57] The railroads also advertised heavily in Northern European newspapers, especially those based in port cities, such as Liverpool, Bremen, and Hamburg, to spread the word about the opportunities to own land in America. Some of these newspapers focused primarily, if not exclusively, on immigration.[58] In 1884, the

Northern Pacific was advertising in 200 American and Canadian newspapers, 68 German language newspapers, and 32 Scandinavian American newspapers, and by the late 1880s, the company's Land Department was advertising in 3,385 different newspapers.[59] The railroad both mailed informational publicity releases to newspapers and cultivated relationships with writers and editors to persuade them to write positive articles about the railroad's lands independently. Free railroad passes for newspaper staff helped to encourage this positive coverage.[60]

The Northern Pacific also engaged in concealed advertising, in which promotional material was written by someone not connected to the railroad but for which the Northern Pacific paid. For example, a lawyer in Sweden, Alex Nilsson, convinced the Northern Pacific to pay for half of the printing costs of a booklet Nilsson wrote about Swedish emigration in 1872.[61] Northern Pacific European agent A. Roedelheimer got the publicity departments of several steamship companies to reprint and distribute 15,000 copies of a four-page pamphlet he had written, thus making the pamphlet appear as if it was a product of the steamship lines, not the railroad.[62]

The most successful effort of concealed advertising was when Jay Cooke & Co. trustee agent A. G. Nettleton convinced the postmasters of several large American towns and cities to give the Northern Pacific the addresses of all letters mailed to Europe within a certain period. The Northern Pacific then mailed promotional material to those addresses in the hopes of convincing the recipients that friends or relatives in the United States were sending them information about land in the United States to encourage them to immigrate.[63]

All of the large railroads opened offices in European cities, mainly London and Liverpool, but also Hamburg and Christiana (Oslo) from which they advertised in European newspapers, sent agents to targeted areas to do promotional speaking, and organized the media campaign from that city or country. Railroads also relied upon U.S. consuls' offices and institutional partners, such as banks and steamship lines, as sites from which information about railroad land grants could be distributed. Jay Cooke was the chief financier of the Northern Pacific Railroad, and so when the Northern Pacific began its promotional activities in the early 1870s, the road's president, Frederick Billings, sent its European agent, George Sheppard, to London to operate out of the office of Cooke's British partner, Jay Cooke, McCullough & Co. The Northern Pacific also had a branch office in Liverpool and hired agents in Paris, Rotterdam, Düsseldorf, Geneva, Gothenburg, and Christiania, and retained a publicist in Berlin.[64] Within four months in late 1872, Sheppard had more than doubled the number of agents working in England and Wales, from 44 to 94, and also had agents working in France, the Netherlands, Germany, Norway, Sweden, and Denmark. These agents, who were freelancers and could be found in such diverse businesses as newspaper offices, booksellers, railroad stations, insurance offices, and notary publics, disseminated information and organized meetings of people interested in immigrating.[65]

In anticipation of the completion of the railroad in September 1883, the Northern Pacific blanketed Europe with promotional material about the company's real estate offerings. By this point, the railroad had 831 agents in Great Britain and another 124 agents working in Sweden, Norway, Denmark, the Netherlands, Germany, and Switzerland. The Northern Pacific distributed 632,590 copies of publications in English, Dutch, Swedish, Norwegian, and Danish from the Liverpool office, and literature produced by the railroad was published in English, German, Dutch, Norwegian, Swedish, and Finnish. Agent Roedelheimer visited Switzerland, the Scandinavian countries, and Bremen and Hamburg to promote immigration to the Pacific Northwest, and in particular, to Oregon and Washington.[66]

Between 1877 and 1884, the Southern Pacific Railroad had an office in London, managed by a New York–born dentist and Texas promoter Dr. William G. Kingsbury. Kingsbury traveled extensively around Europe, visiting every country except for Russia and Turkey, to promote immigration to California.[67]

A wide variety of people worked as railroad agents, but the most common were fellow immigrants who could testify to their own success, ministers, and newspaper writers and editors.

The Northern Pacific recruited a variety of people in the United States and in Europe to serve as agents but found that ministers and successful immigrants were particularly effective in encouraging people to immigrate. Established immigrants could speak to their own experiences and give practical advice to would-be immigrants about conditions and help set expectations about life in America. Ministers were experienced public speakers and already had influence with their congregations and communities. Among the ministers recruited by the Northern Pacific were Dr. J. P. Tustin—a minister who had worked for railroads in Michigan and who visited Sweden, Denmark, and Norway in the summer and fall of 1872, persuading religious leaders to bring their congregations to Minnesota.[68]

Col. Hans Mattson, who also served as the secretary of the Minnesota State Board of Immigration, was another effective agent for the Northern Pacific. In 1872–1873, Mattson traveled to Norway and Sweden and brought large numbers of immigrants back to Minnesota with him.

Mattson also used other, earlier immigrants as assistants to encourage family and friends to follow in their suit and emigrate.[69]

Col. Otto von Corvin, a Prussian journalist and 1848 revolutionary, ran the Northern Pacific's press service in Germany in the early 1870s, while another German, Armand Goegg, spent 200 days in 1872 giving public lectures in Germany and Switzerland and the rest of his time writing and distributing a monthly emigration bulletin on behalf of the Northern Pacific Railroad.[70]

Carl Bernhard Schmidt, the European agent for the Atchison, Topeka & Santa Fe Railroad, was one of those successful immigrants who used his connections and experiences with the Old Country to persuade thousands of Europeans to move to the Midwest. Despite coming from an upper-middle-class family (his father was architect to the king of Saxony) and being university educated, he immigrated to the United States in 1864, settling first in St. Louis, Missouri, a city with a large German community. Schmidt married and moved with his family to Lawrence, Kansas, in 1868, where he owned a grocery store and worked as a correspondent for German newspapers.[71]

The Southern Pacific's first colonization agent was Bernhard Marks, a Jewish immigrant from Poland who had come to California as a young man in 1851 and had had a varied career as a store clerk, prospector, and schoolteacher before pioneering raisin farming in Fresno in the mid-1870s. Marks wrote the booklet "Small-Scale Farming in Central California: The Colonization of the Great Valley of the San Joaquin."[72]

The Southern Pacific Railroad preferred to hire newspaper editors and writers to be land and immigration agents. *Sacramento Record Union* newspaper editor William Mills was hired in January 1883 to be the land agent for the Central Pacific railroad but with oversight over Southern Pacific land sales as well.[73] Mills hired his former agricultural editor at the *Record Union*, Isaac N. Hoag, to be the Southern Pacific's first immigration commissioner. Hoag was sent to Chicago in June 1883 to open an office and supervise a network of agents in American cities as well as in London, Bordeaux, Berlin, and Gottenburg. Hoag also established a permanent display of California agricultural products in downtown Chicago and at the Illinois State Fair; arranged for Eastern writers and journalists to travel to California and write about the state, distributed promotional literature, advertised in newspapers, spoke to various groups, and corresponded with people asking questions about California and the Southern Pacific's property there.[74]

A major site of railroad promotion work was at national and international expositions. One of the first events where the Southern Pacific advertised California products was at the Vienna Exposition in 1873, followed by the Centennial Exposition in Philadelphia in 1876 and the Columbian Exposition in Chicago in 1893. Even smaller regional fairs received railroad attention. The Southern Pacific spent approximately $75,000 to promote California at the Industrial and Cotton Exposition in New Orleans in the winter of 1884–1885.[75] In 1894, the Southern Pacific published "California for Health, Pleasure, and Profit: Why You Should Go There" for the Mid-Winter Exposition in San Francisco.[76]

Extolling the beauty, fertility, and availability of their land grants was not enough; railroads went to great lengths to ensure that prospective customers made it to their regions and not to territory belonging to their competitors. This was particularly an issue for railroads focusing on Europeans who faced long journeys first across the Atlantic and then to their desired location.

To facilitate transportation, the Northern Pacific partnered with steamship companies to get railroad tickets bundled with steamship tickets so immigrants could buy an all-in-one transportation package to their ultimate destination.[77] The railroad also negotiated deals with the major British steamship companies—the Inman, the Cunard, the National, and the Allan lines—whereby Northern Pacific agents in Europe were given blocks of train tickets to distribute to immigrants traveling on those lines to allow these people through transportation to St. Paul or Duluth. The Cunard line agreed to freely distribute Northern Pacific literature in Europe as long as the railroad would not sign an exclusive agreement with any particular steamship company.[78]

Most immigrants traveled on a combination ticket, but for those who bought only a steamship ticket, the railroads had agents in New York City meet arriving steamships, answer immigrants' questions, and try to sell train tickets on their lines and not others.[79]

Railroads did not hesitate to try to divert immigrant passengers to their lines and land grants. Although the Union Pacific Railroad was required by the transcontinental charter to honor reduced-fare tickets on the Central Pacific held by California-bound passengers, it often did not and frequently sought to divert Southern Pacific/Central Pacific passengers to buy land in Nebraska and other areas where the Union Pacific owned property rather than continuing to California.[80]

Since the railroads were primarily in the transportation business, the easiest thing they could do for would-be immigrants was to offer free or discounted travel to their new homes. Immigrants and prospective settlers paid full fare for land exploration tickets, but individuals who bought at least 40 acres within 60 days of buying the ticket received a refund and were entitled to free transportation on the railroad line to the property they had purchased. In addition, parties of five or more were entitled to discounts on fares, which further encouraged group purchase and settlement of railroad land. Buyers of Northern Pacific land could also buy on credit, with seven years to pay back the loan.[81]

To recruit settlers, the Southern Pacific Railroad offered "land-seeker's tickets" through the Pacific Coast Land Bureau in San Francisco. A person with such a ticket could travel along the line and scope out possible homestead sites. If he bought railroad land, he could use the attached voucher as cash when he made his first payment.[82]

The Southern Pacific Railroad also provided special accommodations on its rail cars for immigrants traveling to their homesteads. By 1883, the Southern Pacific had placed emigrant cars or tourist sleepers on its Sunset and Ogden lines for people traveling with a one-way ticket. These cars were arranged to allow people to sleep comfortably on the seats at night with no extra charge. Bedding could be either brought by the passenger or bought at the railroad's eating houses along the way.[83]

So eager were some railroads to get immigrants to their lands, and not to another company's, that they provided temporary housing for immigrants once they arrived to the land grant area. As track was laid across Minnesota and west into the Dakotas, the Northern Pacific built three large reception homes, one each in Duluth, Brainerd, and Glyndon, Minnesota, to house newly arrived immigrants until they could buy their land and build their own homes.[84]

The Southern Pacific also developed "emigrant houses" in Texas, San Antonio, Seguin, and Luling, beginning in 1884. Each emigrant house was managed by a Southern Pacific agent who served as an employment agent, maintaining lists of local people who needed workers and matching them with newly arrived immigrants. Unemployed travelers were allowed to stay a week at the house without charge. Many of these immigrants used the emigrant houses as a way of earning quick money on their way to California.[85]

Railroads were interested in selling their land to anyone with enough cash to at least make the required deposit, but the companies with the largest land grants preferred to sell land to groups, called colonies, in the belief that they would be more successful in quickly developing communities along the companies' lines.

In the colony model, a group of people were recruited to pool their resources to buy land together and shared supplies and other resources when needed. Although individuals owned their own land and homes, they could go into debt to either the colony or the railroad or both and could pay off these debts by sharecropping or tenant farming for wealthier members of the community. The railroads also offered generous terms for mortgage repayment. The colony model was particularly appealing to working-class or lower-middle-class people who did not have large amounts of capital on hand to invest in land and tools.[86]

In "California for Health, Pleasure, and Residence: A Book for Travellers and Settlers," promoter Charles Nordhoff encouraged the formation of colonies of 20 to 50 families, relying on railroad land offices as sources of information about climate and agriculture, hiring a colony agent and/or manager, and practicing diversified agriculture and using irrigation.[87]

Some of the most successful colonies the Southern Pacific Railroad developed in Southern California were the cities of Pasadena, which began as the California Colony of Indiana and the San Gabriel Orange Grove Association; Riverside, formerly Judge J. W. North's Southern California Colony Association; and Long Beach, which started as William F. Willmore's American Colony. Other colonies that were heavily promoted by the railroads and their agents were the Centinela Colony (Inglewood), Westminster, Anaheim, the Chicago Colony (Redlands), Lompoc (in Santa Barbara County), and the Central California Colony and the Washington Colony in what is now Fresno.[88]

When the Northern Pacific was organizing its land sales program in the spring of 1872, it hired Major George B. Hibbard to be its commissioner of emigration in charge of its Bureau of Immigration, based in St. Paul. Hibbard was responsible for all aspects of the company's work in relation to immigration, including planning the itineraries and making the travel arrangements for groups of colonists coming from Europe.[89] The first settlers on Northern Pacific land in Minnesota were English immigrants who arrived in May 1872 and founded the Yeovil Colony at Hawley and the Furness Colony at Wadena the following year.[90] The benefit of the colony plan, according to Northern Pacific financier Jay Cooke, was that "neighbors in Fatherland may be neighbors in the new West."[91]

Thanks in large part to the promotional efforts of the Northern Pacific, the populations of the states and territories through which the railroad passed grew dramatically in the late 19th century.

The population of Minnesota, for example, grew from 439,706 people in 1870 to 1,751,394 residents in 1900, and the percentage of immigrants in the state's population ranged between 29 and 35 percent, depending on the decade. Most of the state's foreign-born residents were German, Norwegian, or Swedish, with these groups making up more than half of all immigrants in the state in the late 19th century.[92]

The Dakota Territory grew from a mere 14,181 residents in 1870 to a combined population of 720,716 people in 1900 (the Dakotas were divided into South Dakota and North Dakota in 1889). The foreign born made up between 28 and 38 percent, depending on the decade. Most of these immigrants came from Norway, Canada, Russia, Germany, Great Britain, and Sweden.[93]

In Montana and Washington, too, the Northern Pacific contributed significantly to those territories' population growth. In Montana, the majority of settlers between 1870 and 1900 were English and Canadian, German, and Chinese; of these, only the Chinese were not recruited by the railroads to be settlers.[94] In Washington, most foreign-born residents were from Canada, Great Britain, and after 1890, increasingly from Germany, Sweden, and Norway, countries where the Northern Pacific had aggressively recruited immigrants.[95]

Kansas also nearly quadrupled its population between 1870 and 1890, from 364,399 residents to 1,427,096 persons, largely thanks to the efforts of the Atchison, Topeka & Santa Fe Railroad. Most immigrants in Kansas were from Great Britain, Germany, and Sweden.[96]

But despite the efforts of the Santa Fe Railroad to develop New Mexico and Arizona, Northern Europeans could not be attracted to the Southwest. The largest immigrant group in New Mexico and Arizona were Mexicans—not surprising, given the territories' location and historical connection to Mexico. New Mexico and Arizona did not gain enough white population to become states until 1912, and most of these white settlers were native-born Americans.[97]

California's population did grow, in part due to the promotional efforts of the Southern Pacific to develop Southern California. In 1870, the combined population of Los Angeles, San Diego, and San Bernardino counties was only 24,248 people.[98]

By 1900, Los Angeles County had grown to 170,298 residents, from 101,454 in 1890, and the City of Los Angeles had more than doubled its population from 50,395 in 1890 to 102,479 in 1900. Several other communities in Los Angeles County experienced explosive growth in the 1890s: the City of Long Beach had grown from 564 to 2,252 residents, Whittier from 585 to 1,590 residents, Rowland from 736 to 2,051 residents, and South Pasadena from 623 to 1,001 residents in 10 years.[99]

Railroads were successful in selling off their land grants to Northern Europeans and white Americans by emphasizing the message of personal and financial independence through property ownership and unlimited opportunity on a safe, limitless frontier. But this message was an easier sell east of the hundredth meridian than west of it, as both Europeans and Americans attempted to establish farms on arid lands frequently plagued by drought and other forms of extreme weather. But with their land grants sold off, railroad corporations could once again focus on transportation, not real estate, and what happened to their former property was no longer the companies' concern.

Religious and philanthropic groups that promoted immigration did not have the railroads' profit motives or incentives and so were interested in the fates of the people they persuaded to immigrate.

CHAPTER FOUR

Selling the Promised Land: Religious and Philanthropic Promotion

In addition to state agencies and railroads, a wide variety of private, corporate, and not-for-profit philanthropic organizations encouraged the immigration of various ethnic and religious groups to the United States in the 19th and early 20th centuries. The most active of these organizations focused on relocating Mormon converts from Great Britain and Scandinavia to Utah and settling Russian Jewish immigrants in rural areas.

These ethnic and religious societies differed from other promotional agencies and organizations in that by focusing on one particular group, they had already decided that members of that community were desirable as immigrants and future American citizens. The messages of ethnic and religious organizations promoting immigration also differed from those of state agencies and railroads.

For members of the Church of Jesus Christ of Latter-day Saints (LDS), a core principle of their faith was living together with other LDS members. European converts were expected to immigrate first to the Mormon community of Kirkland, Ohio, later Nauvoo, Illinois, and then after 1847, to the Territory of Utah. It was not until the mid-1890s that LDS officials in Salt Lake City began to encourage converts to remain and develop congregations in their home countries. An estimated 55,000 British and more than 22,000 Scandinavian (mostly Danish) converts emigrated between

1840 and 1900, many with financial and logistical support from the LDS Church.[1] Although the LDS Church did not use its subsidy of immigration as a way of gaining converts, Mormonism's uniquely American character made immigration an important aspect of LDS missionary work in Europe. LDS missionaries were promoting both a new religion and a new country to prospective European converts, and these ideas were deeply intertwined in LDS theology.

In the case of Jews, in particular, but also with other groups, the idea of religious liberty and its constitutional protection was stressed by promoters. America was a place where people could practice their religions freely, and even Jews could live safely in a predominantly Christian country, unlike in many European countries. But the promotion of immigration among Russian Jews by American Jews was filled with tensions and contradictions: American Jews wished to help their coreligionists being persecuted for their faith in Europe, but they also feared that an increase in Russian Jewish immigration would trigger more anti-Semitism in the United States and result in legislation restricting immigration.

Therefore, American Jewish immigration promotion focused on youth, health, and skills, seeking to recruit only young, healthy, and strong individuals who would be capable of hard manual or skilled labor. Jews who would reinforce the stereotype of the tubercular tailor or the elderly peddler or who would not work on Saturday (the Jewish Sabbath) were not wanted by American Jewish colonization groups.[2]

Mormons and Jews were not the only groups that attempted to immigrate as organized religious groups. Catholics in Great Britain, Ireland, and the Protestant German states; dissenters from Lutheranism in Norway and Sweden; and many other religious minorities throughout Europe suffered discrimination, harassment, and persecution in countries with state churches. Immigration promoters often targeted dissenting ministers in such countries to persuade their congregations to emigrate as colonies. Many of these church members emigrated together but then found it challenging to maintain group unity once in America. The checkerboard pattern of public land and railroad land made it difficult for congregation members to buy property next to one another.

Ironically, religious liberty also encouraged disbursement and assimilation, as the external pressure from European governments and state churches that had previously held congregations together was removed. With church attendance now a personal choice, only the more devoted members stayed in the congregation. Of the many religious groups that immigrated in the 19th century, only tightly organized sects like the Mennonites and Hutterites tended to stay together, primarily because they already had extensive experience with self-segregation and communal living in Europe.[3]

Mormon immigrants were successful in maintaining group unity because they were immigrating specifically as an expression of their faith and entered into a tightly organized religious community, experiencing sometimes intense harassment and persecution in the United States.

Founded by Joseph Smith in upstate New York in the mid-1820s, the LDS is a particularly American religion. The LDS teaches, among other things, that North America is the geographic site of Zion; that the Garden of Eden is located in Jackson County, Missouri; that Jesus visited North America after his resurrection; that North America was settled by ancient Mesopotamians and Israelites; that American Indians are the descendents of these ancient Hebrew tribes; and that Utah will be a place of sanctuary for God's chosen people in the Last Days. In addition, Mormonism as a faith exemplified several core American values: progress, democracy, upward mobility, meritocracy, utopianism, messianism, and pioneering.[4]

Mormonism emerged out of a context of tremendous social change and economic expansion in America and was just one of many religious, utopian, and social movements that rejected the individualism and market capitalism of antebellum American society and sought to reform it through such things as temperance, better diet, and communal living.[5]

In 1837, less than 15 years after founding the LDS Church, Smith sent the first set of missionaries to Great Britain, and these new "apostles" quickly tapped into British people's discontentment with the established Church of England. The LDS missionaries made their greatest inroads among working-class people, who were alienated from the class system within the Anglican Church and who were often already attracted to Methodism and other dissenting faiths.[6] In May 1840, pioneering missionary Parley Pratt started publishing the London-based newspaper *Latter-day Saints' Millennial Star*, which mixed Mormon theology with descriptions of the beauty of the new Eden that was the American frontier. In June 1840, the first shipload of 41 British converts sailed for New Orleans, destined for the Mormon colony of Nauvoo.[7]

The common language and similar culture between the United States and Great Britain made Mormon missionary work there obvious, but the LDS Church also had great success in Scandinavia, particularly Denmark, once that country granted freedom of religion in 1849. But even Norwegian and Swedish government and church harassment of Mormon missionaries in the 1850s worked in the LDS Church's favor, as the theme of persecution for revealing the "true faith" was an important Mormon message in the United States as well as in Scandinavia.[8]

One of the distinctive things about the church Smith was building was its emphasis on communal living. The LDS Church was not just a new faith; it was creating a new society on the American frontier. Upon converting, LDS members were expected to turn their property over to church leaders, who would redistribute it according to each family's needs, with surpluses being used to support the poor and the church's organizational needs.[9] But the poverty of many European converts meant that they could not afford to pay for the trans-Atlantic passage and/or the long journey from Eastern ports to Utah themselves.

To assist with this emigration, the LDS Church established the Perpetual Emigrating Fund (PEF) in 1850. The PEF solicited donations from wealthier church members and loaned transportation money to immigrants, who were expected to pay back the loan once they were settled in Utah, although many never actually did. By the time the fund was dissolved in 1887, it had helped approximately 26,000 European converts travel to Utah out of a total emigration of 85,000 people.[10]

Church members organized all aspects of the immigration, from raising money for the PEF, chartering ships, distributing information about sailings and costs, and providing information about what emigrant converts should bring with them. Missionaries served as passenger agents, cutting out for-profit middlemen, and ensured that emigrants had sufficient food and water on the ships. They also made sure converts got to the docks on time, sailed with them to America, and held daily religious services and other organized activities on board ship to foster a sense of community and congregation among the Mormon passengers. Once the converts reached America, initially New Orleans and later various other Atlantic ports, a church emigration agent met them and arranged for their travel to first a frontier outfitting point and then to Utah. Thousands of British converts walked to Utah from Iowa City, pulling their belongings in handcarts, when the church struggled to outfit wagon trains in the

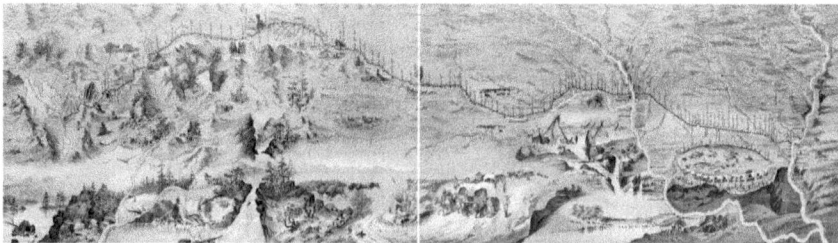

Millroy & Hayes, "Route of the Mormon pioneers from Nauvoo to Great Salt Lake, Feb'y 1846–July 1847," Salt Lake City, c. 1899. (Library of Congress)

1850s. In Utah, church officials provided temporary housing until immigrants could be assigned and escorted to a community.[11]

In its proselytizing in Europe, LDS missionaries did not simply offer a subsidized, easy way to emigrate. They were offering a new life in a new territory, a place where a convert could live his or her new faith as it was intended and wait for the Second Coming of Christ while communally building the Kingdom of God. Many British converts were factory workers who had to reinvent themselves as pioneer farmers in Utah, which meant that this opportunity for radical transformation was real for many people.[12]

As Parley Pratt wrote in the *Latter-day Saint Millennial Star*: "But let it ever be remembered that this is a new country, so that those who come to this place should not be surprised nor murmur if some of them should have to make brick; if some should have to quarry stone, and prepare and put them in their place."[13]

Land ownership through the Homestead Act also became possible after 1862 as the LDS Church eventually abandoned its insistence on communal living and shared property ownership.[14]

But as in other parts of the West, what Mormon settlers considered open, available land had long belonged to other people. When LDS Church leader Brigham Young decided to move his followers to Utah in 1846, the territory was still part of Mexico and largely populated by Ute Indians. In the Mexican-American War of 1846–1848, Mexico lost this territory to the United States, but the Ute never recognized or accepted foreign sovereignty over their land. In 1865, war between Mormon settlers and the Ute broke out when some Ute refused to move south to a reservation in western Colorado.[15]

Although LDS Church leaders wanted to create a separate society in the Salt Lake desert, they still found themselves dependent on the U.S. federal government and its diplomatic and military power to seize Utah away from its Mexican and Ute owners.

Thanks to LDS-organized immigration, Utah's non-Indian population soared from 11,380 residents in 1850 to 143,963 people in 1880, and 30 percent of these were foreign born, mainly from Great Britain, Denmark, and Sweden.[16] Even after the LDS Church ended its formal immigration assistance, the immigration of European converts to Utah continued, as church theology emphasized the idea of a new Zion in the American desert.

The promotion of immigration among European Jews by Jewish colonization organizations was as institutionally organized as the migration to Utah by the LDS Church but much less successful in establishing Jewish communities.

There were two waves of Jewish colonization efforts: the first in the 1880s, in reaction to pogroms in Russia, and the second in the early 1900s, as Jewish immigration to the United States reached record numbers after the failed Russian Revolution of 1905 intensified anti-Semitism in Russia.

After the first large-scale Russian pogroms started in 1881, thousands of Jews fled Russia for the United States, most settling in large Eastern cities, especially New York. Yet a small number were recruited by philanthropist groups to settle on farms. Another small minority of Jewish immigrants already in the United States were assisted in their efforts to relocate to the Midwest and West.

The two main Jewish colonization groups—the Baron de Hirsch Fund and the Alliance Israelite Universelle—were both European and strongly influenced by the idea that agriculture was the fundamental basis for society and economy. These colonization organizations believed that Jews could and should be agricultural people and that it was only medieval anti-Semitic laws that prohibited Jews from owning land that kept Central and Eastern European Jews from practicing agriculture. American Jews connected to the Alliance and the Baron de Hirsch Fund were also influenced by Jeffersonian ideas about the productivity and morality of agriculture in society.

The Alliance was founded by Adolphe Crémieux in Paris in 1860 to protect Jews' civil rights and to encourage education and agriculture among the Jewish diaspora, especially in the Middle East. The Baron de Hirsch Fund acquired land through its Jewish Colonization Association and established Jewish agricultural colonies in Canada, the United States, Argentina, Brazil, and Palestine.[17]

Between 1881 and 1884, more than 200 pogroms against Jews occurred in southwestern Russia (today's Poland and Ukraine), as Jews were blamed for the March 13, 1881, assassination of Czar Alexander II (in fact, the assassins were left-wing Russian revolutionaries, not Jews). The ensuing violence, property destruction, and the repressive May Laws, which severely restricted the few civil rights Jews had in Russia, caused thousands of Jews to leave, mostly to the United States but also to Great Britain. Between 1870 and 1879, there were approximately 35,000 immigrants to the United States from Russia; between 1880 and 1889, 182,700 Russians immigrated (virtually all of them Jewish). Between 1890 and 1919, more than 3 million people emigrated from Russia to the United States, most of them Jews.[18]

This dramatic increase in Eastern European Jewish immigration to the United States overwhelmed existing Jewish charities and caused American

Thomas Nast, "Exiles from Russia–their first day in New York," from a sketch by S.F. Yeager, *Harper's Weekly*, February 18. 1882, p. 109. (Library of Congress)

Jews, most of whom were of German heritage and secular in lifestyle, to worry about the assimilability of the newcomers. German American Jews also feared that a mass immigration of poor, ultraorthodox, very traditional Jews would trigger anti-Semitism in the United States.[19] German American Jews wanted to help their Eastern brethren but feared the social consequences of associating too closely with them.

Jewish colonization schemes were influenced in part by Irish Catholic farm colonies and were based on two principles: "no colony should be organized upon the communistic or co-operative plan, and that the refugees should not be disposed of collectively, but individually," and "colonization must be conducted strictly on business principles and not as a charity," according to Julius Goldman of the Hebrew Emigrant Aid Society in 1882.[20]

This rejection of communal living was the result of the stereotype held by both American Jews and non-Jews that Russian Jews were susceptible to Marxist and other foreign ideas of social organization and because individualism was seen as a core American value that immigrants had to embrace in order to assimilate. The tension between charity and business would also plague Jewish immigration promotion programs. Jewish immigration promoters wanted immigrants who were hardworking, frugal, and eager and able to pay off their debts quickly. Cognizant of the fact that anti-Semitic laws in Russia had prevented Jews from owning land and thus gaining farming experience, Jewish immigration promoters readily embraced the dubious belief that experience was not necessary for success, only hard work and patience. The fertility of the land in America meant that even novice farmers could be successful.

"All practical Western farmers, and all those who have had dealings with them, concur in the opinion that farming in the West on virgin soil requires no previous knowledge or experience. It is mainly a question of observation and imitation, accompanied by such advice as is easily obtained," Goldman insisted after he traveled to Minnesota and the Dakotas in 1882 to investigate the possibility of organizing a colony of Russian Jewish refugees in one of those territories.[21] Although this colony was never developed, the idea that inexperienced city residents could successfully farm persisted among Jewish immigration promoters.

The Alliance Israelite Universelle was primarily interested in establishing schools for Jews in the Ottoman Empire, but the organization did partner with prominent New York Jewish Americans to try to start up Jewish agricultural colonies in the United States. The first, Sicily Island, was established in Louisiana in 1881 with 20 families, who abandoned the colony after a flood in the spring of 1882 washed away their homes and crops.[22]

More successful was Alliance, a Jewish agricultural community established in 1882 in Pitts Grove, Salem County, New Jersey—a hundred miles from New York City and 40 miles from Philadelphia. The Alliance Israelite Universelle, the Hebrew Emigrant Aid Society of New York City, and New Jersey's commissioner of immigration, who happened to be a local real estate agent, partnered together to buy 1,000 acres of land, which was then handed to the Alliance Land Company, which was owned by the initial 43 families settling Alliance.[23] Within a few years, Alliance became the center of a Jewish colonization movement in southern New Jersey, with several hundred Jewish families living and farming in the region. The Alliance Israelite Universelle and other Jewish philanthropies paid for Jewish immigrants' transportation and encouraged them to farm and to develop local businesses, such as canneries and garment factories, to provide nonfarm employment.[24]

The Baron de Hirsch Fund was also active in developing Jewish agricultural colonies in the United States. Baron Moritz von Hirsch auf Gereuth had been born in Munich and was the son of the first Jew allowed to own land in Bavaria. He became a banker like his father and donated large sums to the Alliance Israelite Universelle, among other Jewish charities. In 1891, Hirsch established the Jewish Colonization Association with an endowment of £2 million, a sum that was increased to £11 million in 1899. The purpose of the association was to promote and assist the emigration of Jews from the Middle East and Europe and to establish agricultural colonies of Jewish immigrants in North and South America. The colonization association also funded a wide variety of educational programs and businesses, including model farms, factories, and credit unions and savings and loan banks to help support its colonization efforts.[25]

Hirsch also funded the Jewish Agricultural and Industrial Aid Society (JAIAS) in 1900 with an initial grant of $2.4 million and regular subsidies following. The purpose of the JAIAS was to educate and assist "Hebrew emigrants from Europe" and their children by granting loans to agriculturalists, transporting immigrants from port of arrival to places of employment, training them in mechanics and handicrafts, and offering instruction in English and agriculture.[26]

The colony of Woodbine was the largest agricultural colony promoted by the Baron de Hirsch Fund in the United States. Established in 1892 in Cape May County in southern New Jersey, Woodbine started out with 60 families, who were "South Russians, for it was believed that they would make the best farmers."[27] But of the original 60 families, only 15 had emigrated directly from Russia to Woodbine; the rest had been living in the New York City area for a few years.[28]

To recruit Jews for its colonies, the Baron de Hirsch Fund stationed agents at immigration centers in New York, Baltimore, and Philadelphia to meet steamships when they arrived. It also used its connections to the Alliance and Jewish Territorial Organization's Jewish Emigration Society in Russia to recruit immigrants.

The Baron de Hirsch Fund earmarked $240,000 toward the colony and capitalized the Woodbine Land and Improvement Company with $50,000. The directors of the company were the trustees of the Baron de Hirsch Fund, which held all of the capital stock. The fund bought 5,300 acres for $37,500 and appointed Dr. H. L. Sabsovich, an agricultural chemist, to be the superintendent of the colony. Woodbine was laid out into 30-acre farms, plus town lots and a commercial district, with a layout similar to a medieval English village. Besides farming, the other primary source of income for the colonists was to be the cloak manufacturer Myer Jonasson & Co. of New York City, which employed 150 people.[29]

The original colonists signed contracts that would give them ownership of 30-acre farms after 12 years, with the average cost of a farm being $1,100. For the first three years, the colonists would pay an annual rent of $50; they were to receive a deed to their land after paying $200 and gaining a mortgage for the land and their homes. The Baron de Hirsch Fund and the trustees of the Woodbine Land and Improvement Company expected the immigrants' children to help support their families by working in the cloak factory while the parents cleared the land and developed the farms. The fund anticipated that it would take four years for the agricultural part of Woodbine to be developed, during which time additional factories would be started that would create a local market for the farms' produce.[30]

When in the spring of 1893, 58 of the 60 heads of households refused to sign the leases for the farms in protest of the terms and living conditions at Woodbine, the fund decided to evict the leaders of the colonists' revolt.[31]

Eventually, after the colonists hired lawyers and gained the attention of the New York press, both Jewish and non-Jewish, the Baron de Hirsch Fund agreed to negotiate with the Woodbine residents. The Woodbine Land and Improvement Company provided the colonists with work until their land was cleared and ready for farming; lease terms were modified and interest payments were postponed until October 1894; the price of farmhouses, livestock, clearing, and plowing was reduced; and the company agreed to pay for necessary repairs to people's homes and farm buildings.[32]

Besides the inexperience of its residents in farming, Woodbine faced the additional challenge that the Panic of 1893 had begun just as the colony was getting started. The Myer Jonasson factory, which was to be the economic foundation of the colony until the farms began producing, failed and had to be replaced by another clothing manufacturer, the Guy Haas Company, which demanded that the Hirsch Fund subsidize it by reimbursing it for losses caused by the poor workmanship of inexperienced workers. Despite a subsidy of $160/month for six months, the Guy Haas Company failed in February 1896.[33]

For most of the 1890s, the Baron de Hirsch Fund found itself in the position of having to bribe manufacturing businesses with free or discounted facilities and utilities to relocate to Woodbine and then having to subsidize them further once they had opened shop to provide employment for Woodbine residents.[34]

Unlike many other agricultural colonies, Woodbine survived in large part because its location provided good access to both the Philadelphia and New York City markets for both agricultural and industrial products. Heavy subsidies from the Baron de Hirsch Fund and the Jewish Colonization Association also helped keep Woodbine and its industrial economy afloat. By 1910, Woodbine had nearly 2,400 residents, was incorporated as a municipality in 1903, and was the home of the Baron de Hirsch Agricultural College, established in 1894.[35]

Although a central goal of the Alliance and Baron de Hirsch Fund colonization efforts was to preserve Jewish culture and religion by protecting and relocating Jews, the communities developed by these groups in the United States were more Jewish American than simply Jewish. Architecturally, Woodbine resembled an English village more than a

Russian Jewish village, and its neatly gridded streets were named after American presidents, poets, and other important cultural and political figures and lined with single-family homes. Besides building a school and a synagogue, Woodbine's colonists also built baseball fields and parks, reflecting their embrace of American popular culture.[36] Although Alliance no longer exists as a functioning community, Woodbine is still an incorporated municipality in New Jersey, with approximately 2,500 residents.[37]

The second phase of Jewish agricultural colony development began in the early 1900s, as a new wave of Eastern European Jewish immigration began in reaction to increased anti-Semitism in Russia. Believing that if Jews were better distributed throughout the United States versus clustering in Eastern cities they would assimilate more quickly and undermine anti-Semitic immigration restriction arguments, Jewish American philanthropists, as well as the Baron de Hirsch Fund, began encouraging Jewish immigrants to move to smaller cities in the American interior. The most concerted effort in this area was the Galveston Plan, in which Jewish immigrants were encouraged to enter the United States at Galveston, Texas, versus New York between 1907 and 1914.[38]

The German American Jewish banker Jacob Schiff, along with the European-based Jewish Territorial Organization (ITO) and the New York–based Industrial Removal Office (IRO), developed the Galveston Plan, which was responsible for helping approximately 10,000 Jews enter the United States through Galveston over the course of seven years.[39]

The Jewish Territorial Organization had been founded by the British playwright and Zionist activist Israel Zangwill in 1905 to encourage the creation of a Jewish homeland somewhere in the world. Acting on the suggestion from Schiff, the ITO created an Emigration Regulation Department, which in turn established a Jewish Emigration Society, based in Kiev, Ukraine. The Industrial Removal Office, which had been created in 1901 in reaction to a surge in Jewish immigration from Romania after increased anti-Semitism in that country, established a Jewish Immigrants' Information Bureau (JIIB) in Galveston in January 1907, once that port had been chosen as the best one through which to send the recruited immigrants. IRO manager David Bressler's assistant, Morris D. Waldman, was sent to Galveston to organize the JIIB and establish receiving facilities at the port, after Schiff successfully lobbied secretary of commerce and labor Oscar Straus (the only Jewish cabinet member) to open an immigration station at the Port of Galveston.[40]

Galveston was chosen as the southern port for several reasons: immigration promoters in Charleston only wanted Anglo-Saxon immigrants,

New Orleans was plagued by yellow fever, and most importantly, one of the largest German steamship companies then transporting large numbers of Russian Jews, North German Lloyd, sailed from Bremen to Galveston, via Baltimore, and had done so since the 1880s.[41]

The Jewish Emigration Society established a network of 82 committees throughout the Russian Pale of Settlement where Jews were segregated. These committees distributed literature in Yiddish, describing opportunities in the western United States. Acting under IRO instructions, the Jewish Emigration Society was to focus its propaganda and recruitment efforts on people under the age of 40 as well as ironworkers, carpenters, cabinetmakers, butchers, plumbers, tinsmiths, painters, paper-hangers, shoemakers, tailors, masons, and machinists. Reflecting American Jews' belief that orthodox observation of Judaism was in many ways incompatible with American life, the Jewish Emigration Society was directed to specifically discourage religiously observant people who would not work on the Jewish Sabbath, as well as ritual slaughterers and Hebrew teachers, from immigrating through Galveston, because they were seen as either work-shy or unemployable in America. Schiff and Bressler also wanted the Jewish Emigration Society to discourage peddlers, clerks, and shopkeepers from immigrating because they feared it would be difficult to find such people jobs. People who already had family in America were also not wanted for the Galveston Plan because they were seen as less flexible about where they settled.[42]

Prospective emigrants paid for their train and steamship tickets to Bremen and then to Galveston, although Western European Jewish charities such as the Baron de Hirsch Fund often helped Russian Jews pay for their transportation. The Jewish Emigration Society also provided Galveston-bound immigrants with letters of introduction to the Hilfsverein der deutschen Juden (German Jewish Aid Society) in Bremen and to the JIIB in Galveston. The Hilfsverein was responsible for protecting the emigrants in Bremen and also worked with North German Lloyd to ensure fair treatment of Jews on board ship. Once a ship with Galveston-bound passengers left Bremen, the Hilfsverein wired Bressler in New York City with the name of the ship and the number of emigrants on board, and Bressler forwarded this information to the JIIB in Galveston. Bressler also received a list of expected Jews from the Jewish Emigration Society. The JIIB then determined where to send the emigrants once they arrived in Galveston, using a network of B'nai B'rith fraternal lodges. Immigrants were temporarily housed in a JIIB-owned building near the port until they could be sent to their new homes. To provide an incentive to local Jewish communities to help new arrivals find jobs and housing, the JIIB paid an allowance of 10 dollars per immigrant or 25 dollars per family. The JIIB also employed employment agents at salaries of about 60 dollars a month, plus the allowance, to help immigrants find work. Once a person was settled in a new community, the address was sent to the Hilfsverein and to the ITO, which in turn informed the Jewish Emigration Society in Kiev so other family and friends could join the person in America.[43] The operations of the IRO and the JIIB were paid for by Schiff, who donated $500,000 to the Galveston movement.[44]

To placate Galveston's small Jewish community and gain its support and assistance, very few Russian Jews remained in Galveston but rather were immediately sent to other communities. Out of 10,000 people distributed between 1907 and 1914, fewer than 300 stayed in Galveston.[45]

The Galveston movement faced several significant obstacles in its goal of distributing Jewish immigrants to the interior of the United States. The Panic of 1907, which began in the fall, caused a depression and a decline in available jobs until 1909, just as the Galveston Plan was being implemented by the Jewish Emigration Society in Russia. The Jewish Emigration Society itself faced the problem that the Russian government deemed the promotion of emigration illegal, because so many Jewish men sought to escape compulsory military service by emigrating. Then, in 1910, as the Galveston movement had achieved momentum and was sending hundreds of Russian Jews through Galveston, immigration authorities at Galveston began scrutinizing Jewish immigrants more carefully and deporting many under the vague category of "Liable to Become a Public Charge" if an immigrant did not have at least 25 dollars, although there was no legal minimum amount of money an immigrant was required to have upon entry. Another ground for deportation was on the basis of the even vaguer health diagnosis of "weak physique," which supposedly would prevent the immigrant from being able to earn a living. This increase in deportations in 1910 caused the IRO and the JIIB to call for the temporary suspension of Galveston-bound immigrants from Russia. It was not until 1911 that the Jewish Emigration Society began sending Russian Jews again to Galveston.[46] The percentage of immigrants excluded at Galveston was 5 percent, compared to 1 percent at New York and other ports, a significant difference.[47]

Other problems that the Galveston movement faced were that it took about 23 days to get to Galveston, about one week longer than it took to get to New York, and the absence of large Jewish communities into which people could settle. Most Russian Jewish immigrants wanted to go to New York City, where many people already had friends and family and which was seen as the center of American Jewish life.[48]

The IRO and the JIIB also faced criticism, especially from restriction-ists both within and without the federal government, that their activities constituted immigration recruitment and thus violated contract labor laws. The fact that the JIIB helped Galveston-bound immigrants find jobs caused the federal government to question the entire enterprise. The IRO and the JIIB insisted that it was only "dissuading the weak and the unfit, and directing with information and advice those fit to go, but in no case stimulating or inducing anyone to leave Russia for America. This is an important point and one that the [Galveston] Bureau strictly insisted upon and conscientiously carried out, as it did not wish in the remotest way to appear as an encourager of immigration to this country," IRO man-ager David M. Bressler wrote.[49] American Jewish activists such as Bressler were hypersensitive to any charge of illegality or favoritism on the part of Straus (or other government officials) because of their fear of reinforcing the anti-Semitic stereotype of the manipulative, untrustworthy Jew. The Industrial Removal Office was closely involved with the implementation of the Galveston Plan, but that effort was part of the IRO's larger work to distribute Eastern European Jews out of the Eastern cities and throughout the Midwest and West. The IRO was officially part of the Jewish Agricul-tural and Industrial Aid Society, which had been created by the Baron de Hirsch Fund and the Jewish Colonization Association in 1900, but it operated largely independently of the JAIAS. Relying on B'nai B'rith's national network of lodges, the IRO was a not-for-profit Jewish employ-ment agency. It collected information from local communities about job opportunities in their towns and then advertised in the Yiddish press in New York City, Boston, and Philadelphia, encouraging people to apply to the IRO for help in relocating to those jobs.[50]

The purpose of what the IRO called "distribution" was to help with Eastern European Jews' social and cultural (but not religious) assimilation and reduce Eastern cities' problems of unemployment due to high job competition and overcrowding. Rejecting restrictionists' and eugenicists' arguments that Jews could not assimilate into American society, Bressler, Waldman, Schiff, and other IRO supporters argued that Jews would and could assimilate quickly and easily once they were living outside of New York's Lower East Side and exposed to the "American" way of life.[51]

Applicants seeking IRO help were investigated to determine their suit-ability, both economically and socially, for relocation. Despite the pater-nalism of IRO leaders, the agency received more applications for help than people it ultimately relocated, so there was a relatively high demand for assistance on the part of New York City Jews.[52]

Between 1901 and 1922, the IRO helped "distribute" 79,000 immigrants to Midwestern and Western cities and towns. The states that received the most Jewish immigrants via the IRO were Ohio, Illinois, Missouri, Michigan, California, Pennsylvania, New York, and Wisconsin.[53]

Besides the IRO, the United Hebrew Charities (UHC) also helped relocate Jews west; between 1874 and 1911, UHC helped up to 24,300 immigrants move out of Eastern cities.[54]

But for all of the work and money contributed by both European and American Jews to encourage Eastern European Jews to move out of New York City and settle in small towns and on farms, few Eastern European Jewish immigrants did so. It would be several generations before large numbers of American Jews moved to suburban areas in other states.

Jewish immigration promotion organizations such as the Jewish Agricultural and Industrial Aid Society, the Jewish Colonization Association, and the Industrial Removal Office were well organized and well funded but ultimately failed to encourage large numbers of Russian Jews to settle in rural areas because Jewish immigrants were not interested in, or had no experience with, an agricultural life. The Church of Jesus Christ of Latter-day Saints was much more successful in promoting immigration to America among its European converts because immigration to Utah was understood by converts to be one of the requirements of conversion.

The promotion of immigration to America by state governments was much more common than promotion by religious and ethnic groups. Midwestern states resumed their promotional programs after the Civil War, while Western and Southern states sought to catch up and attract immigrants to their regions.

CHAPTER FIVE

Immigration Promotion in the Midwest, 1865–1914

Midwestern states either resumed or initiated immigration policies after the Civil War within the context of two larger policy goals of the United States: the first was the long-term diplomatic and military effort to force Native Americans off their lands and move them further west and then to segregate them onto ever-shrinking reservations. The second was the redistribution of conquered or ceded Indian land to individuals, states, and railroad corporations through the land grant system and the Homestead Act of 1862. And refusing to stay in the background of all of this population movement was the environmental problem of recurring drought and extreme weather that significantly affected people's ability to transform the Great Plains' portion of the Midwest into an agriculturally productive region.

The immediate post–Civil War period was a busy time for immigration promotion. Immigration had been depressed during the war, and 18 states passed laws in favor of increasing immigration to their jurisdictions between 1866 and 1871, including, in the Midwest, Indiana, Wisconsin, Michigan, the Dakota Territory, Iowa, and Nebraska.

Midwestern states that already had a history of immigration promotion, as Michigan, Wisconsin, and Minnesota did, took advantage of the federal government's land and Indian policies and used their promotional experience to expand their efforts to recruit immigrants to their regions. Other Midwestern states and territories that had not promoted immigration before the Civil War, such as Iowa, Nebraska, and the Dakotas, joined the movement but struggled to compete with their more experienced neighbors.

Yet regardless of a state's experience with immigration promotion, Midwestern state promotional policies lacked consistency, as cost-conscious legislatures and governors cut appropriations, refused to reimburse agents, replaced agents with political favorites, and terminated and then revived agencies, then killed them off again when a new administration entered the governor's mansion or a new faction gained control of the state house. With railroads, newspapers, and private real estate interests all vigorously selling their sections of the Midwest, it was sometimes hard to justify spending taxpayer money on immigration promotion.

During the post–Civil War period of the 19th century, the Republican Party dominated Midwestern politics, except for the early 1890s, when the very unpopular and very high (50 percent) tariff of 1890 and the Panic of 1893–1896 caused Republicans to lose control of several Midwestern states, albeit for only a few years. Although the Democratic Party also supported Indian removal, the United States' policy of land confiscation and redistribution was primarily implemented by the Republican Party, and it was one element of the Republicans' post–Civil War economic program; the abolition of slavery, the subsidization of railroads, an open-door immigration policy, a national banking system, a national currency, and a high tariff on manufactured goods were the others. The Democratic Party had supported immigration promotion and won the support of urban immigrant voters before the Civil War with its rejection of nativism, but the Republican Party positioned itself as the party of immigration, and of immigrants, after the war. Republicans created a winning coalition of Midwestern and Western farmers (many of them immigrants), Midwestern and Eastern urban factory workers (a growing number of them also immigrants), and capitalists that allowed the party to dominate American politics until the 1930s. Immigration promotion at the state level was part of the larger Republican economic program, although support was often fickle, depending on the personalities of the politicians involved.[1]

State immigration promoters stressed the great natural and material wealth of the United States, while at the same time claiming that their particular regions were the most fertile, most prosperous, and most beautiful in the country. Established states argued that they had the best of both worlds: available land and settled society, while less developed states and territories claimed true opportunity for wealth and success was only possible on the frontier. But all of the Midwestern states with immigration promotion policies disseminated the idea that anyone of reasonable intelligence, ambition, and the willingness to work could prosper in America, and that the United States was a unique place of economic and social mobility as well as personal and political freedom.[2]

Greatly facilitating Midwestern states' message of economic opportunity and mobility was the passage of the Homestead Act of 1862, which granted up to 160 acres of public land to individuals willing to reside on and cultivate the acres for five years. Eligibility was generous: for a 10-dollar fee an American citizen—or alien who had filed his first papers stating his intention to become an American citizen—could apply for land. Applicants had to be at least 21 years old, or be the head of a family, or had to have served in the U.S. Army or Navy and had not, or were not currently, engaged in fighting against the Union in the Civil War.[3]

The fact that the Homestead Act and its amendments allowed noncitizens who had taken out first papers to apply for tracts both allowed Europeans to gain access to land and encouraged the naturalization of these new settlers. If a newly arrived immigrant took out his first papers and then immediately filed a claim under the Homestead Act, he could achieve both his citizenship and his ownership of the land after five years.

But the Homestead Act was not, by itself, a major inducement to immigration from Europe; the Civil War discouraged immigration, and Northern European farmers were relatively prosperous in the 1860s. Rather, the Homestead Act and the availability of free or cheap government or railroad land was an important factor in encouraging emigration-minded Europeans to choose the United States over other potential destinations, such as Canada or South America. Many of these Northern European farmers settled in the Midwest, with Michigan, Wisconsin, Minnesota, Iowa, Nebraska, and the Dakotas receiving the largest number of immigrants.[4] The population of non-Indians in Midwestern and Western states and territories grew 488 percent between 1870 and 1900.[5]

Three months after the passage of the Homestead Act in May, the Sioux Uprising of 1862 began in mid-August after the United States was late with annuity payments it owed the tribe as a result of treaties and white traders refused to sell the starving Sioux food supplies on credit. Within 40 days, 800 whites, many of them recent German immigrants, had been killed in Minnesota as the Sioux sought to take advantage of the fact that the U.S. Army and many state regiments were engaged in the Civil War.[6] The Winnebago Indians, who had been relocated to Minnesota from Iowa in 1848, were forced to move again after the Sioux Uprising, this time to Nebraska, along with the Omaha Indians.[7]

In retaliation for the violence in Minnesota, the United States waged war against the Teton Sioux (who had not been involved in the 1862 attacks) in the Dakota Territory in 1863–1864.[8] There was also fighting between the United States and the Cheyenne and Arapaho in Nebraska and Kansas in 1865, 1867, and 1868.[9] Midwestern states were thus developing their immigration promotion policies in the shadow of some of the worst interethnic violence ever to occur in the United States, which was notably missing from state promotional literature.

Midwestern states continued to target Northern Europeans after the Civil War but tended to focus on groups that had immigrated to their areas in large numbers in the antebellum period. This meant Germans, British, Scandinavians (mainly Norwegians and Swedes, sometimes Danes), and Dutch, as well as English Canadians. Minnesota had tried to encourage the immigration of Belgians and French before the war but ceased targeting these groups after the war. Wisconsin did publish literature in French in the 1870s but mainly concentrated on encouraging immigration from Great Britain, Germany, and Scandinavia—the largest countries sending people to Wisconsin.

These states considered Northern Europeans to be particularly desirable based on their previous experiences with these groups before the Civil War. The Iowa Board of Immigration believed, for example, that Germans would be attracted to Iowa because of "a natural love of republican institutions, and to secure homes of their own."[10] Wisconsin's post–Civil War policy was based on the idea of the fostering of chain migration through personal connections in order to get more of the same kinds of people the state had received before the war.[11]

Midwestern immigration promoters also believed that Northern Europeans were better suited to certain kinds of work than Southern or Eastern Europeans. Wisconsin's immigration commissioner argued: "Our state is heavily timbered, and not so easily brought under cultivation as the prairies of our neighboring states, and it needs the industrious, hard-working yeomanry of the old world, men who are able and willing to fell the huge trees and perform other hard labor necessary in clearing the land."[12]

Minnesota's Board of Immigration invited "the honest and industrious, however poor and friendless, to make themselves free homes; also those who have wealth; the well to do class, and those of moderate means."[13] Emphasizing the low cost of establishing a successful homestead (only between $478 and $482), the board declared, "Thus it will be seen that, with the outfit of a few hundred dollars, one can make a start on the new lands of Minnesota; and, if wanting this small capital, he need not be discouraged if he has health and strength; these, with habits of industry and economy, will surely overcome any obstacles. The history of pioneer life abounds in instances of penniless settlers who in a few years acquired a *comfortable independence*."[14]

One group interested in a "comfortable independence" but definitely not desired by Midwestern promoters was blacks. As many as 40,000 so-called Exodusters left the South for Kansas, Oklahoma, and Colorado in the 1870s and early 1880s, a mass movement that accelerated after Reconstruction ended and Southern Democrats regained control of southern state governments and began waging war on black civil liberties. This exodus of black farmers to the Midwest was driven primarily by black ministers and black entrepreneurs and was not encouraged by state immigration promoters.[15]

Midwestern states encouraged immigration using the same methods they had used before the Civil War but intensified those efforts. States created commissions, boards, and bureaus of immigration, opened offices in port cities in the United States and in Europe, took out advertisements in European newspapers, and published and distributed reams of information. But there was a substantial difference between states like Michigan and Iowa, which devoted significant resources to promotion, and Indiana, which refused to even reimburse its agent for his travel, or Nebraska, whose board spent more time arguing about goals and methods than actually promoting immigration.[16]

In 1867, with immigration again on the rise, the Republican governor of Minnesota, William R. Marshall, and the Republican-controlled state legislature established a Board of Immigration, appropriated $10,000 to pay for propaganda literature and agents, and named a Swedish immigrant, Col. Hans Mattson, as commissioner.[17] Mattson made several trips to Sweden to promote Minnesota, and on one trip, in 1869, brought back a group of 800 Swedes to the state.[18]

The Minnesota Board of Immigration sent agents of Swedish, Norwegian, and German backgrounds to New York City, Montreal, and Quebec City to meet newly arriving immigrants, distribute promotional literature, and answer questions about the state. Recognizing the increasingly fierce competition among Midwestern states to attract immigrants, Minnesota's agents began acting as guides, helping people to navigate the long journey to Minnesota in order to keep them from being diverted to other states and territories.[19] Minnesota's agent in New York, E. Page Davis, had an office at 153 Broadway, near the steamship companies' offices, where he exhibited a collection of Minnesota products as an example of what could be produced in the state. Davis also negotiated a deal with the Erie Railroad in 1871 to give immigrants to Minnesota a discount of one-third on their fares and allow them to bring 50 pounds of baggage for free.[20] Immigrants would make up between 28 and 37 percent of Minnesota's population between 1870 and 1900, in part due to these promotional efforts.

Wisconsin also resumed its immigration promotion policy in 1867 with the creation of a Board of Immigration comprised of Republican governor Lucius Fairchild, Secretary of State L. L. Breese, and six other members. The Republican-controlled state legislature appropriated $2,000 for expenses. Unlike the earlier efforts to distribute thousands of pamphlets to newly arriving immigrants in New York City and place advertisements in foreign newspapers, Wisconsin's post–Civil War plan focused on personal connections and the fostering of chain migration. The governor organized committees of three in each county with the charge of collecting lists of names of friends and relatives of county residents living in other states or countries. Pamphlets in English, German, French, Welsh, Dutch, Norwegian, and Swedish were then sent directly to these individuals, encouraging them to move to Wisconsin.[21] These languages were chosen to represent the largest immigrant groups already in the state.

In 1868, the board was expanded to eight members (Gov. Fairchild, Secretary of State Breese, secretary James Ross, and J. A. Becher of Milwaukee, R. G. Fleischer of Madison, J. B. Eugene of Green Bay, Hugh W. Jones of Dodgeville, J. W. Carney of Fond du Lac, and M. A. Fulton of Hudson), and it received a larger appropriation of $3,000.[22] In 1869, two agents, one in Milwaukee and the other in Chicago, were employed for four months to provide information about Wisconsin to immigrants as they arrived from Eastern ports.[23] The Immigration Commission reported that between May and November 1869 more than 14,500 immigrants had arrived in Milwaukee and another 8,300 people (mostly Scandinavians and Germans) had arrived in Chicago intending to continue on to Wisconsin, supposedly due to the efforts of its agents.[24]

The commission also hired a man to create a pamphlet in Norwegian and distribute it among emigration agencies in Norway and Denmark. Pamphlets advertising Wisconsin were also published in English, German, Dutch, French, and Welsh.[25]

Despite the apparent success in attracting immigrants, especially from Scandinavia and Germany, Wisconsin's promotion policy ended in 1870 due to a lack of funding from the Republican-controlled legislature. Republican governor Lucius Fairchild was authorized to send an agent to New York, but the lack of an accompanying appropriation to pay for such an agent meant that no one was sent.[26]

The first state to promote immigration, Michigan, also continued to advertise for immigrants by sending agents to Europe and distributing pamphlets describing the state at entry points, and especially in Detroit, where immigrants entered the United States via Canada. In 1869, the Republican-controlled state legislature appropriated $5,000 to pay for an agent to be based in Germany. East Saginaw lawyer and real estate agent

Max E. Allardt lived first in Frankfurt and then in Hamburg, where he distributed an eight-page pamphlet, *"Der Michiganer Wegwiser"* (The Michigan Guide), in Germany and Austria-Hungary. Iowa's agent, Carl Jaaks, disparaged Allardt's work in Hamburg, saying that the "commissioner of Michigan loiters about the harbor at each starting of an emigrant vessel, like a porter with a plate-mark on his hat."[27] In 1872, Allardt claimed that 2,722 immigrants had settled in Michigan due to his efforts. But Republican governor John J. Bagley did not believe the numbers warranted the cost of maintaining a foreign office and so recalled Allardt in 1874.[28]

In 1870, the Republican-controlled Iowa state legislature passed "An Act to Encourage Immigration," which established a Board of Immigration, with an annual appropriation of $5,000.[29] Besides Republican governor Samuel Merrill, the six other members of the board were Edward Mumm of Keokuk, Lee County; M. J. Rohlfs of Davenport, Polk County; C. L. Clausen of St. Ansgar, Mitchell County; C. Rhynsburger of Pella, Marion County; S. F. Spofford of Des Moines, Polk County; and Marcus Tuttle of Clear Lake, Gordo County; A. R. Fulton of Des Moines, Polk County, was secretary.[30] Several of these board members were state Republican Party activists.

As the new Board of Immigration was developing a promotional program to target Northern Europeans, the U.S. government forced the Potawatomi Indians currently living in Iowa and Kansas to move to Indian Territory (now Oklahoma).[31]

Between June 1870 and May 1871, the Iowa Board of Immigration sent 10 agents to Germany, the Netherlands, Belgium, Great Britain, and Scandinavia, where they advertised in newspapers, distributed pamphlets, gave lectures, met with business and religious leaders, and provided information about immigration to Iowa. The board also sent two agents to Eastern states to perform the same functions. In the spring of 1871, three agents—Louis A. Ochs, the Rev. Alexander King, and Danford Eddy—were recommissioned to go back to Germany, Great Britain, and the American East, respectively. As agent Jaaks noted of his work in Northern Germany, "I contrived to send the respective pamphlets from the most renowned hotels down to the obscurest inns, from the most considerable merchants down to the shop-keepers in villages, owners of mills, and to all those, who by their trade are brought into connection with their neighborhood."[32] Jaaks also left Iowa pamphlets in railroad station waiting rooms, where they could be perused by travelers.

Agents sought to exploit every angle they could to persuade Northern Europeans that Iowa was the best of many options. Agent Ochs, traveling in Southern Germany, found it necessary to hire prominent local people to vouch for him and help advertise his presence before he arrived in a community, because many other agents representing other states, other countries, railroads, and steamships were all circulating in Germany encouraging immigration and/or selling land and train and steamship tickets.[33]

To save money, the Iowa Board allowed railroad companies passing through Iowa to pay for its agents. "Several of the agents commissioned by the Board were working under partial pay from the different railroad companies, so that only $400 of the appropriation has been expended in payment to agents," the Iowa Board reported to the legislature.[34]

The main pamphlet Iowa's agents distributed was the 96-page book entitled "Iowa: The Home for Immigrants being a Treatise on the Resources of Iowa and Giving Useful Information with Regard to the State, for the Benefit of Immigrants and Others," which gave physical, social, historical, educational, and economic descriptions of the state. Some 35,000 copies were printed in English, 15,000 copies in German, 6,000 in Danish, 5,000 copies in Dutch, and 4,000 in Swedish. Secretary Fulton recruited state geologist C. A. White; Dr. J. M. Shaffer, secretary of the State Agriculture Society; and superintendent of public instruction A. S. Kissell to write sections to give the publication scientific and political heft. The book also made careful note of how to establish a homestead on railroad and government lands and the estimated cost of establishing a farm in Iowa.[35]

The Iowa Board of Immigration also published a one-page circular in several Iowa newspapers. To reach people who were most likely to buy land, the circular, which was printed in several European languages, was distributed to bankers in the state with the request that the information be shared with anyone who inquired about immigrating and/or settling in Iowa.[36] Despite these efforts, immigrants only comprised between 13 and 16 percent of Iowa's population between 1880 and 1900.

Promoting the Dakotas was much more difficult than promoting more central Midwestern states such as Iowa or even Wisconsin and Minnesota. Much of the Dakota Territory was unpopulated, and most of the people who lived in the area were Sioux and Chippewa Indians. All of the land west of the Missouri River had been designed as a reservation for the Sioux, and white settlement was specifically prohibited in the Black Hills, in the southwest, in the Treaty of Fort Laramie of 1868.[37]

The white population of the Dakota Territory in 1870 was only 14,181, of which 4,814 were foreign born.[38] Of these, the largest numbers came from Great Britain and British Canada, Norway, Germany, Sweden, and Denmark.[39] So the primary goal of immigration promotion in the

Dakotas was to gain enough white population to achieve statehood, which would not occur until November 1889. During this period, the Republican Party dominated the politics of the Dakota Territory, with only one Independent being appointed governor in 1873 (by Republican president Ulysses S. Grant) and one Democrat being appointed governor in 1887.

In January 1871, the Republican-controlled territorial legislature established a Bureau of Immigration, and Republican governor John A. Burbank appointed James S. Foster, who had already been working as an immigration agent since 1869, as the commissioner.[40] Working without a salary and with a small appropriation to pay for printing costs, Foster wrote pamphlets and traveled to the East Coast to organize emigration societies.[41] The most important promotional guide Foster wrote was "Outlines of the History of the Territory of Dakota, and Emigrant's Guide to the Free Lands of the Northwest" in 1870.[42]

Despite their failure to pay for an agent to go to New York City, Wisconsin state officials were still interested in promoting immigration. In 1871, Wisconsin created the position of commissioner of immigration, initially appointed by the governor, Republican Lucius Fairchild, until a popular election for the two-year position could be held later in November. The 1871 law that created the commissioner position also specified that an office was to be kept in Milwaukee; that a pamphlet describing the state be published each year in English, French, Welsh, German, and Norwegian; that county committees were to be created to work with the commissioner; and that an agent was to be based in Chicago for four months of the year while the commissioner was to work out of the Milwaukee office. In addition, the 1871 act authorized the commissioner to negotiate with the railroads for reduced fares for immigrants traveling to Wisconsin from New York City and Chicago. The first immigration commissioner was Ole C. Johnson of Beloit, who served from 1871 to 1874.[43]

Johnson instituted the practice of having Wisconsin's promotional pamphlets published in foreign countries to save money on the printing and mailing costs. Five thousand copies were published in Belgium in French under the supervision of the U.S. consul in Brussels, A. S. Chettain, who then distributed the pamphlets through his office, giving official weight to the document. Another 10,000 copies were published in Germany in German and distributed by J. A. Becher of Milwaukee, a former member of the Board of Immigration from 1869 to 1870 now serving as an agent for Johnson in Germany. In 1872, 10,000 pamphlets were published in England in English, the same number was published in Norway in Norwegian and Danish, and 4,000 pamphlets were printed in Welsh to attract Welsh miners from Pennsylvania.[44]

Besides sending Becher to Germany, Johnson hired a P. Langland to be the agent in Chicago between May and September 1871, the busy immigration period, and the commissioner also relied on a Mr. Fermann, who served as an unpaid agent for the state in Quebec Province, and upon William Abell of Milwaukee, who acted as assistant commissioner, also without pay.[45]

Johnson claimed that approximately 10,000 immigrants had settled in Wisconsin in 1871 through his office's efforts, most of these Norwegians and Germans, but also Swedes, Danes, English, Irish, Welsh, French-speaking Belgians, Dutch, and Bohemians.[46] He argued that his office needed at least $10,000 for the next year to successfully promote Wisconsin abroad and stressed the competition from other states. "We have as yet done very little to induce immigration as compared with our sister states, when in fact we need to do much and more than they. The broad prairies of Minnesota, Iowa, Kansas, and Nebraska are open and known to everybody, easily travelled over and explored, whilst many portions of our own state are yet a sealed book."[47]

But the Wisconsin state legislature was not convinced and rejected Johnson's request for a larger budget and greater power to regulate hotel recruiters at boarding houses, train stations, and other places where newcomers congregated and could be possibly exploited.[48] Such regulatory activities went way beyond the perceived responsibilities of the state immigration commissioner, whose primary job was to promote immigration, not protect immigrants. In 1874, newly elected Democratic governor William Robert Taylor replaced Johnson as commissioner with Martin J. Argard of Eau Claire, and then, that same year, the legislature abolished the office of commissioner, leaving Argard with no office to hold or policy to implement.[49]

That same year, 1874, gold was discovered in the Black Hills in southwestern Dakota. The invasion of Indian land by white miners prompted the federal government to abandon enforcement of the Treaty of Fort Laramie's prohibition of whites from the Black Hills. Instead, the United States tried to buy the land for $25,000 and relocate the Lakota Sioux to Indian Territory. The Sioux refused to give up their treaty land.[50]

In December 1875, the Dakota territorial legislature reorganized Foster's office, creating a bureau with five members, two of them immigrants, one from Germany, the other from Norway. The German agent traveled between Chicago and New York City and Philadelphia, where he met steamship arrivals and tried to encourage people to move to the Dakotas. The Norwegian agent met steamships in Montreal and Quebec City as well as traveling around the Upper Mississippi Valley promoting the

A Chief forbidding the passage of a train through his country, *Harper's Weekly*, September 19, 1874, p. 773. (Library of Congress)

Dakotas. But the Republican-controlled territorial legislature deemed the Immigration Bureau to be too inefficient and refused to appropriate any more money, causing the agency to cease functioning.[51]

Two months later, at the end of January 1876, the federal government sent the army to the Dakotas to claim the Black Hills for white settlement. The resulting Black Hills War (also called the Great Sioux War) of 1876–1877 belied any claims by territorial or other boosters that the Great Plains, and the Dakotas in particular, was safe for white settlement.[52]

Besides recurring Indian–white violence, the problem of drought severely complicated the Dakota Immigration Bureau's efforts to promote immigration. Between 1870 and 1877, the Midwest, including the Dakotas, suffered from severe drought that devastated crops and made animal husbandry difficult as animals struggled to find adequate water. The Panic of 1873, which ushered in prolonged economic depression and unemployment, and a locust swarm in 1874, also made recruitment to the Dakotas difficult. The region suffered from the brutal winter of 1886 and then another severe drought between 1890 and 1896.[53]

In 1879, Wisconsin renewed its immigration policy again, this time for six years. Instead of a commissioner of immigration, a Board of Immigration was created, comprising of the governor, secretary of state, and three other members; the president of this board was J. A. Becher, who by this point had been involved in promoting immigrant settlement in Wisconsin since the late 1860s. Authorized to encourage immigration from Canada, the Eastern United States, and Europe, the Wisconsin board was given an appropriation of $2,500 for the first year. A secretary, Henry Baetz, was hired, and the county committees were revived.[54] The Board of Immigration produced the pamphlet "Wisconsin, What It Offers to the Immigrant: An Official Report Published by the State Board of Immigration of Wisconsin" in 1879.[55]

In addition to the pamphlet, the Board of Immigration began producing pocket maps of Wisconsin in English, German, and Norwegian; in 1880, 10,000 such maps were printed. The following year, 5,000 maps each were sent to England and Germany. Between 1880 and 1886, more than 100,000 pamphlets were distributed. The board also engaged in extensive advertising in Europe, including newspapers in London and Frome, England; in Orebro, Sweden; in Hanover, Rostock, Gotha, Berlin, Stuttgart, Kaiserlautern, Regen, and other German cities; in Vienna, Austria; and in Berne, Switzerland. In 1882, the board advertised in 41 German and Austrian newspapers.[56]

At the same time that the new Board of Immigration was printing and distributing its pamphlets and maps, the Wisconsin Central Railroad appointed one of its land agents, K. K. Kennan, to serve as the European agent of the board, at the railroad's expense. Kennan immediately set out for Europe, setting himself up in Basel, Switzerland, to avoid German laws against emigration recruitment. Once there, he focused on German and Scandinavian immigrants, advertising extensively in newspapers, distributing the state pamphlet and other state documents, and responded to thousands of letters from prospective immigrants.[57]

In March 1880, the Republican-controlled Iowa state legislature passed another immigration promotion act, this one to create a commissioner of immigration. This commissioner, George D. Perkins, served until 1882.[58] Unlike the earlier Board of Immigration, which had been comprised mainly of successful immigrants, Perkins was an American who had been born in New York. He came to Iowa in 1869 and was a Republican newspaper editor in Sioux City and then a member of Congress from 1891 to 1899.[59]

The new position of commissioner of immigration had an appropriation of $5,000 for two years, but its activities were restricted to the United States. Perkins organized an immigration convention to be held in Sheldon, O'Brien County, in June 1880 and then published the proceedings in a pamphlet, "Information for the Homeseeker." Perkins also wrote or revised several other pamphlets and one-page circulars, including "Iowa as an Agricultural State," "Homes in the Heart of the Continent," and the Dutch *De Volksvriend* (The People's Friend), and he advertised his position as commissioner of immigration for Iowa in several Eastern newspapers. In 1880 alone he distributed nearly 60,000 copies of these pamphlets and 422,000 copies of the one-page sheets using a network of more than a hundred agents around the country.[60]

Finding himself limited in what he could do, since he could not travel or advertise outside of the United States, Perkins noted in his annual report to the legislature that "work in my department must be conducted on the cooperative plan" and that "the real estate dealers and agents, including the land commissioners of the leading land-grant railroads, have been my most serviceable allies."[61]

In the 1870s, most of Iowa's promotional efforts had focused on Germany, the Netherlands, and Great Britain, while in the early 1880s, Perkins's work as immigration commissioner was limited to advertising Iowa to immigrants and other Americans already in the United States. The political turmoil in Germany in the 1870s caused hundreds of thousands of Germans to emigrate, so persuading Germans to leave their homes in this period was not difficult. Yet despite Iowa's efforts to attract Dutch immigrants, people from the Netherlands did not make up a large percentage of the state's immigrant population. Iowa was successful in attracting immigrants, but these immigrants came from the largest sending countries in the late 19th century—Germany, Ireland, Norway, and Sweden.

But Perkins's message was the same as the earlier Iowa Board of Immigration's: Iowa was a place of opportunity for hardworking Northern European farmers.

After letting the position of immigration agent lapse, the Republican-controlled Michigan state legislature revised the post in about 1881, and Col. Frederick Morley, a Detroit newspaper editor, was appointed agent. Between 1881 and 1885, Morley distributed 42,000 copies of a 144-page book, "Michigan and Its Resources," throughout Great Britain, Germany, and the United States, extolling the virtues of Michigan at an annual cost of $11,500.[62]

But the state legislature was no longer willing to spend money for immigration promotion and recruitment. Although Michigan's population continued to grow due to new industrial opportunities in Detroit and nearby cities, many of these new residents were native-born Americans. In addition, the largest immigrant groups in Michigan were Canadian and British, two groups that did not need active encouragement to come to the Upper Midwest. Democratic governor Josiah Begole, who had been elected in 1883, abolished the position of immigration agent in 1885, just before he was replaced by Republican Russell Alger.[63]

Although the Wisconsin Board of Immigration was to have dissolved after six years, in 1885, it managed to maintain political support in the legislature for most of the 1880s and 1890s, even during periods of Democratic Party control of the legislature and the governor's mansion. In 1895, the Board of Immigration was renewed for two years, with an annual appropriation of $5,000, and then again in 1897, for another two years, with an appropriation of $8,000. By this point, the board was made up of the governor and the secretary of state and managed by a salaried secretary.[64] In 1899, the board was extended for another two years, with an annual appropriation of $5,000 and a paid secretary, but was allowed to expire in 1901.[65] In 1905, the state granted county boards of supervisors the right to appropriate money to promote local immigration recruitment efforts. In 1907, the Board of Immigration was once again revived and continued its activities until 1915, when immigration promotion was shifted to an Immigrant Division within the state's Department of Agriculture.[66]

The Dakota Territory's Immigration Bureau was disbanded in 1889 when statehood was achieved and the territory was split into North Dakota and South Dakota. In North Dakota, promotion of immigration was placed in the hands of the commissioner of agriculture and labor, an office held by Republicans between 1889 and 1934, except between 1893 and 1894, and 1917 and 1920. For the next 20 years, this office published and distributed pamphlets and ran articles praising North Dakota's agricultural and stock-raising opportunities in large newspapers in Chicago, Minneapolis, Des Moines, and Indianapolis to try to convince people to move to the state.[67]

Just as North Dakota and South Dakota were achieving statehood, the Sioux Nation made its last attempt to resist the United States' policy of assimilation that dissolved tribes and divided and sold tribal land to individual Indians and whites. The Ghost Dance movement of 1890, which was centered at the Lakota Pine Ridge Agency in South Dakota, encouraged the Sioux and other Great Plains Indians to resist government assimilation efforts through pan-Indian tribal cooperation and cultural revival. The massacre at Wounded Knee on December 29, 1890, in which 153 mostly women and children of the Minniconjou and Hunkpapa bands were killed by the U.S. Army, marked the end of organized Indian resistance to removal and assimilation.[68]

It was not until 1910 that South Dakota revived its immigration promotion policy and created a Bureau of Immigration, comprised of the secretary of state, the governor, the commissioner of schools and public lands, and a commissioner of immigration, all of whom were Republicans. This bureau promoted South Dakota at state land shows, focusing on both agricultural products and the Black Hills region as a tourist destination. The bureau targeted German, Polish, Czech, and Scandinavian immigrants already in the United States, placing advertisements in these foreign-language newspapers, and mailing 10,000 copies in German, 10,000 copies in "Scandinavian" (probably Norwegian), 6,000 copies in Czech, and 6,000 copies in Polish of the pamphlet "Corn Is King" all around the country in response to letters of inquiry. The bureau also produced and distributed 15,000 maps.[69]

Despite the serious environmental and economic challenges of the late 19th century, the Dakotas, and especially North Dakota, were successful in attracting a significant number of immigrants. In 1900, more than 35 percent of North Dakota residents were foreign born, the highest percentage in the country.[70] The fact that the population of the Dakotas increased at all between 1880 and 1900 was in part due to the aggressive efforts of the states' immigration bureaus and the Northern Pacific Railroad, which owned millions of acres in North Dakota.

Midwestern states and territories disseminated a variety of messages and images to Europeans about life in America and life in their states. Immigrants should move to (fill in the blank state or territory) because it was agriculturally fertile and the opportunity to be economically independent and personally free was available to anyone willing to work hard and take a chance in a new country. More established states, such as Michigan, Wisconsin, and Iowa stressed that they had established communities, with schools and churches, and Michigan and Iowa made a point of noting the presence of immigrant communities that newcomers could join. Minnesota and the Dakotas had to emphasize the availability of millions of acres of undeveloped land.

Wisconsin's 1867 pamphlet "Statistics, Exhibiting the History, Climate and Productions of the State of Wisconsin" was typical of the type of immigration promotion propaganda Midwestern states produced in the late 19th century. To give its pamphlet scientific (and thus credible) heft, the Board of Immigration hired Dr. Allen Lapham, who had written one of the first scientific studies of the region, "A Geographical and Topographical Description of Wisconsin," in 1844, to draw the map that served as the frontpiece. In 32 pages, life in Wisconsin was described in detail, with information about "location, topographical features, water power, rivers, small lakes, climate, health, geology, lead mines, zinc, iron ores, clays, peat and marl, native animals, fishes, forests, pine region, agriculture, chief crops of 1866 [the total value of which is placed at

$69,213,544], livestock, farm products, implements, wages, manufactures, occupations, railroads, markets, population, newspapers, churches, principal cities, lands, surveys, the Homestead Law, land tenure, value of property, government, rights, office-holding, rights of married women, revenues of the state, schools, libraries, state institutions, post offices, and routes from the seaboard."[71]

"Michigan and Its Resources," published in 1882, provided similar levels of detail about Michigan's soil and climate, health, finance and taxation, and transportation, as well as state educational and social welfare institutions, various types of land available, and citizenship and voting rights in the state. Michigan also emphasized that it was a settled state that still held opportunity, not a new, undeveloped territory with its many hardships and risks. "We have over four thousand miles of railway; great public buildings for civil, educational, and benevolent purposes, including a new State capitol, and all paid for; nearly 7,000 school-houses, capable of seating nearly half a million of children, are scattered over every county in the State; two thousand churches of almost every known denomination afford conveniences for the stated ministrations of religion," Immigration Commissioner Morley declared.[72]

Like Michigan and Wisconsin, Iowa advertised itself as the best of both worlds: a settled state with many established social and educational amenities but also one with available fertile land and boundless opportunity for hardworking farmers. "In Iowa there is still room for many thousands more who may see proper to come and secure new homes at low prices on our broad rich prairies, with every reasonable assurance of health, wealth, education, and freedom for all who will only exercise ordinary industry," the Iowa Board of Immigration claimed.[73]

But Midwestern states also argued that life in their states represented the pinnacle of American independence and freedom from European wars and political and religious oppression.

The Wisconsin Immigration Commission declared that among its many attributes Wisconsin was a state "where all the rights of man are respected," "where intelligence and education are permanently secured for all future time," "where all of the necessities and most of the comforts and luxuries of life are easily accessible," "where the division of the products of labor between the laborer and the capitalist is equitably made," "where the farmers are the owners of the land they cultivate," "where honest labor always secures a competence for a man and his family," "where land can be obtained almost without price," "where property is constantly increasing in value," and "where every man has a voice in deciding the policy of the government under which he lives."[74]

Minnesota asserted in 1878 simply that "especially is this a favorable opportunity for the emigrant from foreign countries. Grim visaged war at home. Peace, prosperity, happiness, here."[75] In "Minnesota, Her Agricultural Resources, Commercial Advantages, and Manufacturing Capabilities, Being a Concise Description of Minnesota, and the Inducements She Offers to Those Seeking Homes in a New Country," which the Minnesota Board of Immigration published in 1879, the board sought to appeal to landless British and Irish immigrants by stressing that land purchase in the United States was fee simple, property ownership in perpetuity, with no leases or landlords involved.[76]

"Iowa: The Home for Immigrants" noted the state's diverse population, comprised of Germans, Scandinavians, Dutch, and English, but also Irish and Scottish residents, thus assuring those groups that if they too moved to Iowa, they could live near people of their own nationality.[77]

As a frontier state, and one suffering under the stereotype of being ice-and-snow bound for most of the year, Minnesota's promoters used colorful, sometimes florid, language to describe the state. In "Minnesota, the Empire State of the New North-West, the Commercial, Manufacturing and Geographical Centre of the American Continent," published in 1878, the Minnesota Board of Immigration claimed that Minnesota had "inexhaustible prairies," plentiful timber, massive acreage (equal in size to Massachusetts, Connecticut, and Rhode Island), extensive railroad lines, and "unequalled water power."[78]

Tackling Minnesota's greatest negative, its perceived harsh climate, the state board insisted that the weather was comparable to that in Scandinavia and Northern Germany and waxed lyrical about the seasons on the Great Plains. "Nothing can be more enchantingly beautiful than many of her winter days. It is at this season of the year that her atmospheric phenomena are most magnificent. No pen or pencil can portray the grandeur of her sunrises, and the mind can only appreciate by observation the brilliancy of her auroras. It is at this season that her skies are bluest and gemmed at night with the brightest stars, and the pure bracing air fits one for the enjoyment of the beauty surrounding him."[79]

The Dakota territorial legislature also wanted to counter the image of the Dakotas popular in the American (and European) imagination as a harsh and barren country populated by hostile natives. Foster and other boosters of the Dakotas emphasized the region's vast size, the fertility of the soil for both grain and stock raising, and the supposed healthfulness of the climate. Opportunity for grain farmers was as limitless as the prairies themselves.[80] The Dakota Territory's winter air was described as "a robe of arctic furs, which holds in and stimulates the resilient fires of vital heat within the body, imparting in their reaction a sense of elastic vigor and redundant animation."[81]

Midwestern immigration promoters came from a variety of backgrounds, but many of them were successful immigrants from the countries their new homes were now targeting. Wisconsin's first immigration commissioner, Ole C. Johnson, was from Norway and had fought with the Union Army during the Civil War, receiving the rank of colonel; he also served as mayor of his new hometown, Beloit.[82] Minnesota's most active agent, Col. Hans Mattson, was also a Union Civil War veteran and worked for several railroads, including the St. Paul & Pacific Railroad and the Northern Pacific Railroad, in addition to serving as Minnesota's secretary of state in 1870.

Several of Iowa's immigration commissioners and agents were immigrants as well. Iowa's first agent, Nicholas Johann Rusch, had been born in 1822 in Sankt Michaelisdonn, Holstein (then Denmark, now Germany). He attended the University of Kiel before immigrating to the United States in 1847, settling in Scott County, Iowa, near Davenport. Rusch became active in the Iowa state Republican Party and served as second lieutenant governor of Iowa before being appointed immigration commissioner.

Iowa Board of Immigration member Edward Mumm was from the Netherlands and settled in Iowa in 1849. He became a bookkeeper and then deputy clerk of both county and federal courts before starting his own law practice. He also served as deputy recorder and deputy auditor of Lee County and sat on the Keokuk City Council.[83]

Mathias Rohlfs emigrated from Schleswig-Holstein (then Denmark, now Germany) in 1847 and was active in local politics in Davenport and Polk County, serving on the County Board of Supervisors at the same time he was on the Board of Immigration.[84]

Claus Clausen had been born in Denmark but had been active in promoting Norwegian immigration first to Wisconsin and then to Minnesota and Iowa from the time he first immigrated with a group of Norwegians to Milwaukee in 1843. A Lutheran minister, he was a founder of the Norwegian Evangelical Lutheran Church and also edited an influential Norwegian American newspaper, *Emigranten*, as well as a monthly Lutheran church paper. He was a founding member of St. Ansgar, which was the center of the Norwegian community in Mitchell County and the surrounding area.[85]

Claude Rhynsburger was also from the Netherlands, immigrating in 1855 to Marion County, where he farmed and then opened a mercantile business in Pella in 1861.[86]

Iowa's immigration agents were also immigrants. Alex. A. Wise was from London; Carl Jaaks was from Hamburg, Germany; and L. W. Hasselman and Henry Hospers were from the Netherlands; Hospers was also the mayor of Pella, Iowa, where board member C. Rhynsburger also lived.[87]

Other boosters were American-born and active in local and state politics. S. F. Spofford was originally from New Hampshire, moving first to Michigan in 1824 and then to Iowa in 1855. He owned a hotel, the Des Moines House, was a director of the Citizens National Bank of Des Moines, and was active in Des Moines politics, serving as mayor in 1864 and on the city school board. He was also active in the state agricultural society and helped establish the county's farm for the poor.[88]

Marcus Tuttle had been born and raised in New York. He moved to Iowa in 1855 and was a founder of Clear Lake, where he farmed, dealt in real estate, and ran a mercantile business. He was active in Iowa Republican state politics and sat in the state Senate between 1867 and 1871.[89]

The secretary of the Iowa Board of Immigration, Alexander Robert "A. R." Fulton, was from Ohio and had trained initially as a civil engineer. He moved to Iowa in 1851, where he was a partner in, and then owner of, the *Fairfield Ledger*, served as a surveyor and judge for Jefferson County, and was active in Iowa Republican state politics. In 1868, he became the assistant editor and traveling correspondent for the Des Moines–based *Iowa State Register*. While secretary of the Board of Immigration, Fulton wrote the book "Free Lands of Iowa," and in 1882, he wrote one of the first studies of American Indians on the Great Plains, "The Red Men of Iowa."[90]

The Dakotas' immigration commissioner, James Foster, had been born in Connecticut and raised in New York and had come to the Dakotas in 1864 as the leader of a colony of 60 New York farm families looking to relocate to the Midwest. He became involved in local politics and was appointed the first territorial superintendent of schools in 1864 before being named immigration commissioner. He had a real estate business in Mitchell, North Dakota, and Foster County, North Dakota, is named for him.[91]

The decades that Midwestern states were most active in encouraging immigration from Northern Europe were a period of recurring drought and extreme weather, especially on the Great Plains. These environmental problems, which also affected the West, were most severely felt in western Minnesota and the Dakotas, but also in Kansas, Nebraska, and what was known as Indian Territory, Oklahoma. These states and territories suffered prolonged droughts between 1856 and 1865, 1870 and 1877, and 1890 and 1896, causing thousands of homesteads to fail and the near

W. Emerman, "A supply train in a snow-storm" (top); P. Frenzeny, "Distributing supplies to the Indians" (bottom), *Harper's Weekly*, February 11, 1882, p. 89. (Library of Congress)

collapse of the cattle industry. An estimated 600,000 people, of the 1 million who took out homesteads between 1862 and 1900, left the Great Plains, and Kansas and Nebraska lost between one-quarter to one-half of their populations in the 1890s.[92] In addition, major blizzards in January 1873, which affected Wisconsin, Minnesota, parts of Iowa, Nebraska, and southwestern Kansas, and the Great White Winter of 1886, which froze the Dakotas and the rest of the Great Plains, caused many people to rethink settlement in the Northern Midwest.[93]

But despite the serious environmental and economic challenges of the late 19th century, the Midwest as a region was successful in attracting a significant number of immigrants. The foreign born comprised 22 percent of Michigan's and South Dakota's populations, 25 percent of Wisconsin's population, 28 percent of Minnesota's population, and more than 35 percent of North Dakota's population in 1900, the highest in the country. In Iowa and Kansas, the percentage of foreign born was much lower, only 13 percent and 9 percent, respectively, but Nebraska, which did little to no promotion, was 16 percent foreign born in 1900.[94] And by 1900, the children of immigrants made up a large minority of Midwestern states' native-born population.

Midwestern states continued their antebellum immigration promotion policies after the Civil War because their prewar activities had been reasonably successful and because the federal Homestead Act of 1862 provided a major new incentive for people to immigrate to the still undeveloped lands of the Midwest. But established states, particularly Michigan, Wisconsin, and Iowa, had an easier time encouraging immigrants to move to their areas than new states and territories did, because they could present themselves as having both civilization and opportunity. New states and territories, such as Minnesota and the Dakotas, faced the challenge of convincing immigrants that they possessed opportunity while downplaying the hardship and challenge of frontier life. Yet, even these new states were successful in attracting immigrants. Western states and territories, however, faced greater challenges of an often inhospitable environment and high levels of interethnic violence to overcome in their efforts to promote immigration to their areas.

CHAPTER SIX

Immigration Promotion in the West, 1865–1914

Immigration promotion in the West was part of a larger national effort to transform territory long populated by American Indians and Mexicans into organized states settled by white Americans and Northern Europeans.[1] The presence of Chinese immigrants in Western states and territories (and their refusal to behave as guest workers and return to China) and ongoing hostility with American Indians added a level of urgency to these efforts.

But unlike Midwestern states, Western states and territories sought to increase and whiten their populations on the cheap: advertising was done primarily in the United States versus Europe, and agents were not sent abroad to organize colonies and escort immigrants to their new homes as Midwestern states did. Instead, immigration agencies in Oregon, Washington, Wyoming, Idaho, Colorado, New Mexico, and Arizona often partnered with private interests, mainly railroads, to attract Northern Europeans and white Americans to their territories. In the case of California, the state developed no official promotion policy and instead relied completely on the Southern Pacific Railroad to encourage immigration.[2]

This cheapness was in part due to the structure and nature of territorial governments: once a territory had been organized by Congress, the president appointed a territorial governor who governed without a legislature until he organized elections for a representative government. Territories were expected to be economically self-sufficient to demonstrate their capacity for statehood.[3] The Republican Party controlled most Western state and territorial governments, but unlike in the Midwest, these Republicans were less willing to spend public money on immigration promotion.

Indian nations' resistance to removal, segregation, and assimilation policies also complicated Western promotional efforts and often resulted in violence. Western states and territories depicted their corner of America as a contained wilderness, an Edenic land of mild climate, fertile soil, and opportunity without significant hardship, danger, or risk. Yet in actuality, the West was plagued by interethnic violence until the United States finally crushed Indian resistance in the late 1880s.[4]

Complicating the dissemination of this largely false image of a safe frontier was the natural environment of the West, particularly of the High Plains. This territory between the Rocky Mountains and the Cascades to the hundredth meridian—dubbed the "Great American Desert" by the first American explorers in the early 19th century—is semiarid, arid, or desert and receives much less rainfall and has much less humidity than the eastern and southern United States. Eastern Washington, eastern Oregon, and all of California are also dry and receive most of their precipitation in the winter. In the 1870s–1890s, this region was aggressively promoted by state and territorial agencies and railroads with the pseudoscientific argument that "rain follows the plow," or that agriculture and homesteading had a permanent effect on the climate, making it more humid.[5] A series of droughts in 1856–1865, 1870–1877 (which brought Rocky Mountain locusts), and 1890–1896, plus the Great White Winter of 1886, which killed up to 75 percent of the cattle grazing on the Great Plains, belied this theory and made selling the West even harder.[6]

But despite these challenges, immigrants and their American-born children came to comprise a large percentage of Western states' populations by the early 20th century, and many of these immigrants were the pioneer founders of their communities.[7]

As in the Midwest, the most desired immigrant groups for Western states and territories were Germans, Scandinavians, British, and English Canadians, all undeniably white and predominantly Protestant nationalities. Other immigrants who arrived without encouragement—such as Irish, French, and Italians—were tolerated but not actively recruited by Western promotional agencies. Chinese, Mexicans, and Southern and Eastern Europeans were recruited by private labor contractors to be guest workers but were not viewed as desirable settlers and future citizens by immigration promoters.

Although all of the Western states and territories that engaged in immigration promotion targeted Northern Europeans, some groups were desired more than others by some states and territories. Wyoming was

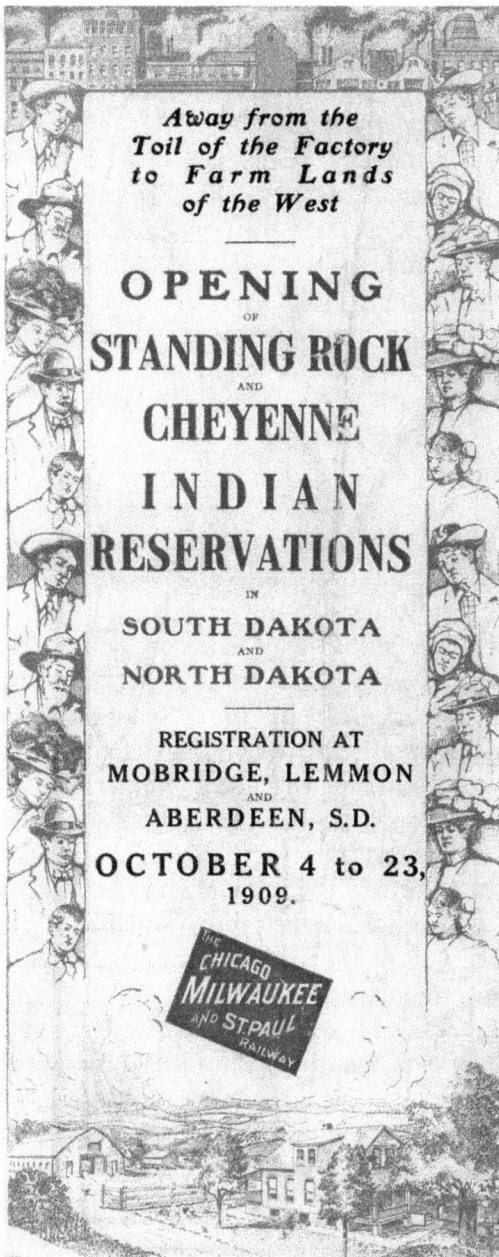

"Away from the Toil of the Factory to Farm Lands of the West, Opening of Standing Rock/Cheyenne Indian Reservations in South Dakota and North Dakota," promotional poster, 1909. (South Dakota Historical Society)

interested in attracting British and Germans.[8] Oregon and Washington focused on Germans and Scandinavians in the belief that immigrants from those countries were predisposed toward farming, dairying and animal husbandry, fishing, and timber harvesting, all important industries in those states.[9] Washington was explicit in its desire for experienced farmers, saying, "What is wanted is intelligent farmers with enough money to commence in business. Such men, by thrift and industry, can soon acquire and improve the best of homes in this state."[10]

Colorado took advantage of the drier air in the Rocky Mountains and marketed itself to people with allergies and other respiratory diseases. Dr. F. J. Bancroft, whom the Board of Immigration hired to write about the alleged health benefits of Colorado's climate, claimed: "The healthfulness of Colorado arises from its pure, dry air; its altitudes; its many bright sunshiny days; its uniform and highly electrified atmosphere, and its brilliant and grant scenery, which produces cheerfulness and a contented frame of mind."[11] Arizona and New Mexico also advertised the many health spas that had developed in those territories in the late 1890s, particularly in Santa Fe.[12]

As was common across the country, the promotion policies developed by Western states and territories operated in fits and starts, and Arizona, Oregon, Washington, and Wyoming all passed multiple acts intended to encourage immigration. States and territories frequently passed legislation but then refused to fund an agency, and/or terminated a policy when a new governor or new political party took over state or territorial government. The transition from territory to state was the point at which promotional policies ended or began. In the West, only Oregon and California were organized as states before the Civil War (Nevada entered the Union in 1864); for the rest of the region, immigration promotion was part of the effort to gain white population for statehood.

Western states and territories developed immigration promotion policies in a period of political and economic turbulence after the Civil War. With the Confederacy defeated, the U.S. federal government turned its attention back to its ongoing military and diplomatic conflict with American Indian nations, which were continuing to resist U.S. pressure to move them farther and farther west. The few white residents of the West found that the completion of the Central Pacific–Union Pacific transcontinental railroad in 1869 caused both unemployment and wages to drop as the railroad brought new workers to the region. The Panic of 1873, which began in the United States in September, was caused in part by the overdevelopment of railroads, particularly in the West. The mining economies of Nevada, Colorado, and Idaho were also negatively affected by the federal government's decision to end bimetallism with the Coinage Act of 1873. Promoters' claim that the West was the true frontier of opportunity in America was seriously in question in the 1870s through the 1890s.

Colorado was one of those territories where these disparate factors— Indian wars, railroad expansion, economic depression—all came together. Whites had rushed to Colorado in large numbers in the 1857 gold rush to Pike's Peak in the Rocky Mountains, and as a result, Colorado was organized as a territory out of Cheyenne lands in 1861. The combination of railroad development in eastern Colorado and gold and silver mining in the west created frequent opportunities for violence between white settlers and Indians for much of the 1860s. The worst interethnic violence was in the spring of 1864, when the Cheyenne raided several ranches in the Box Elder Creek area, prompting the Colorado territorial militia to retaliate and massacre more than one hundred Cheyenne at Sand Creek on November 29, 1864.[13]

Wyoming was also the site of clashes between the Cheyenne and Arapaho and the U.S. Army, particularly the Battles of Platte Bridge (on July 26, 1865) and of Tongue River (on August 29, 1865).[14] The discovery of gold at South Pass in 1867 enabled Wyoming to gain enough white population to become its own territory, carved out of the Dakota Territory, but the continued encroachment of whites on Indian land only led to more violence.[15] Oregon also experienced recurring violence between the Paiute Indians and the United States in 1866 and 1867.[16]

The interethnic tensions of the 1860s prompted Colorado and Wyoming territorial leaders to develop formal policies to encourage more whites to settle permanently in their areas. In February 1872, Colorado governor Edwin M. McCook, a Ulysses S. Grant appointee, established the first of several boards of immigration to promote Colorado in the late 19th century.

This board developed and distributed 25,000 copies of a one-page circular, "Official Information on the Resources of Colorado," and another 25,000 copies of a 26-page pamphlet, "Statement of Facts," in Europe and the United States. In 1873, the "Statement of Facts" was translated into German, and the board disseminated 20,000 copies of the pamphlet "Resources and Advantages of Colorado." The Board of Immigration also relied heavily on free advertising in the *Rocky Mountain News* and newspaper articles written by local journalists to advertise the territory.[17] The Union Pacific, Kansas Pacific, and Atchison, Topeka & Santa Fe railroads also brought Eastern journalists to Colorado on sightseeing tours to encourage them to write favorable stories.[18] The Colorado Board of Immigration claimed that 25,000 people had moved to Colorado in

1872–1873 and anticipated another 30,000 people in 1874 because of its promotional efforts.[19]

Wyoming was also desperate for white American and European settlers. The territory only had about 9,000 non-Indian residents spread out over 97,814 square miles (253,340 sq km), of which one-third were foreign born, mainly British and Irish, but the gold rush and the building of the Northern Pacific Railroad across Wyoming in 1873 had also attracted Chinese immigrants from other Western states and territories.[20]

Wyoming Territory leaders could not have picked a worse time to initiate an immigration promotion program. Indian–white violence intensified in early August 1873, when the U.S. Army skirmished with the Sioux at the Battle of Yellowstone, after the Sioux attacked soldiers guarding surveyors for the Northern Pacific Railroad, and then with the Northern Arapaho at the Battle of Bates a year later on July 4, 1874, near Wind River. The Powder River section of Wyoming, the main part of the territory the Northern Pacific Railroad was interested in developing for agriculture, was the site of the Battle of Red Fork, between the United States and the Cheyenne on November 26, 1876, as part of the larger Great Sioux War of 1876–1877 that engulfed the Great Plains.[21]

Then in September 1873, Jay Cooke & Co., the main financial backer of the Northern Pacific Railroad, failed, causing an international depression, widespread unemployment, and immigration to drop significantly and remain at low levels until 1880. The Northern Pacific, one of the largest recipients of Indian land from the federal government, teetered on the brink of bankruptcy, and construction and land sales in its land grant temporarily ceased between fall 1873 and 1875.

It was in this context of growing hostilities with the Plains Indian nations and economic panic that Republican governor John Allen Campbell established the Wyoming Board of Immigration in December 1873, with an appropriation of $4,000, half of which was to pay for the activities of a Board of Immigration and the other half to pay for a commissioner of immigration.[22] The board published a booklet, "The Territory of Wyoming, History, Soil, Climate, Resources, Etc.," in 1874 but did little else.[23]

The pressure to reduce Chinese immigration was very strong in Western states like California, Nevada, and Oregon, where Chinese were the largest or second-largest immigrant group between 1870 and 1890.[24] To counter this awkward demographic fact, the Republican-controlled Oregon state legislature passed an act in October 1874 to create a state Board of Immigration Commissioners but then refused to appropriate any funding for it. The board was thus dependent on private contributions from wealthy Portland residents, but it managed to publish the pamphlet "Oregon. Facts

Regarding Its Climate, Soil, Mineral and Agricultural Resources, Means of Communication, Commerce and Industry, Laws, Etc., Etc., for Use of Immigrants, with Map" in both English and German.[25] New editions of this pamphlet were expanded and released every few years.[26]

Although the purpose of the Oregon Board of Immigration was to encourage immigration to Oregon by publishing and distributing useful information about the state to would-be settlers, the board was also to maintain a record of public and private land for sale, maintain a labor bureau, and "procure at the request and at the expense of any citizen desiring it, whatever agricultural or skilled labor he may wish from abroad, through the State's honorary commissioners, and forward to them conditions for settlement of small colonies wished by citizens."[27]

In March 1875, as the depression and unemployment worsened, a Republican-controlled Congress passed the Page Act, which required that immigration from Asian countries be "free and voluntary."[28] Although most Chinese immigrants arrived in America with a labor contract, they were not enslaved or "coolie" laborers, as American lawmakers and nativists assumed and argued. This was the first in a series of anti-Chinese laws adopted by the United States in response to pressure from organized labor, much of it based in Western states and territories.

Chinese immigration was not as great a concern in Washington Territory, where most immigrants were British and English Canadian, but territorial leaders still desired more white American and European population to help Washington gain statehood. In November 1875, Republican governor Elisha Peyre Ferry created a Board of Immigration Commissioners out of the private Emigration Society and allocated funds to print 5,000 copies of a promotional pamphlet. In its first year, the board distributed 4,000 pamphlets and 16,000 circulars and answered 550 letters of inquiry, often relying on prominent citizens to mail circulars themselves. The board also used the railroads as a means of distributing information about Washington Territory.[29]

But white settlement of Washington and Idaho was complicated by the refusal of the Nez Perce to cede their remaining land in eastern Washington and northern Idaho after the United States violated the terms of the 1855 Camp Stevens Treaty and allowed whites to settle in the Nez Perce reservation after gold was discovered in the area in 1860. The Battle of White Bird Canyon on June 17, 1777, in Lewis County, Idaho, was a great defeat for the U.S. Army and the beginning of the Nez Perce War that ranged from eastern Washington north and east through Idaho to Canada before the Nez Perce finally surrendered in October 1877 and were moved to Indian Territory.[30]

Idaho also experienced white–Indian violence when the Shoshoni and Bannock Indians began raiding rural communities in the Salmon River area in the Sheepeater War of 1879 before finally surrendering to the U.S. Army in early October and removing to the Fort Hall Reservation.[31]

Between 1871 and 1887, the United States passed several laws designed to weaken Indian nations' collective power and finish redistributing Indian land to whites. The Indian Appropriation Act of March 3, 1871, declared that tribes would no longer be recognized by the United States as independent nations and individual Indians would be considered wards of the federal state. The Dawes Severalty Act, or the General Allotment Act of 1887, broke up the remaining communally held Indian land and allocated it in 160-acre plots to individual Indians on the condition that they live separately from their former tribes in Anglo-American-style nuclear families and practice Euro-American agriculture. Land not allocated to Indians was declared surplus and sold to white settlers, railroads, and other corporations. Because of these policies, American Indians lost control of most of the territory they still controlled in 1887 before the Dawes Act was repealed in 1934 and tribes were allowed to reorganize.[32]

In 1882, after heavy lobbying by Western politicians and labor organizations, especially the Knights of Labor, the United States passed the Chinese Exclusion Act, which barred Chinese laborers from entering the United States for the next 10 years and required that Chinese immigrants who had entered between November 17, 1880, and May 1882 be deported. Those Chinese who were allowed to remain in the United States were required to register with the federal government. They were then issued identification certificates that they had to carry with them to prove their right to be in the country.[33] The Chinese Exclusion Act would be renewed in 1892 (the Geary Act) and made permanent in 1902 (the Scott Act). Although the Chinese Exclusion Act would cause Chinese immigration to drop drastically, there was still the fact that more than 100,000 Chinese immigrants lived in the United States in 1880, mostly in Western states and territories.[34]

The Oregon Board of Immigration Commissioners had ceased functioning by the early 1880s. By 1881, German investor Henry Villard, who had been active in railroad development in Oregon, Washington, and California since 1874, had gained control of the Northern Pacific Railroad and begun to reorganize its immigration promotion efforts.[35] In the spring and summer of 1883, in anticipation of the completion of the road's construction at Helena, Montana, in September, the Northern Pacific's European department blanketed Northern Europe with advertisements about land in the Pacific Northwest, particularly in Oregon and Washington.[36]

In February 1885, the Republican-controlled Oregon state legislature passed another "Act to Provide for the Appointment of a Board of Immigration Commissioners." This Board of Immigration worked very closely with the Northern Pacific's land offices in Portland, Oregon, and Boston, and the relationship between the two organizations became so close that the railroad's Boston office served as the Oregon state commission's Eastern branch.[37]

The state board relied on the Northern Pacific's immigration bureau to produce an English-language pamphlet explaining and extolling life in Oregon and to advertise in English, German, Norwegian, and Swedish newspapers. Favorable responses to these advertisements prompted the railroad to produce copies of its pamphlet in German and the Scandinavian languages, and offices were opened in England and Scotland. The Northern Pacific's Boston immigration office distributed approximately 20,000 of a short circular and 20,000 copies of the English version and 5,000 copies of a German version of the pamphlet. In response to queries, the immigration bureaus sent grain samples as evidence of the types of crops that could be successfully grown in Oregon.[38] While the Northern Pacific assumed responsibility for promoting Oregon in Europe, the Board of Immigration Commissioners produced the 65-page pamphlet "Oregon, as It Is" in 1885.[39]

In Wyoming and Washington, the efforts to whiten the territories' populations were more direct. On September 2, 1885, white miners destroyed the Chinatown in Rock Springs, Sweetwater County, Wyoming, murdering 28 and injuring 15 Chinese residents.[40] In Seattle, members of the Knights of Labor rioted and forcibly evicted more than 200 Chinese residents of the city in a race riot that lasted from February 6 to 9, 1886. White mobs drove out Chinese immigrants in other Washington towns as well. To make it clear that Chinese immigrants were unwelcome in Washington, the territorial legislature amended the territorial constitution to bar "aliens ineligible for citizenship" (meaning Asians) from owning property. As a result of this violence, the Chinese populations of Wyoming and Washington dropped dramatically.[41]

At the same time that white Washingtonians were driving out Chinese immigrants, the Republican territorial governor, Watson C. Squire, was turning his reports to the secretary of the interior into promotional literature. The territorial legislature paid to have 10,000 copies of Squire's 1885 report "Resources and Development of Washington Territory" printed and then distributed throughout the United States and in Europe by the Northern Pacific Railroad and Washington real estate interests. The territorial secretary, N. H. Owings, also produced a statistical report on the economic benefits of Washington in 1888.[42]

In Oregon, despite the Board of Immigration commissioner's insistence that it was recruiting settlers to be farmers, the newly elected governor, Sylvester Pennoyer, a populist Democrat and anti-Chinese immigration activist, began campaigning against the board, arguing: "If the early pioneers of forty and fifty years ago could find Oregon without a trail through the forests or over the deserts, immigrants that desire to come here now can undoubtedly already, without artificial aid."[43]

In the Southwest, the demographic problem was the presence of American Indians and Mexicans. Arizona began its immigration promotion policy during a period of ongoing Indian–white violence in the territory, as the U.S. Army and the Apaches engaged in tit-for-tat retaliations in the 1870s and early 1880s.[44] Arizona also faced the problem that its largest immigrant group was Mexicans. So, in 1881, over territorial governor John C. Frémont's veto, the territorial legislature designated *Tombstone Democrat* editor Patrick Hamilton commissioner of immigration, with a salary of $2,000. Hamilton produced four editions of the pamphlet "The Resources of Arizona" and also wrote the pamphlets "Arizona for Homes," "The Arizona Outlook," and "Irrigation, Its History in Different Counties."[45] Hamilton's successor, Cameron H. King, wrote the pamphlets "Resources of Apache County," "The Citrus and Fruit Belt of Southern Arizona," and "Yavapai's Wealth" between 1887 and 1888.[46]

Despite a relatively high level of productivity, the Arizona commissioner of immigration became the center of a series of political battles between Democrats and Republicans in the territory between 1887 and 1890. During these years much political plotting and very little immigration promoting was done in Arizona.[47] The agency was abolished in 1891, revived in 1895, and then allowed to lapse after 1896.[48] During this period, most immigration promotion work in Arizona was done by railroads, especially the Atchison, Topeka & Santa Fe and the Southern Pacific.

Colorado had become a state in August 1876, and the new Republican-controlled state legislature allowed the Board of Immigration to lapse. In 1889, the Colorado legislature, still in the hands of Republicans, revived its promotional policy and created a Bureau of Immigration and Statistics, which designated assessors in each of the state's 55 counties to be deputy superintendents of immigration and operated until 1897.[49]

Immigration promotion in the West became less ambitious in the 1890s, as territories gained statehood and the pressure to gain white population decreased with Chinese exclusion and successful U.S. wars against

American Indian nations. Another significant drought, this one from 1890 to 1896, which straddled the Panic of 1893–1899, also made promotion more difficult, as thousands of Western residents abandoned their homesteads and businesses and moved back East.[50] The Panic, which caused the bankruptcies of the Union Pacific, the Northern Pacific, and the Atchison, Topeka & Santa Fe railroads, among others, also cut into promotional efforts, since so many Western states depended on railroad assistance or subsidy.

In Washington, which finally became a state in 1889, the Republican-controlled state legislature created a Bureau of Statistics, Agriculture, and Immigration in 1895 but failed to appropriate funds for the bureau between 1897 and 1899. The bureau managed to submit one annual report, in 1896, most of it recycled statistics from the 1890 Census and what data on agriculture and industrial prospects could be gathered from boosters in local communities. Realty agent D. B. Ward had been hired as an immigration agent and so promoted Washington alone until he retired in 1901.[51]

As the economy improved and immigration began to increase in 1900, some Western states again began passing immigration promotion laws. But increasingly immigration promotion was tied to the collection of economic and social statistics and their distribution versus the active recruitment of new settlers.

Idaho had been content since the 1860s to allow discoveries of gold and silver in the territory to attract residents without any formal policy. But finally on the verge of statehood (in 1890), Republican territorial governor George Laird Shoup created a Bureau of Immigration, Labor, and Statistics on March 2, 1899, and allocated $5,000 per year to pay for immigration promotion. This bureau distributed 120,000 maps, pamphlets, and circulars advertising Idaho between 1899 and 1903 and claimed responsibility for 21,000 to 23,000 property owners moving to Idaho.[52]

The Washington Bureau of Statistics, Agriculture, and Immigration produced the pamphlets "The Resources and Industries of Washington, the Advantages and Opportunities of the State of Washington for Homebuilders, Investors and Travelers" and "Agricultural, Manufacturing and Commercial Resource and Capabilities of Washington" in 1901, reissuing the second publication every two years for the next several years.[53] The bureau also biannually published "A Review of the Resources and Industries of Washington," beginning in 1905, and a series of publications on irrigated lands, manufacturing opportunities, and tourism in Washington State in the 1910s.[54]

Wyoming, which gained statehood in 1890 and was dominated by the Republican Party, created a Department of Immigration, to be comprised of the commissioner of public lands, the state geologist, and the state engineer, in 1907. In 1909, Colorado, under a brief period of Democratic Party control, established a State Board of Immigration and a commissioner of immigration, which worked with local communities to publicize information about the opportunities to be had in their areas, but both the Wyoming Immigration Department and the Colorado Board of Immigration operated more as statistics collection agencies than as promotion bureaus.[55]

Only in Oregon did the state devote significant resources to immigration promotion in the 1910s (after years of financial neglect in the 1870s and 1880s). The Oregon Immigration Commission had a budget of $25,000 in 1911 and $50,000 in 1914 and used these funds to publish 250,000 pamphlets describing Oregon's agricultural opportunities in German, Norwegian, Swedish, and English.[56]

Western states disseminated a variety of messages about themselves, but the primary image was one of agricultural bountifulness. Challenges such as desert heat, drought, or Indian attacks were rarely, if ever, mentioned by promoters. Although Americans were increasingly discovering the mineral wealth of the West, mining required large amounts of capital and equipment to be successful, and so while promoters noted mineral wealth where it existed (especially in Idaho, Colorado, and the Southwest), they emphasized agriculture, and to a lesser extent stock raising, in their promotional literature.[57]

Oregon, in particular, took advantage of the commonly held (mis)perception that all of the state was as wet as the coastal region and emphasized its mild and moderate climate and plentiful rainfall (which only existed on the coast), fertile soil, and extensive timber (which also only existed in the western part of the state).[58]

In such hefty pamphlets as the 88-page "The Pacific Northwest: Facts Relating to the History, Topography, Climate, Soil, and Agriculture ... Etc., of Oregon and Washington Territory ... Also an Appendix Containing Suggestions to Emigrants, a Short Description of the Several Counties... Issued for the Information and Guidance of Settlers and Others" and the 68-page "Oregon as It Is, Solid Facts and Actual Results, for the Use of and Information of Immigrants," the Oregon Board of Immigration overwhelmed would-be settlers with information about Oregon's natural environment, agricultural and timber economy, land law, taxation, educational and religious institutions, and transportation systems, and profiled its cities and towns. It challenged the belief that the Pacific Northwest had cold winters and instead claimed that the climate was more like that of Northern Europe. Noting that settlement of both Oregon and Washington had been slow until the arrival of railroads in the late 1870s, the board declared in 1882: "All that now is wanting is more brain, muscle and capital for the Pacific Northwest to weave from the warp and woof of its destinies a great and wonderful future."[59]

Relying on experts to provide "scientific" information about climate and agriculture was a common tactic of state immigration promoters. The Washington Bureau of Statistics, Agriculture, and Immigration's pamphlet "Agricultural, Manufacturing and Commercial Resource and Capabilities of Washington" presented itself as a scientific document, with entries on history, geology, dairying, and stock raising written by professors at the University of Washington and the state's agricultural college, while the section on climate was written by the director of the U.S. weather bureau in Seattle, and the material on timber was written by the secretary of the Pacific Coast Lumber Manufacturers Association.[60]

Colorado covered all its bases and advertised itself as a farming-mining-stock raising state, a place with something for everyone.[61] The 126-page pamphlet "The Natural Resources and Industrial Development and Condition of Colorado," which the Bureau of Immigration and Statistics published in 1889, was designed to convince immigrants that Colorado was not just a mining state but one where both farming and stock raising were profitable.

Although the Colorado board did acknowledge the Panic of 1873, one thing it did not discuss in its promotional material was the problem of drought and the recurrent swarms of Rocky Mountain locusts that devoured crops in Colorado and other Great Plains territories between 1873 and 1877.[62]

Selling Wyoming as an agricultural bread (or fruit) basket was more difficult, but the Wyoming Board of Immigration tried to do so. In 1874, the Board of Immigration published "The Territory of Wyoming, History, Soil, Climate, Resources, Etc.," in which it claimed, among other things, that fruits and vegetables could be grown on Wyoming's arid prairies without irrigation.[63] The opportunities for success in farming in Wyoming were as endless as the horizon, according to the Wyoming board.

After Congress passed the Enlarged Homestead Act of 1909, which doubled the size of initial homesteads in semiarid areas to 320 acres, Wyoming began to aggressively promote dry farming (deep plowing to help the soil retain moisture) as well as irrigation.[64] In "Wonderful Wyoming, the Undeveloped Empire," published around 1910, Wyoming's commissioner of public land, Robert P. Fuller, devoted considerable attention to how one could establish a homestead using the Federal Desert (Carey) Land Act of 1894, which allowed corporations to develop irrigation systems and profit off of the sale of water.[65]

Arizona also struggled with its undeniable desert image. Immigration commissioner Thomas Edwin Farish insisted that, with irrigation, Arizona's "trackless desert" could be made "anew in its emerald garnitures of restored productiveness."[66] Another Arizona pamphlet, "Arizona: The Land of Sunshine and Silver, Health and Prosperity, the Place for Ideal Homes," from 1891, acknowledged Arizona's "barren mountains and alkali desserts," but this was unusual; boosters of Arizona rarely even acknowledged the Southwestern desert heat.[67]

Unlike Midwestern promoters, most Western immigration promoters were native-born Americans and themselves pioneers in their states and territories. Some were also Democrats in a time and a region dominated by the Republican Party.

The first Wyoming Board of Immigration had only one immigrant member, L. Abrams, of Albany County, originally from Baden, Germany.[68] M. E. Post had a grocery business in Cheyenne, while P. L. Smith and William McDonald were county commissioners in Carbon and Uinta Counties, respectively. James Kime was originally from Pennsylvania and came to Wyoming in 1866 after spending time in Nebraska and Colorado. He followed the construction of the Union Pacific across Wyoming, establishing freight and passenger service and then a transfer and express business in Cheyenne. In the 1870s, he ran a store and was postmaster in Sweetwater County as well as having a cattle and horse ranch. He was active in local Democratic Party politics and was elected to the territorial legislature in 1886 and to the state Senate in 1892.[69]

The first Colorado Board of Immigration was similar to Wyoming's in its makeup. The members were all successful businessmen and newspaper editors.[70] David C. Collier published the influential *Tri-Weekly Miners Register*, while William N. Byers was editor of the *Rocky Mountain News*.[71] Byers was originally from Ohio but moved to Kansas and then Nebraska in the 1850s, where he was active in territorial and state politics, and then settled in Colorado in 1859, bringing the first printing press west of Omaha with him. He was active in promoting Colorado statehood and the railroads.[72] Jesse M. Sherwood was originally from New York and was a pioneering rancher in Larimer County.[73]

The only immigrant on the Colorado Board of Immigration was Fred Z. Salomon, who had been born in Posen, Prussia, and was one of the first Jews to settle in Denver. Immigrating in the 1840s, he and his brother Hyman had a successful peddling business selling supplies to miners and homesteaders in the Kansas and New Mexico territories before arriving in Denver in 1859 during the gold rush. Besides running a successful grocery dry goods business, Salomon also opened a brewery and a water company. He served on the Denver City Council and was treasurer of the Denver Chamber of Commerce.[74]

The early Arizona immigration commissioners were predominantly newspaper men, people who already had a vested interest in encouraging migration to the territory and who were experienced wordsmiths.[75] Arizona's second commissioner, Thomas Edwin Farish, later served as Arizona's first state historian in 1909, writing the eight-volume *History of Arizona*, published in 1915.[76]

Only Oregon's first state Board of Immigration Commissioners, which was active between 1874 and 1885, had more than one member who was an immigrant.[77]

Christian A. Leinenweber was a German immigrant from Bavaria who came to Oregon in 1866 and settled in Astoria. By 1881, he owned a tannery, the Astoria Boot and Shoe Company, and the John Badollet & Co. cannery, which he had cofounded with Badollet. Active in local and state politics, Leinenweber was a delegate to the state Democratic convention in 1873, and he served in the Oregon House of Representatives in 1884.[78]

Bernard Goldsmith was also from Bavaria, from Munich, but he was Jewish. In 1847, when he was 15, he immigrated to the United States and apprenticed with a watchmaker. He moved first to California in the 1850s, opening several jewelry stores in Northern California before moving to Portland in 1861. Besides owning a mercantile store with several of his brothers, who had also immigrated to Oregon, Goldsmith began speculating in the risky wheat and cattle markets and foreign currencies and investing in mines in Idaho. He also invested in the Willamette River Navigation Company and the Willamette Falls Locks and Canal Company as well as being a founding member of the Portland Stock and Exchange Board in 1865. Goldsmith was elected the mayor of Portland in 1869 as a Democrat and was the first Jewish mayor of the city.[79]

The board's secretary, William Reid, was from Scotland. He had been made U.S. vice-consul in Dundee, despite not being a U.S. citizen, as the result of meeting and impressing Mary Todd Lincoln. He served from 1869 to 1874 and then immigrated to the United States, settling in Oregon. He had already written the pamphlet "Oregon and Washington as Fields for Capital and Labor" in 1873 and then cofounded the Oregon and Washington Trust Investment Company with the Earl of Airlie as president and Reid as secretary. Upon arriving in Portland, he helped organize the Board of Trade and became its first secretary. A few months later, in

September, he was named to the Board of Immigration and became its secretary. He wrote the board's pamphlets, had them translated into various languages, and then circulated them at the 1876 Paris and Philadelphia expositions.[80]

The other members were William S. Ladd and Henry Winslow Corbett. Ladd was a former mayor of Portland (in 1854–1855 and 1858) and a successful merchant and banker. Born in Vermont, he came to Oregon as a young man, arriving in Portland in 1851, shortly after the city had been founded.[81] Corbett was another Oregon pioneer and was originally from Westboro, Massachusetts. After training as a store clerk in New York, he arrived in Portland in 1851 when it was a village of 400 people. After working for his old employer for a few years, Corbett opened his own general merchandise business, H. W. Corbett, in about 1854 (this became Corbett, Failing & Co. in 1871). Corbett was also active in banking and railroad development in Oregon and the Northwest, serving as a director of the Oregon Railroad and Navigation Company, among others. A Republican, he served as a U.S. senator for Oregon from 1867 to 1873.[82]

Less is known about Oregon's second Board of Commissioners, appointed in 1885.[83] The board's president was Charles H. Dodd of Portland. Dodd was a native of New York City and had moved to Oregon in 1966, where he opened a hardware store in Salem. He became successful in business, with his Charles H. Dodd & Co. hardware and machinery business opening branches in several cities throughout the Northwest. He was active in the Portland Chamber of Commerce and the Oregon Republican Party.[84]

Although Western states and territories did not devote as much resources to immigration promotion as Midwestern states, they were, in general, successful in attracting immigrants and white Americans to the region, especially after the tumultuous 1890s.

Although the U.S. Bureau of the Census declared the frontier officially closed in 1890, the high point of homesteading was between 1900 and 1913, during which 1 million homestead claims were filed, a rate twice that of the period of 1862–1900. In 1913 alone nearly 60,000 homesteads covering nearly 11 million acres were claimed from the federal government.[85] Oregon's population grew from 90,923 in 1870 to 413,536 residents in 1900, but Chinese still continued to be one of the state's largest immigrant groups.[86]

Washington, meanwhile, experienced significant population growth between 1870 and 1900, and most of its immigrants were of the desired Northern European or English Canadian background.[87]

Colorado's population grew—more slowly than Oregon or Washington's—but Colorado was able to attract Northern Europeans as its immigration boards had hoped.[88]

Idaho's population also grew slowly, from 14,999 in 1870 to 161,772 in 1900, but most immigrants were from Northern Europe, and Idaho was successful in reducing the number of Chinese immigrants in its population.[89]

Wyoming struggled to gain population in the late 19th century, and the few European immigrants who did come, especially Finns, Italians, Basques, and Greeks, were often recruited by labor contractors, not by the state, and worked in the mining industry or for the railroads.[90]

Western states and territories sought to encourage both immigration and general population movement to their regions but did so as cheaply as possible. Western immigration boards did not spend as much on promotion as Midwestern states did, and Western promoters worked closely with railroads and real estate interests to distribute costs and to take advantage of private corporate networks. The West was also the site of ongoing conflict between the United States and American Indians, as the federal government often resorted to military force to expropriate Indian land and redistribute it to whites through the Homestead Act and railroad land grants. In addition, Western promoters faced significant challenges in countering the often accurate image of their areas as barren, drought prone, and extremely hot or cold. The weather in the late 19th century in the West often did not cooperate, and it was not until significant federal subsidy of irrigation that much of the West became suitable for agriculture.

CHAPTER SEVEN

Immigration Promotion in the South, 1865–1914

The promotion of immigration to America was not limited to undeveloped, "empty" Midwestern and Western states and territories. Southern states also actively recruited new white settlers after the Civil War. But while Midwestern and Western states still faced the problem of removing American Indians and replacing them with white Americans and Northern Europeans, the South had solved its "Indian problem" in the 1830s by forcing the Five Civilized Tribes (the Creek, Cherokee, Choctaw, Chickasaw, and Seminole) to move west of the Mississippi River to Indian Territory.

Instead, the South's main challenge after the Civil War was one of labor, as slavery was abolished and black workers took advantage of their freedom to leave the region in pursuit of better working conditions and higher wages in Northern and Midwestern states. Southern promoters saw European immigration as the solution to the region's dependence on black labor, but Southern leaders could not decide whether they wanted immigrants to be settlers or simply cheap foreign labor to replace freed slaves. As a result, Southern immigration promotion was inconsistent, underfunded, and often more talk than action. Only Texas, a frontier state with a long history of promoting immigration, was successful in recruiting large numbers of immigrants, and this was because it had plentiful land to offer and welcomed immigrants as future citizens, not simply as guest workers.

Southern states engaged in just as much hyperbole as other states and territories promoting immigration but could not mask the region's real economic, political, and social problems after the Civil War. Southern states could not compete with Midwestern and Western states and territories offering immigrants free government and cheap railroad land, subsidized transportation, temporary housing, and high wages.

The primary images of the South that Southern states conveyed in their promotional material were long growing seasons and the supposed healthfulness due to a warmer climate. Some states also claimed that land was particularly cheap in their areas, and South Carolina, Mississippi, and Tennessee specifically charged their immigration commissioners with registering, advertising, and selling land, while Georgia and Florida explicitly combined the sale and development of state land and immigration. Most Southern immigration agencies were either linked or subsumed within state departments of agriculture, reflecting the assumption that most immigrants would engage in farming, either as farm laborers or farm owners.

Every Southern state passed at least one immigration promotion law between 1866 and 1880, and West Virginia, Georgia, and South Carolina passed multiple acts in this period. Another high point of Southern state immigration promotion was 1906–1907, when Mississippi, Kentucky, Tennessee, North Carolina, and Alabama adopted laws in response to the federal government's efforts to clarify federal rules against advertisements encouraging immigration for the purpose of contract labor.[1] By this point, Southern states were more interested in attracting immigrants as guest workers than as permanent settlers.

Like Midwestern and Western states, Southern states were primarily interested in attracting clearly white, Protestant Europeans, although Louisiana attempted with a small degree of success to encourage French immigration. Texas was interested in continuing the immigration of Germans, Norwegians, Czechs, and Poles that it had been receiving since the Mexican period because the state considered these groups particularly hardworking and productive.[2] Missouri also focused on attracting Germans, Swiss, Hungarians, Czechs, and Poles in the belief that according to the "isothermal laws of migration," it could not attract immigrants from Scandinavia or even Great Britain and Canada.[3] Maryland and West Virginia targeted Germans and Swiss in particular, in the belief that they were "a moral, ingenious, and industrious people" and well suited for farming mountainous environs.[4] Tennessee was also particularly interested in recruiting Germans.[5] Mississippi claimed it simply wanted "thrifty and industrious settlers."[6] Florida also desired "population from every state in the Union, and from every country in Europe" and stressed, "We do not want immigrants for subordinate positions, but, on the contrary, invite them to locate, and become the owners of their homes in fee simple forever."[7]

In the Midwest and West, immigration promotion was primarily developed by the Republican Party, but in the South, both Republicans and Democrats supported promotion. Republicans, especially Radicals, wanted to undermine the political and economic power of the larger planters but worried that increased immigration would undercut black labor.[8] Southern Democrats saw immigration promotion as a way of replacing a subservient black labor force with a foreign one or prompting enough competition between blacks and immigrants to drive down the wages of both groups. In March 1864, even as the Civil War still raged, the newly created state of West Virginia passed a law authorizing the governor to appoint a commissioner of emigration to publicize the advantages of the state in Europe and to recruit immigrants from Germany, Austria, Sweden, Switzerland, and Great Britain.[9] Republican governor Arthur I. Boreman appointed Joseph H. Diss Debar, an immigrant from Strasbourg, Alsace (now France), to be the state's first commissioner of emigration.[10]

Debar wrote and mailed off 3,000 copies of a short (eight-page) pamphlet in English and German and began networking with large European newspapers, consulate officials, and businessmen connected to immigration, particularly in the steamship industry, to persuade them to distribute literature about West Virginia in Europe. Debar also hired an official from the Interior Department of Württemberg, C. Lautenschlager, to be an agent in southern Germany and Switzerland, while Debar based himself at Castle Garden in New York City.[11]

In 1865, Debar distributed another 8,000 copies of his pamphlet as well as copies of the state constitution, maps, and other literature about the state, and promoted West Virginia aggressively among miners who were interested in working in the newly developing coal fields as well as capitalists interested in investment. For the first time, the Republican-controlled state legislature was persuaded to appropriate $1,000, which paid for printing costs, but still refused to grant Debar a salary.[12]

Finding that encouraging individuals to immigrate was tedious, Debar focused on trying to encourage large-scale colonization projects, and he helped to organize an emigration company managed by several wealthy West Virginia businessmen, the State Immigration and Improvement Company. But this company failed to get off the ground and was particularly hindered by state law that prohibited corporations from buying or selling land for profit.[13]

In February 1865, Missouri, which had not seceded from the Union, created a five-member Board of Immigration, two of whom were the governor, Thomas C. Fletcher, and the secretary of state, Francis Rodman, both Republicans. The other members were Amade Valle; Frederick Muench, a long-time promoter of German immigration to Missouri; and board secretary Isidor Bush, the president of the German Emigrant Aid Society of St. Louis. The board was granted an appropriation of $6,000 for its first two years and was authorized to hire agents in the Eastern United States and in Europe. The board also solicited nearly $4,500 in private contributions, which it put into an "immigration fund" to support its charge of both promoting immigration and advising and assisting immigrants.[14]

The Missouri Board of Immigration hired a handful of agents to write and distribute literature, travel around the country giving speeches, and assist immigrants in their journeys to Missouri.[15] The board also hired Berlin writer John I. Sturz, the former German consul to Brazil and Uruguay, to promote immigration to Missouri in Germany and used board member Muench's relationship with the editor of the Bremen-based *Auswanderer Zeitung*, H. M. Hautschild, to publish material about the state.[16] The board also negotiated with railroads to secure reduced fares for immigrants on both travel and baggage, although not all of the roads in the state were willing to give discounts.[17]

The Board of Immigration distributed 10,000 copies of an English-language circular, "Free Missouri," and paid to mail copies of Muench's pamphlet, "The State of Missouri: A Handbook for German Emigrants," to Germany. The board also distributed copies of "The Resources of Missouri," by S. Waterhouse, and "A Handbook of Missouri and Geological Map," by N. H. Parker. In addition, information about the board was included in Daniel Hertle's book, "The Germans in North America and Struggle of Freedom in Missouri," of which 500 copies were distributed in Germany.[18]

Because board secretary Bush was the president of the German Emigrant Aid Society of St. Louis, the Missouri Board of Immigration partnered with several emigrant societies and used their connections to further encourage immigration. The Board of Immigration also encouraged the creation of local auxiliaries, which the board hoped would serve as a source of information about job and real estate opportunities in various communities.[19]

Missouri was unusual in its recognition of the nature and function of chain migration and of the importance of encouraging the development of such chains. "Wherever the immigrant can find society, people from his native home, where he can speak the language of his childhood, can visit the church in which he had been brought up, can sing with friends the tunes of known melodies, can dance and play the games of his youth, can drink his long cherished beverages—there he will much sooner feel at home again, and will invite others to join him," the Board of Immigration argued.[20]

But most Southern states were not interested in immigrant communities developing within them. "We want people from all the great nationalities to come and be with us and of us, but when they come we want them to be no longer Germans, or Scandinavians, or Irishmen, but purely and grandly American," asserted Robert Gates, the vice president of the Southern Immigration Association in 1884.[21]

On April 9, 1865, Confederate general Robert E. Lee surrendered at Appomattox Court House in Virginia, but fighting between Union and Confederate forces continued until June 23, 1865. Confederate states fell under military governance and Republican political control between 1863 and 1877, as the Union Army conquered and occupied Confederate territory, and the federal government instituted Reconstruction policies to abolish slavery, re-establish republican government, and protect newly freed slaves' civil rights. Although all of the former Confederate states were readmitted to the Union by 1870, military occupation of Florida, Louisiana, and South Carolina continued until early 1877. Reconstruction was a period of extreme political turmoil and racial violence as blacks and whites and Democrats and Republicans fought over fundamental questions of political and economic power.

On March 17, 1866, the Democratic-controlled Louisiana state legislature passed "An Act to Organize a Bureau of Immigration" and appropriated funds to pay the bureau chief an annual salary of $3,500.[22] J. C. Kathman, an attorney and a dealer in coke and charcoal, was the first head of the Louisiana Bureau of Immigration, from 1866 to 1868.[23] Kathman wrote (or compiled) a pamphlet, "Information for Immigrants into the State of Louisiana," published in 1868, and sent at least one agent to Europe to promote Louisiana.[24]

Unlike in Midwestern states, which sought to recruit immigrants with enough capital to start farms and businesses, the Louisiana Bureau of Immigration accepted requests from Louisianans looking for wage workers and functioned as much as a labor bureau as a state marketing agency.[25]

Kathman resigned in the spring of 1867 after the state legislature refused to pay him for his work.[26] His replacement, James O. Noyes, was originally from New York and took over in 1868. In February 1869, Noyes recommended that the Bureau of Immigration be reorganized into a Commission of Immigration and that it open a labor exchange along the lines of the one operated at Castle Garden by the New York State Board of Commissioners of Emigration. Republican governor Henry C. Warmoth accepted this recommendation and created a six-member Commission of Immigration and named Noyes as its president and chief agent. The purpose of the commission was to bring the "employer and the laborer" and the "seller and buyer" of land together, not recruit immigrants as settlers. This commission survived until 1873, when it was defunded by the state legislature.[27]

Kathman and Noyes managed Louisiana's Immigration Bureau during a period of extreme political volatility in the state. Louisiana had three military governors between mid-1865 and 1868 and two contested elections that resulted in two competing legislatures being sworn in and sitting, one Democrat and the other Republican, between 1872 and 1874, and two competing governors being inaugurated in 1877. All of this political chaos was marked by fraud and increasing violence by whites against blacks. Part of the Compromise of 1877, which formally ended Reconstruction and military occupation of the former Confederacy, recognized Democratic control of Louisiana state government.

South Carolina began promoting immigration in late 1866. In December, at the urging of German immigrant and Confederate general John A. Wagener, the Democratic-controlled state legislature passed an act creating the office of commissioner of immigration and appropriated $10,000 for the commissioner to register state land for sale and advertise this property in Northern Europe. Military governor James Lawrence Orr, a Democrat and former Confederate congressman, appointed Wagener to be commissioner in February 1867.[28]

Wagener wrote the pamphlet "South Carolina: A Home for the Industrious Immigrant" and distributed 5,000 copies in English, 5,000 copies in German, 2,000 in Swedish, and 2,000 in Danish. In May 1867, a Mr. Ferler sailed for Scandinavia, while a Captain Melchers went to Germany to promote South Carolina. Wagener had hired a Major Ryan to be the agent for Ireland, but Ryan changed his mind at the last minute and left for new opportunities in Texas, and so South Carolina was left without an agent for Ireland or Great Britain.[29] Such were the challenges of promoting immigration to the South in the late 1860s.

Besides registering both public land and private land planters were willing to sell, Wagener organized immigration societies at the local and county levels to support his promotion efforts and lobbied the European steamship companies to sail directly from Bremen, Hamburg, and

Glasgow to Charleston. On November 29, 1867, a ship of 152 immigrants from Germany arrived at Charleston, but few of these Germans actually stayed in South Carolina.[30]

Southern legislatures' efforts to *de facto* re-enslave blacks through Black Codes and increasing white-on-black violence caused Radical Republicans in Congress to pass the Reconstruction Acts in July 1867, which divided the Confederacy into five military districts and abolished the Democratic-controlled state governments elected in November 1866. In late 1868, Radical Republicans took control of the South Carolina state government and abolished the immigration commissioner's office in the belief that its purpose was to undercut black labor and because Wagener's promotional efforts had been largely unsuccessful: only about 400 immigrants had settled in the state.[31]

Tennessee was another state that sought to combine immigration promotion and land sales. A border state under Republican Party control between 1865 and 1869 and the first Confederate state to rejoin the Union in 1866, Tennessee first passed a state Senate resolution calling for a Committee on Immigration in October 1865 and then created a five-member Board of Immigration in early December 1867, appropriating $2,000 to pay for a commissioner and the publication of a pamphlet. Besides the governor, Radical Republican W. G. Brownlow, and the secretary of state, A. J. Fletcher, the other board members were the Hon. R. B. Cheatham, Dr. J. M. Kerchival, and Gen. John Eaton Jr., the state's superintendent of public instruction and former assistant commissioner of the Freedmen's Bureau. German immigrant and minister Hermann Bokum was appointed immigration commissioner. Bokum was charged with documenting the resources of each county and land available for sale and for keeping records of people interested in buying land in the hopes of matching sellers and would-be buyers. He sent agents to Germany and Switzerland and advertised in Northern American and German newspapers. Bokum also hired an agent in New York City, C. E. Evans, who issued train tickets to immigrants traveling from New York to Tennessee via Norfolk, Virginia, on the Virginia and Tennessee Railroad.[32]

Under both Republican Party control and military occupation in 1869, Florida created a Bureau of Immigration, which published the pamphlets "Florida: Its Climate, Soil, and Productions, with a Sketch of Its History, Natural Features and Social Condition: A Manual of Reliable Information Concerning the Resources of the State and the Inducements to Immigrants" and "The Florida Settler; or, Immigrants' Guide."[33] But the bureau lacked the resources to hire an agent in New York or advertise or send anyone to Europe, so the bureau instead focused on trying to persuade people in the Northwest and far West to move back east and south to Florida.[34]

Unlike other Southern states, Texas had a long tradition of promoting immigration since the Mexican period, through the Texas Republic, and into the post-Civil War period. Radical Republican governor Edmund Davis was so eager to establish a Bureau of Immigration that he appointed Gustav Loeffler superintendent in 1870, even before legislation creating the bureau was passed. In fact, Loeffler's first report specifically urged the passage of legislation enabling the bureau's work, which finally occurred on May 23, 1871.[35]

The Republican-controlled Texas state legislature also granted Loeffler a salary of $2,000 per year for the next four years, and he hired as agents J. H. Lippard, who started in New Orleans but quickly moved to St. Louis, Missouri; William H. Parsons, who had an office in New York City; Dr. Theodore Hertzberg, who was based in Bremen, Germany; and John T. McAdam, who worked out of Manchester, England.[36] Loeffler also negotiated with several railroad and steamship companies to get special rates for immigrants and their luggage through the Port of Galveston.[37]

After the turbulent 1860s, as former Confederate states experienced military occupation and evolving Reconstruction policies, Southern immigration promotional efforts became less ambitious, with few states sending agents to Europe. Immigration promotion agents struggled to gain funds or even to stay in office. Increasingly, in the 1870s through 1890s, immigration promotion in the South was about printing propaganda and little else. This was due to Southern state leaders' realization that regardless of their efforts, immigrants were not moving to the South in large numbers.

In West Virginia, the legislature passed a new law in February 1871 charging the Board of Public Works to develop a plan to recruit "sober and industrious immigrants, with their families" from other states and Europe. Debar was fired and a new commissioner of immigration was to be appointed who would implement the board's policy.[38] But the legislature refused to appropriate funds, and so little actual promotion work was done between 1871 and 1879.

Under Republican Party control between 1870 and 1875, Mississippi created a Department of Agriculture and Immigration in 1873 and appointed Richard Griggs as commissioner. Griggs was a freed slave who had been sold 18 times before Emancipation and at one point had been owned by Confederate general Nathan B. Forrest, a founder of the Ku Klux Klan.[39] Griggs published "A Guide to Mississippi" in 1874 but lacked the funds to do anything else.[40]

Keppler & Schwarzmann, "The new South—the triumph of free labor," *Puck*, v. 38, No. 972, October 23, 1895, centerfold. (Library of Congress)

In 1873, Democrats gained control of the Texas state legislature and then the governorship in 1874. Governor Richard Coke replaced Gustav Loeffler with Jerome B. Robertson as superintendent of the Bureau of Immigration. Robertson headed the Bureau of Immigration for two years before the agency was defunded and disbanded by the new state constitution adopted in 1876.[41]

During this period, Robertson and the Bureau of Immigration attempted to challenge the image of Texas as a wild, lawless place by insisting that "law and order are rigidly maintained, and crime as properly punished as in any of the States."[42] Yet, in fact, Texas was plagued by raids by the Kiowa, Comanche, and Cheyenne on ranches as well as by outlaw gangs who rustled cattle and robbed settlers. The United States' Red River Indian War of 1874 against Comanche, Cheyenne, and Kiowa directly challenged Texas officials' claims that the state was free from Indian violence.[43]

Under Democratic Party control since 1872, Georgia created a Department of Agriculture in 1874, and it was this agency that was primarily involved in promoting immigration to Georgia, through such publications as "A Manual of Georgia for the Use of Immigrants and Capitalists" and "Georgia, from the Immigrant Settler's Stand-Point" until 1879, when the legislature passed another act calling for the encouragement of immigration.[44]

The Georgia Department of Agriculture attempted to encourage chain migration by collecting the names of residents who were either immigrants or from the North and sending circulars to these people so they could in turn provide information about their communities designed to appeal to immigrants. But of the 13 letter writers referenced, only one was from an immigrant, a man from Great Britain.[45]

Reconstruction, and Republican Party control of state government, ended in Mississippi in 1876 with a great deal of white-on-black violence, which greatly damaged the reputation of the state among both Northerners and immigrants. Thousands of black Mississippians left the state for Kansas and other border states to escape white terrorism. A yellow fever epidemic in 1878 sickened 16,000 and killed more than 4,000 people, further discouraging immigration. On March 4, 1878, the Democratic-controlled state legislature passed an act establishing a Board of Commissioners of Immigration and Agriculture and appointed Major E. G. Wall as commissioner.[46] The other members of the Board of Agriculture and Immigration were Governor John Marshall Stone, state treasurer W. L. Hemingway, and Attorney General Thomas C. Catchings, all Democrats. Promotional work was left to Wall, whose experience was publishing "Wall's Manual of Agriculture, for the Southern United States" in 1870.[47]

On March 10, 1879, West Virginia passed another immigration promotion act, this one authorizing the appointment of a state agent of immigration and appropriating $500 to pay him. The legislation also specified that the agent was to be Charles E. Lutz of Randolph County and the land agent for Helvetia, a Swiss colony in Randolph County founded in 1869.[48]

Ever since the Louisiana Bureau of Immigration was dissolved in 1873, sugar planters had lobbied for its revival and/or strengthening as large numbers of black residents left the state for the Midwest and better living and working conditions. Finally, on May 23, 1880, the Democratic-controlled state legislature passed a bill to create a Bureau of Agriculture and Immigration, but it was not until 1885 that Democratic governor Samuel McEnery appointed William Harris commissioner of agriculture and immigration and J. C. Morrison immigration agent; no salary was appropriated for either man. To pay for the publication of a pamphlet, Morrison solicited funds from parish police juries.[49]

The Louisiana Bureau of Agriculture and Immigration focused on distributing information about agricultural conditions in the state through a network of railroad agents, representatives at fairs and expositions, and real estate salesmen. The Illinois Central Railroad, which had a terminus in New Orleans, paid for the cost of printing and distributing several thousand handbooks in 1894.[50]

On December 24, 1880, the Democratic-controlled South Carolina state legislature made another effort at promotion, passing "An Act to Aid and Encourage Immigration into this State by Returning the Amount of Taxes Paid by Immigrants upon all Real Estate Purchased by Them, and upon the Capital Used in Improvements thereon, Except the Two Mills School Tax, for a Period of Five Years, and by Authorizing the Department of Agriculture to Use the Funds under Its Control, in its Discretion for that Purpose." This act placed the responsibility for promotion in the hands of the Agricultural Department and its commissioner of agriculture, rather than in a separate commissioner of immigration as it had been under Wagener, and funded promotion through the real estate taxes paid by immigrants instead of a direct appropriation. Dr. E. M. Boykin, a Civil War Confederate Army veteran, was appointed commissioner.[51]

But under Boykin, the Agricultural Department focused on recruiting European farm labor for planters versus encouraging immigrants to come and settle permanently in the state. The Agriculture Department also did not promote or facilitate land sales.[52]

Between 1881 and 1883, South Carolina spent approximately $8,895 on immigration promotion and managed to recruit 860 immigrants, at a cost of about 10 dollars per head, or the cost of transporting a person from New York City to Columbia. Planters seeking to recruit immigrant labor reimbursed the state for its advertising and other promotional efforts. Boykin offered employment to 1,000 German families, prepaying passage and guaranteeing 18 dollars per month wages.[53]

After briefly ending its promotional work in 1882, the South Carolina Agriculture Department, under the management of Commissioner Col. Andrew P. Butler, resumed the immigration promotion campaign in 1883.[54] Butler wrote several pamphlets and handbooks, worked with officials at Castle Garden, and arranged for the construction of a temporary home for the few newcomers who arrived in Charleston.[55]

Alabama had passed immigration promotion laws in February 1866 to "encourage immigration and to protect immigrant labor," and in February 1875 to create a commissioner of immigration and a Board of Commissioners and Directors, but nothing came of these efforts. In February 1887, Alabama initiated another promotion policy, passing an act to "encourage immigration and investment of capital" in the state. The Democratic-controlled legislature appropriated $2,000 to buy the copyright to booster Benjamin Franklin Riley's book "Alabama as It Is: Or, the Immigrant's and Capitalist's Guide Book to Alabama" as well as another $1,500 to distribute 5,000 copies of it.[56]

In 1888, Virginia created a Committee of Immigration and Labor Statistics within its Department of Agriculture, and this agency functioned into the 1950s. It conceded the failures of promoting immigration to Virginia in the past and instead concentrated its efforts on encouraging young Virginians to stay at home versus leave in search of work elsewhere and to encourage people already in the United States to move to Virginia "rather than repeat the efforts to turn upon us a stream of promiscuous population from abroad."[57]

The federal Immigration Act of 1891, which established Ellis Island and other immigration stations, also banned the assistance or encouragement of immigration through advertisements printed and published in a foreign country but specifically exempted states from this prohibition.[58]

Southern immigration agencies took advantage of this exemption and increasingly focused on recruiting European labor versus promoting the immigration of permanent settlers. In February 1904, the South Carolina state legislature passed "An Act to Establish a Department of Agriculture, Commerce, and Immigration," whose commissioner, Ebbie Julian Watson, was authorized to encourage immigration by offering to pay immigrants' passage out of a state fund made up of state appropriations and private contributions.[59]

Louisiana's Bureau of Agriculture and Immigration also began targeting Southern Europeans, particularly Italians, by partnering with the private Louisiana Immigration League, which sent agents to New York to try to divert Italians to Louisiana.[60]

In an effort to bring European workers directly to South Carolina, Commissioner Watson negotiated with North German Lloyd to make an experimental trip to Charleston after recruiting textile workers from Belgium, Germany, and Austria-Hungary. In November 1906, 450 steerage passengers sailed on the S. S. *Wittekind* to Charleston, where they were interviewed by federal Bureau of Immigration inspectors who made a special trip to South Carolina since the Port of Charleston did not have an immigration station.[61]

The arrival of the *Wittekind* in Charleston and Louisiana's recruitment efforts in New York triggered a larger debate about the legality of such policies. Organized labor alleged that South Carolina mill owners were the money behind the state's immigration fund and were using the state to import foreign labor to work in their mills. Secretary of commerce and labor Oscar S. Straus ruled that South Carolina's recruitment of immigrants and payment of transportation did not violate federal contract labor laws. But a year later, in response to protests from Northern congressmen and the amending of the immigration laws in February 1907,

Attorney General Charles J. Bonaparte announced that states were only allowed to advertise the benefits of immigration, not pay for or subsidize transportation.[62]

This decision largely ended South Carolina's immigration program. But Louisiana continued to help planters get around the contract labor ban. The Louisiana Bureau of Agriculture and Immigration created a fund into which planters could deposit $160 to pay for the transportation of an immigrant family for whom the state would pay transportation. When the immigrants arrived, the state would collect the deposit as a fee for its costs.[63] The bureau also granted labor recruiter Frank Missler the right to import workers from Europe to Louisiana's sugar plantations and lumber camps. In July 1907, Missler sent 1,000 Bulgarians to Louisiana and split the two dollars per head fee the bureau charged each immigrant upon arriving at the Port of New Orleans with state immigration commissioner Charles Schuler.[64]

The federal ruling on states engaged in contracting immigrant labor meant that the few Southern states interested in doing any more than publishing pamphlets could not. Maryland's Bureau of Immigration got creative and gave the names of everyone who had applied for information about the state to licensed real estate agents to try to facilitate land sales.[65] And the bureau's secretary, Herman Badenhoop, visited Germany and Switzerland in 1907 to try to persuade "gentlemen farmers" to move to Maryland and toured several Midwestern states in 1908 with the same purpose.[66] But most Southern states ended their promotional programs after 1907.

Confronted with an economy wrecked by war; a lack of large amounts of available, undeveloped, and fertile farmland; and the challenge of replacing slave labor with free and/or wage labor, Southern immigration promoters focused on the region's warmer weather, longer growing season, and plentiful water and rainfall to try to sell the South to Europeans and white Northerners. Florida and Georgia also claimed their states had particular health benefits, while Louisiana asserted a cosmopolitan culture. Despite the significant poverty of the South in the postbellum period, the region's immigration promoters projected an image of abundance, even overabundance, and an environment of inexhaustible resources. Virtually all Southern states insisted, especially during the Reconstruction period, that hostility toward Northerners and foreigners was absent.

The description C. Menelas, a Greek immigrant to Mississippi, gave of his adopted state was typical of Southern claims about the benefits of the Southern environment for agriculture: "The attractions that Mississippi offers to the industrious and intelligent immigrant are innumerable. He will live in a land of plenty, where the climate is salubrious, the air balmy, the summers have unfailing breezes, the winters are mild, and where the soil, under judicious tillage, can produce crops almost the year round."[67]

Southern promoters reminded immigrants of the droughts, blizzards, and even locusts that the Midwest and West suffered in the 1870s and 1880s. "More people have frozen to death in Northwest Iowa and Western Minnesota than were ever murdered by Indians in those countries since their settlement," according to a veteran of Iowa winters, whose views the Kentucky Bureau of Immigration was happy to share with would-be settlers.[68]

For those who thought the Southern climate excessively hot, especially in the summertime, Southern immigration promoters insisted that "*as a matter of fact*, the thermometer rises *higher* in New York, Boston and Montreal than in St. Augustine, Tampa and Key West."[69] Georgia's agricultural commissioner, Thomas J. Janes, explained this was because New York's northern latitude caused the city to have an extra hour of daylight in the summer, thus allowing more heat to be generated.[70]

By contrast, the South was not only warm, it was supposedly geographically (and presumably also culturally and spiritually) comparable to Biblical civilizations. For those who thought Florida a swampy backwater, the commissioner of the Florida State Bureau of Immigration, A. A. Robinson, reminded his readers: "Her territory is included in the same zone in which, according to the most ancient of books, the human race had its origin, and in which the Garden of Eden was said to be situated. This zone embraces the territory of the ancient civilizations of Egypt, Babylon, Greece and Rome."[71] Janes insisted of Georgia: "We have the winter climate of Rome, and the summer climate of Jerusalem."[72] The Texas Bureau of Immigration proclaimed Texas's climate "superior to that of Italy."[73]

The chief benefit of the Southern climate was short, mild winters, which meant a longer growing season, an important factor for farmers. South Carolina immigration commissioner John Wagener, who was responsible for advertising land for sale, emphasized the mild climate and long growing season possible for a wide variety of crops in a state where cotton had been the dominant crop for generations.[74]

Florida boosters, of course, highlighted fruit growing, especially of citrus and other exotic, tropical fruits, and provided information about how to start an orange grove.[75] Florida was a place of "light work and ample leisure," where luxury fruits and vegetables could be grown in one's spare time, unlike the hard labor of "ordinary farming" done in Western and

Northern states.[76] Alabama's pamphlet "Farm Lands for Sale in the South," published in 1895, also emphasized the opportunities for small farmers, especially of fruits and vegetables.[77]

Although the South lacked large amounts of public land to distribute to homesteaders, Southern immigration promoters insisted that privately owned land was cheap and that Southern planters were eager to sell to European farmers. Land was described as being particularly cheap in West Virginia and Florida.[78] In Louisiana, the 1867 pamphlet "Information for Immigrants into the State of Louisiana" provided information about land for sale and reprinted letters from Louisianans interested in selling their farms and other properties to immigrants.[79] In the early 20th century, the Louisiana Bureau of Agriculture and Immigration published a "List of Louisiana Lands for Sale" every two years after 1902.[80] The 1874 "Guide to Mississippi" included a long list of state lands available for purchase by county, and the 1875 pamphlet "Texas, the Home for the Emigrant, from Everywhere," presented information about lands for homestead, sale, or lease.[81]

Yet, in reality, land in the South was often expensive or else unimproved. In South Carolina, property registered with the Immigration Bureau was priced up to 15 dollars per acre for land that sold for only one or two dollars at public auction.[82] In Louisiana, only 18.2 percent of land in the state was improved and ready for immediate occupancy, 9.5 million acres were "swamp and over-flow land," and large planters owned most of the state's good farmland. New farmers would have to clear and drain their land before they could even begin planting, and then they faced the problem of tight credit controlled by the large planters.[83]

The supposed healthfulness of the South was also a selling point for promoters. Like Colorado and New Mexico, which stressed the benefits of desert air and plentiful sunshine, Georgia advertised the health benefits of its many mineral springs.[84] Florida's boosters claimed that the state was particularly healthy not just because of its warm climate but because of the large quantity of ozone generated by its extensive coastline and pine forests (in fact, excessive ozone can cause cell damage).[85] In Texas, invigorating health and purified air were attributed to the electricity found in strong wind storms called Texas Northers.[86]

New Orleans, which had long suffered from yellow fever and cholera outbreaks, was instead described by the Louisiana immigration commissioner as a particularly healthy city that people visited or moved to in order to improve their health.[87] Florida promoters also reassured would-be immigrants that yellow fever was not endemic in Florida and that even malaria in Florida was milder than elsewhere in the country.[88]

Virtually every Southern immigration promoter in the 1870s made reference to the Civil War and insisted that Southerners were welcoming of Northerners and of foreigners in general: "We say come here and settle, and labor for the interests of the State and for yourselves, be you Republicans or Democrats, or of no politics at all, and you will meet a cordial welcome. It is not the question to be asked by Republicans, are you rich? Are you a Methodist, or are you a Baptist? Are you a Republican or Democrat? But, are you honest, industrious and truthful and fair-dealing in your intercourse with your fellow man. All are welcome; all are needed. If you have capital, good; if you have no capital excepting your strong muscles and hard hands, still well and good. You are welcome to the best you can earn for yourself in the State. You are more than welcome; your presence is desired," declared Mississippi's first immigration commissioner, Richard Griggs.[89]

Mississippi's second immigration commissioner, E. G. Wall, was more willing to acknowledge Mississippi's racial problems but attempted to reassure Europeans that there was no competition between blacks and whites in Mississippi because "the white man has the advantage and preference in all work requiring skill and management."[90]

Tennessee's immigration commissioner, Hermann Bokum, assured Germans that few black Tennesseans lived in the eastern part of the state and added, "I know of no cases where the colored people are in so disorganized a state as to make it unsafe to live amongst them."[91]

South Carolina's commissioner of immigration, Wagener, insisted that "habits of industry, frugality, honesty, and thrift" were valued in the South and that South Carolina was a "liberal and enlightened community," unlike Northern states that had been plagued by nativism before the Civil War.[92]

Louisiana made the unique argument that its relaxed attitude toward public morality made it "European" and thus welcoming to immigrants: "The laws of Louisiana have always been more liberal than those of any other State in the Union. We have had no sumptuary laws, no Sunday laws, no Maine liquor laws, no laws against hunting or fishing. The theatres, the ball rooms, the beer gardens, the coffeehouses, the billiard saloons and the churches of every sect, are all open and are allowed equal privileges on Sundays," Commissioner Kathman declared.[93]

But Europeans were more familiar with Louisiana's practice of lynching and mob violence, which made international news repeatedly in the 1890s and early 1900s. On March 14, 1891, eleven Italians were lynched in New Orleans for supposedly shooting the New Orleans police superintendent. Three Italians were lynched in Hahnville for alleged murder in 1895, and five others were murdered in Tallulah for injuring a doctor in 1899.[94] These incidents discouraged many immigrants from settling in Louisiana or even going there for seasonal work.

Although most states devoted most of their resources to highlighting what they considered to be their chief assets (and downplaying or ignoring their deficiencies and problems), some Southern states devoted significant attention to what they saw as the deficiencies of other states. Maryland, for instance, criticized Western promoters who swindled immigrants and portrayed the West as an "earthly paradise," when in fact it was "a desert region, endless wastes and prairies, without trees or water, where winter reigns supreme for nine months and raging heat renders the short summers almost unendurable."[95]

Kentucky also contrasted itself sharply with the West in the 1881 pamphlet "Information for Emigrants: The Climate, Soils, Timbers, &C., of Kentucky, Contrasted with Those of the Northwest."[96]

Southern immigration promoters tended to be successful immigrants themselves, most of them German, or wealthy planters interested in solving the South's postwar labor problems. Several of these German promoters had been involved in founding German colonies in the South before the Civil War.

In West Virginia, Debar was the son of the manager of the estates of the Prince Cardinal de Rohan and was educated in France and Germany. He immigrated to the United States in 1842, settling in Parkersburg, Virginia. In 1846, he was hired to be the land agent for a 10,000-acre tract in Doddridge County in western Virginia owned by the Boston financier James Swann. He also bought land in the region and helped to develop a colony of Swiss immigrants, Santa Clara. A Unionist during the Civil War, Debar was elected to the newly created state legislature and then appointed commissioner of emigration.[97]

South Carolina's first agent, John Wagener, had been born in Sievern in northern Hanover in 1816, the son of a store-and-inn keeper. He immigrated first to New York in 1831 and then moved to Charleston in 1833. He was very active in founding German organizations in Charleston, including the newspaper *Der Teutone*; the German Jägerkorps (hunting corps); the Deutsche Feuerwehr-Compagnie (German Fire Protection Company) of Charleston; and a literary and musical society, the Teutonenbund, from which the Freundschaftsbund (Friendly Society) emerged in 1853. He was also the founder of the German town of Walhalla, Oconee County, in 1848. He organized a German Colonization Society, bought land, and laid out the community. Unlike most Germans, who opposed slavery and supported the Union, Wagener fought for the Confederacy, leading a regiment almost entirely manned by Germans, and was made a brigadier general in the Confederate Army. After the Civil War, he served as mayor of Charleston between 1871 and 1873.[98]

Missouri Board of Immigration member Frederick Muench was also German, from Hesse-Darmstadt. A Lutheran minister, Muench and a friend, attorney Paul Follen, were inspired by the pioneer promoter Gottfried Duden to found the Giessener Auswanderungsgesellschaft (Giessen Emigration Society) in 1833, and they brought a group of 500 Germans to Missouri, where they settled in Dutzow, Warren County, near Duden's farm. Muench was a leader in Missouri's abolitionist and antisecession movements and served in the state legislature during the Civil War.[99]

Muench's colleague, Isidor Bush (born Busch), had been born in Prague, Austria-Hungary (now the Czech Republic) into a wealthy German Jewish family. He worked in a Jewish publishing firm owned by his father in Vienna and became involved in liberal and radical politics. After the failed democratic revolutions in 1848, he fled to New York in early 1849 and made his way to St. Louis, where he managed a general store and became active in the Jewish fraternal order B'nai B'rith, and the antislavery and antisecession movements. He was Union general John C. Frémont's aide-de-camp during the Civil War and then worked as a freight and passenger agent for the St. Louis and Iron Mountain Railroad Company while also running the German Emigrant Aid Society in St. Louis.[100]

Another German was Tennessee's immigration commissioner, Hermann Bokum, who also worked for the State of Washington's Bureau of Immigration from 1862 to 1867. Bokum had been a strong supporter of the Union before the Civil War and barely escaped arrest by prosecessionists in 1861.[101]

Texas's first immigration superintendent, Gustav Loeffler, was also from Germany. He initially immigrated to New Orleans but quickly settled in Houston, where he was active in Houston's large German community, serving as president of the city's Turn-verein (athletic club) in 1866. By 1873, he was working as a cotton factor while also serving as immigration superintendent. He served as superintendent from 1870 to 1874 and then returned to dealing in cotton until his death in 1877.[102]

Texas's second superintendent of immigration, Jerome B. Robertson, was born in Kentucky, where he apprenticed to a hatter and then attended medical school. He moved to Texas in 1836 to fight in the Texas rebellion against Mexico. He served in the Texas state house from 1847 to 1849 and the state Senate from 1849 to 1851 and worked as a coroner and postmaster for Washington County. A "rabid secessionist," he fought for the Confederacy during the Civil War, ending with the rank of general.[103]

Benjamin Franklin Riley was a native of Alabama as well as a Baptist minister, president of Howard College (now Samford University) from 1888 to 1893, and the author of several religious histories and guides to Alabama and the South.[104]

Despite several decades of work, immigration promotion in the South was an overwhelming failure. Of all the Southern states that developed promotion policies, only Texas, Louisiana, and Florida attracted European immigrants in significant numbers, and even then, only 6 percent of Texas's population and 4 percent of Louisiana's and Florida's population was foreign born in 1900. Furthermore, the largest immigrant group in Texas in the late 19th and early 20th centuries was Mexican, while in Louisiana, it was Italian, and in Florida it was Cuban, all groups recruited as guest workers, not permanent settlers.[105]

Southern immigration promoters faced several major challenges in persuading Europeans to immigrate to the South. The first was that there were no direct steamship lines that sailed from Europe to Southern ports, and Southern ports did not have reception facilities like Castle Garden or later Ellis Island where immigrants could receive information about work and housing and make train connections to interior destinations.[106] The South wanted the federal government to open an immigration station in at least one Southern port, although, of course, states differed as to which one. Louisiana argued for New Orleans, while South Carolina and Texas lobbied for Charleston and Galveston, respectively. Galveston was designated an immigration station in 1906 and New Orleans in 1913. The German steamship company North German Lloyd did sail from Bremen to Galveston via Baltimore between 1884 and 1888 but ceased this service between 1888 and 1897. And while the trip to Galveston was cheaper than to New York, it was also up to a week longer, which discouraged many immigrants.

West Virginia lacked even the ability to lobby for a Southern immigration station. As a land-locked state with no ocean or river ports, West Virginia was dependent entirely on railroads to transport immigrants to the state, and the Appalachia Mountains had long been a major barrier to interstate transport. Debar was granted a free pass by the Baltimore and Ohio Railroad (B&O), the main railroad that passed through West Virginia, but the B&O made his recruiting work at Castle Garden difficult because it refused to pay Castle Garden officials a per capita commission on immigrants directed to West Virginia. Without this commission (or bribe), Castle Garden managers discouraged immigrants from traveling to West Virginia and instead directed them to travel to western Pennsylvania on the Pennsylvania Central railroad, which did pay the commission.

Eventually, the B&O had to cut its ticket prices by 50 percent in order to make travel to West Virginia attractive.[107]

Another major problem was that the perception of the South in the minds of Europeans had long been negative, and so the lack of immigration before the Civil War meant that the South had few immigrant communities to attract new immigrants.

"Throughout the Old World, the idea prevails even among the educated, that south of Mason & Dixon's line there is naught but cotton-crested fields belted by dismal swamps and choked with malaria—a land that denies ingress to all but the hot-blooded Southerner and the swarthy African," lamented Col. A. J. McWhirter, commissioner of agriculture, mining, and immigration for Tennessee and the president of the Southern Immigration Association, at the Cotton Planters' Association of America's annual convention in December 1883.[108]

Louisiana agent B. F. White reported from Zurich that Europeans had strong stereotypes and biases against the South. "They were told that the heat was so severe that laborers could not live; that diseases of all kinds and of the severest types reigned there without any control, and carried off to the grave all newcomers; that the Southern citizens would and could enslave them and their children."[109]

Southern states sought to encourage immigration but were always conflicted as to whether they wanted new residents and future citizens or cheap white labor. This tension, coupled with the many serious economic, political, and social problems the South faced after the Civil War, caused most immigrants to avoid the region in favor of the Midwest and the West.

Conclusion

Since the beginning of English colonization of North America, migration—be it voluntary or forced—has been central to American labor policy. The question for early English colonization corporations was how to persuade people to leave the known world of Europe for the great unknown that was America. These corporations offered would-be colonists a share of company profits, free land, low taxes, and political and religious freedom to attract them to a dangerous environment populated by natives not interested in ceding their lands to Europeans. As labor shortages continued, English colonizers imported large numbers of African slaves and European indentured servants to do the heavy work of developing colonies. But most of the early European settlers were servants of investors, not investors themselves, and much obfuscation and deception was involved in convincing these servants to go to America, especially the deadly morass that was 17th-century Virginia and the Carolinas.

After the American Revolution, immigration became not just a means of gaining a labor force but of gaining new citizens to populate an aggressively expanding country. When the new United States embarked on its experiment of democratic republican self-government in the late 18th century and allowed all "free white men" to become citizens, this question of who would be allowed to immigrate, and then naturalize, became crucial to the survival and success of the American democratic republic.

In the 19th century, the new nation engaged in two far-reaching demographic policies: the removal of American Indians from their lands and their replacement with white Americans and European immigrants who were deemed desirable because their whiteness made them eligible for American citizenship. The United States alternated between a strong foreign policy against Indian nations and a weak immigration policy for most of the 19th century.

This selective use of state power was due mainly to the federal government's unwillingness to define the nature of American citizenship beyond whiteness and maleness in the first half of the 19th century. The federal government only involved itself in immigration regulation when immigration from China threatened American understandings of citizenship as white at the same time that the Civil War and the status of freed slaves was forcing the United States to develop a new definition of citizenship. The racial foundations of American citizenship were first cracked with the Fourteenth Amendment's granting of citizenship to freed slaves in 1868, but it would be another one hundred years before the glue that bound "white" and "citizen" would be finally broken, and during that period, Asians were explicitly denied the right to both immigrate and naturalize. The federal government's unwillingness to develop a regulatory immigration policy was also a product of the debate about the role of state in the economy and society. For most of the 19th century in the United States, subsidy—through constitutional protection and federal expenditures—of various forms of labor (i.e., slavery) and development (canals, roads, railroads) was tolerated and even expected, but regulation and restriction of private property rights was deemed intolerable. When Eastern states and cities attempted to tax shippers to pay for the consequences of mass immigration, the shippers successfully sued in 1849, using the argument that only the federal government had the ability and right to regulate interstate commerce (and that immigration was part of interstate commerce). But then the federal government refused to act upon this power for more than 50 years in the area of immigration. For the federal government to regulate or even restrict immigration would have required greater exertion of power and the development of greater government capacity (and its corresponding administrative costs) than most Americans were willing to endure in the 19th century.

Even when the federal government did begin to develop a regulatory administration in regards to immigration in the late 19th century, it paid for it through head taxes and by shifting administrative costs to private shipping companies by requiring them to screen passengers for undesirable characteristics before allowing them to sail.

But the United States' willingness to exert real power (and spend significant amounts of money) to divest American Indians of their lands should not be surprising. Americans of all backgrounds and classes believed in their manifest destiny to control most, if not all, of the North American continent, and the incompatibility of white and Indian civilizations had been apparent since the early 17th century. What was surprising was the federal government's efforts at assimilation through the Dawes

Act of 1887 after decades of waging war on Indian nations and segregating the survivors on reservations.

With the federal government refusing to involve itself in most immigration matters, the promotion of immigration was left to Midwestern and Western states and territories being carved out of Indian Territory. These states and territories portrayed their areas and the United States in general as a prosperous, expanding, vigorous country, full of opportunities for people willing to work hard and take risks. Established states argued that they had the best of both worlds—available land and settled society— while less developed states and territories claimed true opportunity for wealth and success was only possible on the frontier.

In Western states and territories this argument about the frontier being a safe wilderness was complicated by recurring Indian violence, hazardous weather, and a large number of undesirable Chinese and Mexican immigrants. In order to whiten their populations and gain enough white citizens for statehood, Western territories partnered with railroads to promote immigration from Europe and migration from the Eastern United States. Recipients of millions of acres of Indian land from the federal government, the railroads promoted an image of America that emphasized fertility and opportunity. Working aggressively to sell their land grants to people who would establish farms and businesses and become permanent customers, the railroads offered Europeans the upward mobility that came with property ownership.

Southern states also promoted immigration to their region after the Civil War, but to fix their black labor "problem" after the abolition of slavery. Yet Southern leaders could not decide whether they wanted immigrants to be settlers or simply cheap foreign labor to replace freed slaves. Severely hindered by a war-devastated economy, the South could only rely on a warmer climate and its longer growing season as selling points.

State-level immigration promotion was also part of the northern wing of the Democratic Party's support for westward expansion and yeoman-style agriculture before the Civil War and the Republican Party's larger economic plan to subsidize industry and agriculture and settle and develop the Midwest and West after the war. The Republican Party had always been more comfortable than the national Democratic Party about using government power to achieve economic goals; it was only in the post-Reconstruction South that Democrats sometimes promoted immigration, and then only to replace or undermine the South's black labor force.

But regardless of the region, or state versus corporate entity, or political party, all immigration promoters desired Northern Europeans, particularly Germans, British, and Scandinavians, all undoubtedly white and predominantly Protestant. Other European groups, such as Southern and Eastern Europeans and the Catholic Irish, were neither desired nor recruited but were tolerated in varying degrees because of their whiteness. Non-white groups, such as Chinese and Mexicans, were recruited as guest workers but were never welcomed as settlers and future citizens.

Northern European immigrants were desired because of white Protestants' cultural biases, ethnoracial and religious prejudice, and pseudoscientific ideas about the racial superiority of whites, especially Anglo-Saxons. The "isothermal theory of migration" was just one of the scientifically racist theories promoters used to justify targeting certain groups and not others. But immigration promoters were often confused about whether Northern Europeans could successfully settle any environment or whether they were biologically limited to certain geographical areas (and thus less superior than other groups). This confusion meant that immigration promoters continued to target Northern Europeans such as Germans, British, and Scandinavians long after those groups' immigration rates had slowed or been surpassed by Southern and Eastern Europeans in the late 19th and early 20th centuries. Promoters rarely carried out the "isothermal theory" to its logical conclusion, which might have resulted in their having to promote immigration in such countries as Spain, Portugal, Italy, or Greece to territory west of the hundredth meridian.

Northern Europeans were also targeted because they were believed to be experienced farmers. An important difference between immigration promotion and labor recruitment was promotion's focus on attracting farmers and selling agricultural land. Promoters did sometimes discuss stock raising and even mining, and very occasionally noted the conditions of wage labor markets, but in general, promotion revolved around the encouragement of agriculture. This focus on agriculture was because the basis of the U.S. justification for seizing Indian land was that the Indians were not using it productively because they did not farm. Agriculture, and especially the raising of crops, was deemed the most economically productive and morally superior form of labor in 19th-century America, and the assimilation of Indians was measured by whether they farmed like white Americans. Herding cattle was not that different from herding buffalo, and white Americans did not want to suggest that Indians had any legitimate claim to American territory. In the West, mining regions would attract workers through various gold and silver rushes, and so no promotion to those areas was needed. Later, mining corporations would recruit labor, not promote immigration.

Despite significant differences between 17th-century labor recruitment and 19th-century immigration promotion, there were commonalities.

The image of America as a new Garden of Eden, a place of opportunity for upward mobility, of fertility and unlimited natural resources, of vast size and natural beauty, was surprisingly consistent between the centuries. Exaggeration, poetic license, and outright falsehoods were common in both periods.

The methods of immigration promotion were also diverse, but the printed word was the most common. Seventeenth-century promoters printed some of the earliest propaganda pamphlets and printed sermons that were to be read both privately and aloud from the pulpit. Nineteenth-century promoters published pamphlets, guidebooks, and circulars in the millions. But like their 17th-century counterparts, 19th-century promoters also hired agents to give speeches about their regions to prospective immigrants in Europe. The most aggressive states organized colonies and transported them from Europe, helping groups of immigrants navigate the rail system and giving them temporary shelter while they built homes.

Immigration promotion was closely connected to the development of advertising, and railroad posters for land were among the first advertisements to use images as a form of salesmanship. Promoters also placed thousands of ads in newspapers, and as immigration increased in the 19th century, specialized newspapers focusing on emigration developed, with some promoters, particularly railroads, even publishing emigration newspapers themselves as a way of selling their lands to Europeans.

It is clear that the promotion of migration in the 17th century was successful in that by the early 18th century Great Britain had settled and controlled all of the Eastern seaboard of North America. But it is necessary to question how successful immigration promotion was in the 19th century. Most Midwestern and several Western states were successful in increasing the number of immigrants among their populations. Immigrants were always in the minority of the population, but in some states they made up a large minority, and when combined with their American-born children, half of the settlers in the West and about 45 percent of the settlers in the Midwest were members of immigrant communities. Only in the South was immigration promotion unsuccessful, and this was mainly because the region's dependency on slave labor discouraged immigrants from settling there in the early 19th century, and so no subsequent chains of migration for immigrant groups could be established.

One thing that remains to be determined, however, is how successful land redistribution programs such as the Homestead Act of 1862 were for immigrants versus native-born Americans. Of the 1.6 million homesteads claimed between 1862 and 1934, the number filed and then claimed by immigrants versus Americans is unknown. A clear answer to this question would significantly further our understanding of the mechanisms of upward mobility for immigrants and their children, particularly in the late 19th and early 20th centuries.

It is also important to question the accuracy and honesty of immigration promoters' message that America was a land of fertility and opportunity, and if so, for whom, and where? The answer is that the United States was a land of opportunity, but only for some, mainly those Northern Europeans promoters most aggressively encouraged, and it was a land of fertility, but only in the Midwest east of the hundredth meridian. The fruit basket of California was only possible with irrigation, and for most of the rest of the West, agriculture even with irrigation was not financially or environmentally feasible without significant government subsidy. Despite the roller-coaster nature of the American economy in the 19th century, the United States was a place of opportunity and upward mobility for many immigrants, particularly those who were able to take advantage of the cheap or free land available in non-arid parts of the Midwest and West. But given the tendency of promoters to exaggerate, immigrants who came to America with middling expectations were more often pleased than those who came with very high expectations of success in the New World. Promotional literature often provided useful information, but it was the wise immigrant who took such information and imagery with a grain of salt.

Appendix: Tables

Table 1   Top 10 Sending Countries of Immigrants to the United States, 1820–1920

Country	Total
Germany	5,500,000
Ireland	4,400,000
Italy	4,190,000
Austria	3,700,000
Russia	3,250,000
England	2,500,000
Sweden	1,000,000
Norway	730,000
Scotland	570,000
France	530,000

Source: U.S. Department of Homeland Security, Bureau of the Census.

Table 2   Immigration by Country, 1820–1869 (Top Five Sending Countries)

	1820–1829	1830–1839	1840–1849	1850–1859	1860–1869
Total (all countries)	128,502	538,381	1,427,337	2,814,554	2,081,281
Germany	5,753	124,726	385,434	723,734	751,769
United Kingdom (England, Scotland, Wales)	26,336	74,350	218,572	445,322	532,956
Ireland	51,617	170,672	656,145	1,029,486	427,419

(*continued*)

Table 2 (*Continued*)

	1820–1829	1830–1839	1840–1849	1850–1859	1860–1869
Canada and Newfoundland	2,297	11,875	34,285	64,171	117,978
Norway-Sweden	91	1,149	12,389	22,202	82,937

Source: U.S. Department of Homeland Security, Bureau of the Census.

Table 3 **Immigration by Country, 1860–1919 (Top 10 Sending Countries)**

	1860–1869	1870–1879	1880–1889	1890–1899	1900–1909	1910–1919
Total (all countries)	2,081,261	2,742,261	5,248,568	3,694,294	8,202,388	6,347,380
Italy	9,853	46,296	267,660	603,761	1,930,475	1,229,916
Austria-Hungary	3,375	60,127	314,787	534,059	2,001,376	1,154,727
Russia	1,670	35,177	182,698	450,101	1,501,301	1,106,998
Canada and Newfoundland	117,978	324,310	492,865	3,098	123,067	708,715
United Kingdom	532,956	578,447	810,900	328,759	469,518	371,878
Greece	51	209	1,807	12,732	145,402	198,108
Norway-Sweden	82,937	178,823	586,441	334,058	426,981	192,445
Mexico*	1,957	5,133	2,405	734	31,188	185,334
Germany	723,734	751,769	1,445,181	579,072	328,722	174,227
Ireland	427,419	422,264	674,061	405,710	344,940	166,445

*Note: Countries sending fewer than 100,000 persons over the noted period not included; no data available for Mexico between 1886 and 1893.

Source: U.S. Department of Homeland Security, Bureau of the Census.

Table 4 **U.S. Population, Native versus Immigrant and Percentage, 1850–1910**

	1850	1860	1870	1880	1890	1900	1910
Total	23,191,876	31,443,321	38,558,371	50,189,209	62,979,766	76,212,168	92,228,496
Native	20,947,274	27,304,624	32,991,142	43,475,840	53,372,703	65,653,299	78,456,380
Foreign	2,244,602	4,138,697	5,567,229	6,679,943	9,249,547	10,341,276	13,515,886
Percentage	9.7	13.2	14.4	13.3	14.8	13.6	14.8

Source: U.S. Department of Homeland Security, Bureau of the Census.

Table 5   Michigan Population, 1850–1900

Michigan	1850	1860	1870	1880	1890	1900
Total state population	397,654	749,113	1,184,059	1,636,937	2,093,990	2,420,982
Foreign born	54,703	149,193	268,010	308,588	543,880	541,658
Foreign born by nationality	N/A					
Austria*		660	795	1,025	3,639	6,949
Belgium		597	833	979	2,232	2,647
Bohemia*			1,179	1,780	2,311	2,160
British America/ Canada		36,482	89,590	148,866	181,416	151,915
Denmark		192	1,354	3,513	6,353	6,390
England		25,743		48,202	55,354	43,839
Finland†					18,910	18,910
France		2,446	1,627	3,203	5,182	2,500
Germany‡		38,127	64,143	89,085	135,039	125,074
Holland		6,335	12,559	17,177	29,410	30,406
Ireland		30,019	42,013	43,413	39,065	29,182
Norway		440	1,516	3,520	27,366	7,582
Poland		112	974	5,421	15,669	28,283
Russia		68	194	1,560	11,880	4,138
Scotland		5,705	8,552	10,731	12,068	10,343
Sweden		266	2,406	9,412	27,366	26,956
Switzerland		1,260	2,116	2,474	2,502	2,617

*Note: The census of 1870 is the first one to list Bohemia, Austria, and Hungary separately.

†Note: The census of 1900 is the first to list Finland.

‡Note: In the census of 1860, Austria is included in the tally for "German states," so this number is that total minus Austria.

Source: U.S. Department of Homeland Security, Bureau of the Census.

Table 6   Wisconsin Population, 1850–1900

Wisconsin	1850	1860	1870	1880	1890	1900
Total state population	305,391	775,861	1,054,670	1,315,497	1,686,880	2,069,042
Foreign born	110,471	276,927	364,699	405,425	519,199	515,971
Foreign born by nationality						
Austria*		7,081	4,486	4,601	4,850	7,319
Belgium		4,647	4,804	5,267	4,567	4,412
Bohemia*			10,570	13,848	11,909	14,145
British America/ Canada		18,146	25,666	28,965	33,163	23,860
Denmark		1,150	5,212	3,797	13,885	16,171
England		30,543	28,192	24,916	23,028	17,995
Finland†						2,198
France		2,446	2,704	2,412	2,069	1,637
Germany‡		116,798	162,314	184,328	250,810	242,777
Holland		4,906	5,990	5,698	6,252	6,496
Hungary			237	447	486	1,128
Ireland		49,961	48,479	41,907	33,300	28,544
Italy		103	104	253	1,123	2,172
Luxembourg*			1,593	2,232	325	480
Norway		21,442	40,046	49,349	65,696	61,575
Poland		417	1,290	5,263	17,660	31,789
Russia		95	102	312	2,270	4,243
Scotland		6,902	6,590	5,770	5,494	4,569
Sweden		673	2,799	8,138	20,157	26,196
Switzerland		4,722	6,096	6,288	7,181	7,666
Wales		6,454	6,550	5,352	4,297	3,356

*Note: The census of 1870 is the first one to list Bohemia, Austria, and Hungary separately, and to include Luxembourg.

†Note: The census of 1900 is the first year to list Finland.

‡Note: The census of 1860 included Austria in the tally for "German states," so this number is that total minus Austria.

Source: U.S. Department of Homeland Security, Bureau of the Census.

Table 7   Minnesota Population, 1850–1900

Minnesota	1850	1860	1870	1880	1890	1900
Total state population	6,077	172,023	439,706	780,773	1,301,826	1,751,394
Foreign born	1,977	58,728	160,697	267,676	467,356	505,318
Foreign born by nationality						
Austria*		860	2,647	2,607	5,168	8,872
Belgium		597	622	515	910	957
Bohemia*			2,166	7,759	9,655	11,147
British America/ Canada		8,023	16,698	29,631	43,580	35,915
Denmark		170	1,910	6,071	14,133	16,299
England		3,462	5,670	8,495	14,730	12,022
Finland†						10,727
France		867	1,743	1,351	1,800	1,449
Germany‡		17,540	41,364	66,592	116,956	117,007
Holland		391	1,855	1,581	1,796	2,717
Hungary*			203	356	1,256	2,182
Ireland		12,831	21,746	25,942	28,011	22,428
Luxembourg*			1,173	2,949	670	430
Norway		8,425	35,940	62,521	101,160	104,895
Poland		127	246	2,218	7,503	11,358
Russia		59	109	2,272	7,233	6,907
Scotland		1,079	2,194	2,964	5,315	4,810
Sweden		3,178	20,987	39,176	99,913	115,476
Switzerland		1,035	2,162	2,828	3,745	3,258

*Note: The census of 1870 is the first one to list Bohemia, Austria, and Hungary separately, and to include Luxembourg.

†Note: The census of 1900 is the first year to list Finland.

‡Note: The census of 1860 included Austria in the tally for "German states," so this number is that total minus Austria.

Source: U.S. Department of Homeland Security, Bureau of the Census.

Table 8 Dakota Territory/North and South Dakota Population, 1850–1900

Dakota Territory	1850	1860	1870	1880	1890	1900
Total state population	-	4,837	14,181	135,177		
Foreign born	-	1,774	4,815	51,705		
Foreign born by nationality						
Austria*			171	31		
British America/Canada		1,458	906	10,678		
Bohemia*			153	1,337		
Denmark		-	115	1,447		
England		35	248	2,311		
Germany[†]		22	563	5,925		
Ireland		42	888	4,104		
Norway		129	1,179	13,245		
Russia		1	4	6,403		
Scotland		23	77	940		
Sweden		-	380	3,177		
Switzerland		1	33	286		
American Indian				1,391		
North Dakota[‡]						
Total state population					182,719	
Foreign born					81,461	
British America/Canada					23,045	25,694
Denmark					2,800	3,953
England					3,309	2,909
Germany[†]					8,943	11,546
Ireland					2,967	2,670
Norway					25,773	30,206
Russia					4,098	14,979
Sweden					5,583	8,419
South Dakota[‡]						
Total state population					328,808	
Foreign born					91,055	
British America/Canada					9,463	5,906
Denmark					4,309	5,038

Table 8 (*Continued*)

Dakota Territory	1850	1860	1870	1880	1890	1900
England					5,111	3,802
Finland[§]						1,175
Ireland					4,774	3,298
Germany					18,188	17,873
Norway					19,257	19,788
Russia					12,398	12,365
Sweden					7,746	8,647

*Note: The census of 1870 is the first one to list Bohemia, Austria, and Hungary separately.

†Note: The census of 1860 included Austria in the tally for "German states," so this number is that total minus Austria.

‡Note: The Dakota Territory was divided into North and South Dakota in 1889.

§Note: The census of 1900 is the first year to list Finland.

Source: U.S. Department of Homeland Security, Bureau of the Census.

Table 9   Oregon Population, 1850–1900

Oregon	1850	1860	1870	1880	1890	1900
Total state population	13,294	52,465	90,923	174,178	313,767	413,536
Foreign born	1,022	5,123	11,600	30,503	57,317	65,478
Foreign born by nationality						
Austria*		17	53	317	664	893
Belgium		18	38	95	261	298
Bohemia*			36	109	79	231
British America/Canada		663	1,187	3,019	6,460	6,634
Denmark		50	87	385	1,288	1,663
England		690	1,344	2,896	5,668	5,663
Finland[†]						2,131
France		198	308	514	842	775
Germany[‡]		1,061	1,875	5,034	12,475	18,292
Holland		15	39	127	244	324
Ireland		1,266	1,967	3,650	4,891	4,210
Norway		43	76	574	2,271	2,789
Poland		39	65	92	96	313

(*continued*)

Table 9   (*Continued*)

Oregon	1850	1860	1870	1880	1890	1900
Russia		22	67	379	2,583	1,753
Scotland		217	394	1,129	2,242	2,283
Sweden		56	205	983	3,774	4,555
Switzerland		71	160	730	2,083	2,677
Mexico§		26	45	40	49	53
China		425	3,326	9,472	9,465	9,367
Japan			-	2	29	2,522

*Note: The census of 1870 is the first one to list Bohemia, Austria, and Hungary separately.

†Note: The census of 1900 is the first to list Finland.

‡Note: The census of 1860 included Austria in the tally for "German states," so this number is that total minus Austria.

§Note: no data is available for Mexico between 1886 and 1893.

Source: U.S. Department of Homeland Security, Bureau of the Census.

Table 10   Wyoming Territory/Wyoming Population, 1870–1900

Wyoming Territory	1870	1880	1890	1900
Total state population	9,118	20,789	60,705	92,531
Foreign born	3,513	5,850	14,914	17,415
Foreign born by nationality				
Austria*	23	23	232	1,046
Belgium	5	7	19	29
Bohemia*	8	10	31	58
British America/Canada	339	542	1,314	1,098
Denmark	54	188	630	884
England	555	1,080	3,147	2,596
Finland†				1,220
France	57	61	127	183
Germany‡	652	801	2,037	2,146
Holland	5	16	17	18
Ireland	1,102	1,098	1,900	1,501
Norway	28	74	345	378
Poland	17	14	18	79

Table 10   (*Continued*)

Wyoming Territory	1870	1880	1890	1900
Russia	5	19	794	90
Scotland	260	432	1,380	1,258
Sweden	109	249	1,357	1,727
Switzerland	60	49	106	199
Wales	58	154	533	398
Mexico§	-	40	23	58
China	143	913	474	424

*Note: The census of 1870 is the first one to list Bohemia, Austria, and Hungary separately.

†Note: The census of 1900 is the first to list Finland.

‡The census of 1860 included Austria in the tally for "German states," so this number is that total minus Austria.

§*Note:* no data is available for Mexico between 1886 and 1893.

Source: U.S. Department of Homeland Security, Bureau of the Census.

Table 11   **New Mexico Territory Population, 1850–1900**

New Mexico Territory	1850*	1860*	1870	1880	1890	1900
Total state population	61,547	93,516	91,874	119,565	153,193	195,310
Foreign born	2,151	6,723	5,620	8,051	11,259	13,625
Foreign born by nationality						
British America/Canada		76	125	280	681	680
Denmark		9	15	23	54	57
England		145	120	389	1,258	968
France		108	124	167	284	298
Germany†		564	582	729	1,413	1,360
Holland		6	3	6	46	99
Ireland		827	543	795	966	692
Italy		11	25	73	355	661
Norway		2	5	17	42	33
Poland		13	12	22	24	76
Russia		2	12	16	73	99
Scotland		49	36	110	436	427

(*continued*)

Table 11 (*Continued*)

New Mexico Territory	1850*	1860*	1870	1880	1890	1900
Spain		24	16	12	23	27
Sweden		3	6	39	149	244
Switzerland		27	42	54	122	123
Mexico‡		4,815	3,907	5,173	4,504	6,649
American Indian				9,772		

*Note: Arizona Territory was carved out of New Mexico Territory in 1863, so population for 1850 and 1860 includes both Arizona and New Mexico.

†Note: The census of 1860 included Austria in the tally for "German states," so this number is that total minus Austria.

‡Note: no data available for Mexico between 1886 and 1893.

Source: U.S. Department of Homeland Security, Bureau of the Census.

Table 12 **California Population, 1850–1900**

California	1850	1860	1870	1880	1890	1900
Total state population	92,597	379,994	560,247	864,694	1,208,130	1,485,053
Foreign born	21,802	146,528	209,831	292,874	366,309	367,240
Foreign born by nationality						
Austria*		727	1,078	1,948	3,687	5,256
Belgium		299	291	1,092	683	785
Bohemia*			90	239	243	504
British America/ Canada		5,437	10,660	18,889	26,028	27,408
Denmark		1,328	1,837	3,749	7,764	9,040
England		12,227	17,685	24,657	35,457	85,746
Finland†						2,763
France		8,462	8,063	9,550	11,855	12,256
Germany‡		20,919	29,699	42,532	61,472	72,449
Holland		439	452	694	760	1,015
Ireland		33,147	54,421	62,962	63,138	44,476
Italy		2,805	4,660	7,537	15,405	22,777
Norway		715	1,000	1,765	3,702	5,060
Poland		730	804	1,026	914	1,320

Table 12   (*Continued*)

California	1850	1860	1870	1880	1890	1900
Portugal		1,459	2,495	4,705	9,850	12,068
Russia		260	540	1,018	3,140	3,421
Scotland		3,670	4,949	6,465	9,290	9,467
Spain		470	402	572	836	896
Sweden		1,405	1,944	4,209	10,923	14,519
Switzerland		1,714	2,927	5,308	9,743	10,974
Wales		1,262	1,517	1,212	1,800	1,949
China		34,935	48,790	73,548	71,066	40,262
Japan			32	133	1,224	10,264
Mexico§		9,150	8,978	8,648	7,164	8,086
South America		2,250	1,956	1,797	1,386	1,137

Note: The census of 1870 is the first to list Bohemia, Austria, and Hungary separately.

†*Note:* The census of 1900 is the first to list Finland.

‡*Note:* The census of 1860 included Austria in the tally for "German states," so this number is that total minus Austria.

§*Note:* no data is available for Mexico between 1886 and 1893.

Source: U.S. Department of Homeland Security, Bureau of the Census.

Table 13   Utah Territory/Utah Population, 1850–1900

Utah Territory	1850	1860	1870	1880	1890	1900
Total state population	11,380	40,273	86,786	143,963	297,905	276,749
Foreign born	2,044	12,754	30,702	43,994	53,064	58,777
Foreign born by nationality						
British America/Canada		647	687	1,036	1,222	1,203
Denmark		1,824	4,957	7,791	9,023	9,132
England		7,084	16,070	10,654	20,899	18,879
France		21	63	129	205	220
Germany*		107	358	885	2,121	2,860
Holland		12	122	141	254	523
Ireland		278	502	1,321	2,045	1,515
Italy		40	74	138	347	1,062

(*continued*)

Table 13   *(Continued)*

Utah Territory	1850	1860	1870	1880	1890	1900
Norway		150	613	1,214	1,854	2,128
Poland		2	11	16	20	65
Russia		-	13	54	290	119
Scotland		1,228	2,391	3,201	3,474	3,143
Sweden		196	1,790	3,750	5,986	7,025
Switzerland		78	509	1,040	1,336	1,469
Wales		945	1,783	2,390	2,387	2,41
China		1	445	502	808	544

Note: The census of 1860 included Austria in the tally for "German states," so this number is that total minus Austria.

Source: U.S. Department of Homeland Security, Bureau of the Census.

Table 14   **South Carolina Population, 1850–1900**

South Carolina	1850	1860	1870	1880	1890	1900
Total state population	668,507	703,708	705,606	995,577	1,151,149	1,340,316
Foreign born	8,707	9,986	8,074	7,686	6,143	5,528
Black	393,944	412,820	415,815	604,332	689,141	782,321
Foreign born by nationality						
British America/ Canada		86	77	545	159	173
Denmark		38	50	98	36	55
England		757	610	670	594	474
France		219	143	131	138	84
Germany*		2,893	2,742	2,846	2,502	2,075
Holland		25	32	16	7	6
Ireland		4,906	3,262	2,526	1,665	1,131
Italy		59	63	84	166	180
Norway		4	-	5	23	49
Poland		142	66	128	63	103
Russia		19	31	29	178	316
Scotland		502	309	354	293	239

Table 14 (*Continued*)

South Carolina	1850	1860	1870	1880	1890	1900
Spain		34	30	48	25	15
Sweden		36	60	63	60	65
Switzerland		33	45	73	47	36

Note: The census of 1860 included Austria in the tally for "German states," so this number is that total minus Austria.

Source: U.S. Department of Homeland Security, Bureau of the Census.

Table 15   Louisiana Population, 1850–1900

Louisiana	1850	1860	1870	1880	1890	1900
Total state population	517,762	708,002	726,915	939,946	1,118,587	1,331,625
Foreign born	68,233	80,975	61,827	54,140	49,747	52,903
Black	262,271	350,373	364,210	483,655	560,192	650,804
Foreign born by nationality						
Austria*		399	433	275	571	765
Belgium		299	220	193	275	315
Bohemia*			23	24	14	30
British America/ Canada		830	714	726	762	781
Denmark		309	290	285	232	216
England		3,980	2,792	2,582	2,456	2,068
France		14,938	12,288	9,992	8,437	6,500
Germany†		24,215	18,912	17,475	14,625	11,839
Holland		262	232	170	76	78
Ireland		28,207	17,068	13,807	9,236	6,436
Italy		1,134	1,884	2,527	7,767	17,431
Norway		63	76	78	136	189
Poland		196	198	164	100	168
Portugal		145	122	141	112	94
Russia		84	165	158	345	692
Scotland		1,051	814	659	465	399
Spain		1,806	1,116	987	880	583
Sweden		193	358	270	328	359

(*continued*)

Table 15 (*Continued*)

Louisiana	1850	1860	1870	1880	1890	1900
Switzerland		878	873	674	521	523
Mexico[‡]		320	409	424	404	488
China		10	65	609	334	544
Cuba[§]			994	449		319
West Indies[§]		1,154	748	568	648	224

*Note: The census of 1870 is the first to list Bohemia, Austria, and Hungary separately, and to include and Cuba.

†Note: The census of 1860 included Austria in the tally for "German states," so this number is that total minus Austria.

‡Note: no data is available for Mexico between 1886 and 1893.

§Note: The census of 1890 lists Cuba and the West Indies as one country, but the censuses of 1870, 1880, and 1900 list them as separate countries.

Source: U.S. Department of Homeland Security, Bureau of the Census.

Table 16   Texas Population, 1850–1900

Texas	1850	1860	1870	1880	1890	1900
Total state population	212,592	604,215	818,579	1,591,749	2,235,523	3,048,710
Foreign born	17,681	43,422	62,411	114,616	152,956	179,357
Black	58,558	182,921	253,475	393,384	589,588	620,722
Foreign born by nationality						
Austria*		730	1,748	3,474	8,758	6,870
Belgium		30	73	109	216	244
Bohemia*			780	2,669	3,215	9,204
British America/ Canada		458	597	2,472	2,866	2,549
Denmark		150	159	489	649	1,089
England		1,695	2,020	6,528	9,441	8,213
France		1,383	2,226	2,653	2,730	2,025
Germany[†]		19,823	23,976	35,347	48,843	48,295
Holland		76	54	228	130	262
Ireland		3,480	4,031	8,103	8,201	6,173
Italy		67	185	539	2,107	3,942
Norway		326	403	880	1,313	1,356

Table 16   (*Continued*)

Texas	1850	1860	1870	1880	1890	1900
Poland		783	448	995	1,591	3,343
Russia		42	62	279	977	2,259
Scotland		524	620	1,659	2,172	1,952
Spain		59	149	240	259	280
Sweden		153	364	1,293	2,806	4,388
Switzerland		453	598	1,203	1,711	1,709
Mexico‡		12,443	23,020	43,161	51,559	71,062

*Note: The census of 1870 is the first one to list Bohemia, Austria, and Hungary separately.

†Note: The census of 1860 included Austria in the tally for "German states," so this number is that total minus Austria.

‡Note: no data is available for Mexico between 1886 and 1893.

Source: U.S. Department of Homeland Security, Bureau of the Census.

Table 17   West Virginia Population, 1860–1900

West Virginia	1860	1870	1880	1890	1900
Total state population	376,688	442,014	618,457	762,794	958,800
Foreign born	16,545	17,091	18,265	18,883	22,451
Black	-	17,980	25,868	32,717	43,499
Foreign born by nationality					
Austria*		59	62	221	1,025
Belgium		21	8	36	79
Bohemia*		1	34	6	27
British America/Canada		207	295	374	639
Denmark		21	38	44	60
England		1,810	2,051	2,760	2,622
France		223	230	213	298
Germany†		6,231	7,029	7,202	6,537
Holland		174	19	22	22
Hungary*			5	39	810
Ireland		6,832	6,459	4,799	3,342
Italy		34	48	632	2,921
Norway		1	3	7	19

(*continued*)

Table 17 (*Continued*)

West Virginia	1860	1870	1880	1890	1900
Poland		4	18	69	638
Russia		11	19	126	721
Scotland		746	622	914	855
Sweden		5	21	72	182
Switzerland		325	810	610	696
Wales		321	369	394	482

*Note: The census of 1870 is the first one to list Bohemia, Austria, and Hungary separately. In addition, the census of 1870, Table 1, does not list the black population for 1860, although the census does list native and foreign-born population for West Virginia in 1860 in Table VI.

†Note: The census of 1860 included Austria in the tally for "German states," so this number is that total minus Austria.

Source: U.S. Department of Homeland Security, Bureau of the Census.

Notes

Introduction

1. Winthrop D. Jordan, *The White Man's Burden, Historical Origins of Racism in the United States* (New York: Oxford University Press, 1974), Chapter 14, "Toward a White Man's Country," 205–216; Matthew Frye Jacobson, *Whiteness of a Different Color, European Immigrants and the Alchemy of Race* (Cambridge, MA: Harvard University Press, 1998), Chapter 1, "Free White Persons in the Republic, 1790–1840," 15–38.

2. William J. Novak, "The Myth of the 'Weak' American State," *American Historical Review* 113.3 (June 2008): 752–772.

3. Jacobson, *Whiteness of a Different Color*, Chapter 1, "Free White Persons in the Republic, 1790–1840," 15–38; Ariela Gross, "Beyond Black and White: Cultural Approaches to Race and Slavery," *Columbia Law Review* 101.3 (April 2001): 681; Peter Kolchin, "Whiteness Studies: The New History of Race in America," *Journal of American History* 89.1 (June 2002). Retrieved from https://pantherfile.uwm.edu/gjay/www/Whiteness/kolchinreviewessay.htm, on March 9, 2016. This provides a critical historiography of whiteness literature.

4. The Naturalization Act of January 29, 1795, changed the waiting period to five years from three; this was changed to fourteen years in the Naturalization Act of June 18, 1798, and then changed back to five years in the Naturalization Act of April 14, 1802. The period between declaration and naturalization was changed from three years to two years in the Act of May 26, 1824. The Declaration of intention became voluntary and has no longer been required since the Act of December 24, 1952.

5. The newly created French Republic was the first nation to grant universal (male) suffrage without property requirements in 1792. The United Kingdom, by comparison, did not achieve universal male suffrage until 1918 and universal suffrage until 1928.

6. During the John Adams presidency, the length of the residency requirement was lengthened from three years to fourteen years in the Naturalization

Act of June 18, 1798, but this was changed back to five years in the Naturalization Law of April 14, 1802. Chinese immigrants were deemed "aliens ineligible for citizenship" by the 1870 Naturalization Act, which limited citizenship to "white persons and persons of African descent," and the Chinese Exclusion Act of 1882 was made permanent in 1902.

7. Report of the Commissioners of Emigration of the State of New York, made to the Legislature January 23, 1850 (New York: Casper C. Childs, 1850); Annual Report of the Commissioners of Emigration of the State of New York, for the year ending December 31, 1855 (New York: William C. Bryant & Co., 1856). In 1849, in *Smith v. Turner* and *Norris v. Boston*, 48 U.S. 283 (1849) (the "Passenger Cases"), the Supreme Court ruled that states did not have the right to impose a head tax on immigrant passengers. Also please see Gerald L. Neuman, "The Lost Century of American Immigration Law (1776–1875)," *Columbia Law Review* 93.8 (December 1993), 1846–1857 on states' efforts to regulate the entry of paupers and other poor people into their jurisdictions; Benjamin J. Klebaner, "State and Local Immigration Regulation in the United States Before 1882," *International Review of Social History* 3.2 (August 1958): 269–295.

8. Aristide R. Zolberg, *A Nation by Design: Immigration Policy in the Fashioning of America* (New York: Russell Sage Foundation, 2006), 145–147, 153–160, argues that minimum space requirements and the requirement that the travelers be fed at least one hot meal per day, adopted in 1847 and 1855 respectively, had restrictive intentions and outcomes, yet these laws had little effect on the numbers of entries in the antebellum period.

9. Allan Kraut, *Silent Travelers: Germs, Genes, and the "Immigrant Menace"* (Baltimore, MD: Johns Hopkins University Press, 1994), 66.

10. The Office of Superintendent of Immigration (later changed to Bureau of Immigration) reported on Chinese immigration and exclusion separately from immigration because it did not consider immigration from China to be immigration but rather violations of the Exclusion Act.

11. Peter Skerry, "Many Borders to Cross: Is Immigration the Exclusive Responsibility of the Federal Government?" *Publius* 25.3, *The State of American Federalism, 1994–1995* (Summer 1995): 76.

12. Arkansas was the last state to ban noncitizens from voting, in 1926, Jamin B. Raskin, "Legal Aliens, Local Citizens: The Historical, Constitutional and Theoretical Meanings of Alien Suffrage," *University of Pennsylvania Law Review* 141.4 (April 1993): 1391–1470. Retrieved from http://www.jstor.org/stable/3312345?origin =crossref&seq=1#page_scan_tab_contents *on January 5, 2016.*

13. Jack Ericson Eblen, *The First and Second United States Empires, Governors and Territorial Government, 1784–1912* (Pittsburgh: University of Pittsburgh Press, 1968), especially Chapter VIII, "Indian Affairs," 237–270.

14. Table, "Indian Wars, Their Cost, and Civil Expenditures," covering military expenditures from July 4, 1776, to June 30, 1890, Department of the Interior, Census Office, *Report on Indians Taxed and Indians Not Taxed in the United States* (except Alaska) (Washington, DC: Government Printing Office, 1894,

reprinted by Norman Ross Publishing, 1994), 641. The only year in which less than $1 million was spent on Indian affairs was in 1843.

15. For example, in the Treaty of Mendota, Minnesota, which the United States signed on August 5, 1851, with the Minnesota Sioux, the Sioux ceded huge territory in Minnesota and Iowa for $1,410,000, to be invested with 5 percent interest to be paid over 50 years. While this was financially generous, most treaties paid much less for acreage, and the Sioux also gave up millions of acres.

16. Eblen, *The First and Second United States Empires*, 3–11 and 237–270; Raymond J. DeMallie, "Touching the Pen: Plains Indian Treaty Councils in Ethnohistorical Perspective," 38–53, in *Ethnicity on the Great Plains*, edited by Frederick C. Luebke (Lincoln: University of Nebraska Press, 1980).

17. Claude F. Oubre, *Forty Acres and a Mule: The Freedmen's Bureau and Black Land Ownership* (Baton Rouge: Louisiana State University Press, 1978), 188.

18. Eblen, *The First and Second United States Empires*, 5.

19. Ibid., 237–270.

20. Please note: Montana, Wyoming, Idaho, and Colorado are being included in the definition of the West while the Dakotas are considered to be part of the Midwest.

21. From *America to Norway, Norwegian-American Immigrant Letters, 1838–1914*, Vol. 1, 1838–1870, edited and translated by Orm Overland (Northfield: Norwegian-American Historical Association, University of Minnesota Press, 2012); *The Land of Their Choice: The Immigrants Write Home*, edited by Theodore C. Blegen (Minneapolis: University of Minnesota Press, 1955); *Letters from the Promised Land: Swedes in America, 1840–1914*, edited by H. Arnold Barton (Minneapolis: University of Minnesota Press, 1975); David A. Gerber, "Acts of Deceiving and Withholding in Immigrant Letters: Personal Identity and Self-Presentation in Personal Correspondence," *Journal of Social History* 39.2; *Kith and Kin: Interpersonal Relationships and Cultural Practices* (Winter 2005): 315–330; Annemieke Galema, "A New Start, A New World. Dutch Migrants and the Image of the United States, 1880–1914," 243–266, in *On Distant Shores: Proceedings of the Marcus Lee Hansen Immigration Conference*, Aalborg, Denmark June 29–July 1, 1992, edited by Birgit Flemming Larsen, Henning Bender, and Karen Veien (Danes Worldwide Archives in collaboration with the Danish Society for Emigration History in Aalborg, Denmark, 1993).

22. Richard White, "It's Your Misfortune and None of My Own," *A History of the American West* (Norman: University of Oklahoma Press, 1991), 196; John C. Hudson, "Migration to an American Frontier," *Immigrants on the Land: Agriculture, Rural Life, and Small Towns*, edited by George E. Pozzetta (New York: Garland, 1991), 86–87, article originally printed in *Annals of the Association of American Geographers* 66.2 (June 1976): 242–265; Sig Mickelson, *the Northern Pacific Railroad and the Selling of the West* (Sioux Falls, SD: The Center for Western Studies, 1993), 145–152. B. Boneva and I. Frieze, "Toward a Concept of a Migrant Personality," *Journal of Social Issues* 57.4 (Winter 2001): 477–491; Aidan S. Tabor,

Taciano L. Milfont, and Colleen Ward, "The Migrant Personality Revisited: Individual Differences and International Mobility Intentions," *New Zealand Journal of Psychology* 44.2 (September 2015): 89–95, examines the theory of a "migrant personality" that argues there are personality traits that are predictors of migration. But this theory has not been applied to historic migration or to large groups.

23. Frederick Luebke, editor, *The European Immigrants in the American West, Community Histories* (Albuquerque: University of New Mexico Press, 1998), x–xi.

24. Mary Poovey, *A History of the Modern Fact: Problems of Knowledge Production in the Sciences of Wealth and Society* (Chicago, IL: University of Chicago Press, 1999).

25. Stephen R. Fox, *The Mirror Makers: A History of American Advertising and Its Creators* (Chicago: University of Illinois Press, 1997), 22, 50.

Chapter 1

1. Herbert S. Klein, *A Population History of the United States* (Cambridge, UK: Cambridge University Press, 2012), 40–43, says that 160,000 Europeans migrated in the 17th century while another 307,000 migrated between 1700 and 1775, while 31,000 Africans were brought between 1619 and 1700 and 251,000 Africans were transported between 1700 and 1775. Carville Earle, "Pioneers of Providence: The Anglo-American Experience, 1492–1792," *Annals of the Association of American Geographers* 82.3; *The Americas before and after 1492: Current Geographical Research* (September 1992), 485–486, asserts that 375,000 English migrated to the English colonies between 1607 and 1700. Both cite Henry A. Gemery, but Klein uses "The White Population of the Colonial United States, 1607–1790," in Michael R. Haines and Richard H. Steckel, eds., *A Population History of North America* (Cambridge, UK: Cambridge University Press, 2000), 170–171, while Earle uses Henry A. Gemery, "Emigration from the British Isles to the New World, 1630–1700: Inferences from colonial populations," *Research in Economic History* 5 (1980): 179–231.

2. Sigmund Diamond, "From Organization to Society: Virginia in the Seventeenth Century," *American Journal of Sociology* 635 (March 1958): 459–460; Franklin D. Jones, "Historical Development of the Law of Business Competition," *Yale Law Journal* 36.1 (November 1926): 42–55.

3. George Louis Beer, "The Early English Colonial Movement," *Political Science Quarterly* 23.1 (March 1908): 86 (see footnote 1), and 87.

4. Allan Kulikoff, *From British Peasants to Colonial American Farmers* (Chapel Hill: University of North Carolina Press, 2000), especially Chapter 1, "From England to America," 39–72.

5. S. Douglas Beets, "Critical Events in the Ethics of U.S. Corporation History," *Journal of Business Ethics* 102.2 (August 2011): 196, Table II, "Critical Events in the Ethics of Corporation History (CEECH)," and 199–200.

6. Theodore K. Rabb, "Investment in English Overseas Enterprise, 1575–1630," *Economic History Review* 19.1 (1966): 72, 79.

7. Rabb, "Investment in English Overseas Enterprise, 1575–1630," 73.

8. L. D. Scisco, "The Plantation Type of Colony," *American Historical Review* 8.2 (January 1903): 264–265.

9. Jones, "Historical Development of the Law of Business Competition," 42–43; Diamond, "From Organization to Society," 461–462.

10. Beer, "The Early English Colonial Movement," 93.

11. David W. Galenson, "The Rise and Fall of Indentured Servitude in the Americas: An Economic Analysis," *Journal of Economic History* 44.1 (March 1984): 4, 6.

12. Rabb, "Investment in English Overseas Enterprise, 1575–1630," 73. Peter Laslett, "The Gentry of Kent in 1640," *Cambridge Historical Journal* 9.2 (1948): 160–163 notes the predominance of Kent County gentry in the initial colonizers of Virginia.

13. "West, Thomas (1577–1618)," Albert Frederick Pollard, *Dictionary of National Biography, 1885–1900* 60 (London: Smith, Elder & Co., 1889), 344–345; Diamond, "From Organization to Society," 461; also Jones, "Historical Development of the Law of Business Competition," 42–43. This one-page flyer advertises shares in the Virginia Company: "Considering there is no publicke action . . . which tendeth to the generall good . . . of this common-wealth, but . . . is also beneficiall . . . to euery particular member thereof, we thought it therefore requisite, to impart vnto you . . . how many wayes it hath pleased God to encourage vs to goe on, in that great worke and enterprize of planting colonies of our English nation in those parts of America, which wee commonly call Virginia, or Noua Britannia" (London, 1609).

14. Diamond, "From Organization to Society," 466.

15. "Richard Hakluyt (1552–1616)," M. Fuller and B. Wolfe *Encyclopedia Virginia* (2014). Retrieved from http://www.EncyclopediaVirginia.org/Hakluyt_Richard_1552-1616 on December 15, 2015; David B. Quinn, "Thomas Hariot and the Virginia Voyages of 1602," *The William and Mary Quarterly* 27.2 (April 1970): 280; please also see a digital copy of Hariot's book at Digital Commons, University of Nebraska–Lincoln. Retrieved from http://digitalcommons.unl.edu/cgi/viewcontent.cgi?article=1020&context=etas on December 15, 2015.

16. Andrew Fitzmaurice, "The Civic Solution to the Crisis of English Colonization, 1609–1625," *The Historical Journal* 42.1 (March 1999): 34; and Andrew Fitzmaurice, "The Commercial Ideology of Colonization in Jacobean England: Robert Johnson, Giovanni Botero, and the Pursuit of Greatness," *The William and Mary Quarterly* 64.4 (October 2007), 793, argue that civic virtues and establishing commonwealth were the main goals of colonization.

17. Jones, "Historical Development of the Law of Business Competition," 42–43.

18. Kulikoff, *From British Peasants to Colonial American Farmers*, 47–52.

19. Max Roser, "Literacy" (2015). Published online at OurWorldInData.org. Retrieved from http://ourworldindata.org/data/education-knowledge/literacy/, on December 17, 2015. See also Stanley Johnson, "John Donne and the Virginia

Company," *ELH: A Journal of English Literary History* 14.2 (June 1947): 127–138; "Foure sermons vpon speciall occasions" (London: Thomas Iones, 1625).

20. Beer, "The Early English Colonial Movement," 75–94; Fitzmaurice, "The Commercial Ideology of Colonization in Jacobean England," 795. Nova Britannia has been digitized and is available at https://archive.org/details/novabritannia of00john. Located on December 17, 2015.

21. Robert Johnson, "Nova Britannia" (1609).

22. "For the plantation in Virginia. Or Nova Britannia" (London: Iohn Windet, 1609).

23. "For the plantation in Virginia. Or Nova Britannia" (London: Iohn Windet, 1609).

24. Diamond, "From Organization to Society," 462.

25. Edmund S. Morgan, "The Labor Problem at Jamestown, 1607–18," *American Historical Review* 76.3 (June 1971): 595–611.

26. Councell of Virginia, "A true declaration of the estate of the colonie in Virginia" (London: [by Eliot's Court Press and William Stansby] for William Barret, 1610), 17, 31 (quote).

27. Councell of Virginia, "A true declaration of the estate of the colonie in Virginia" 32 (quote).

28. Glenn T. Trewartha, "Types of Rural Settlement in Colonial America," *Geographical Review* 36.4 (October 1946): 590.

29. Diamond, "From Organization to Society"; Edmund S. Morgan, "The First American Boom: Virginia 1618 to 1630," *The William and Mary Quarterly* 28.2 (April 1971): 171; see also Wesley Frank Craven, "The Dissolution of the London Company for Virginia," *American Historical Review* 37.1 (October 1931): 17–19.

30. Jon Kukla, "Order and Chaos in Early America: Political and Social Stability in Pre-Restoration Virginia," *American Historical Review* 90.2 (April 1985): 283; Trewartha, "Types of Rural Settlement in Colonial America," 586. *Discourse of the Old Company Source: The Virginia Magazine of History and Biography* 1.2 (October 1893): 155–167. This is a reprint of a document submitted to the English Crown in 1625.

31. This image was disseminated for several decades. The quote is from Anon, "A perfect description of Virginia" (London: Prind [sic] for Richard Wodenoth 1648), 9.51. Morgan, "The First American Boom," 175–176, notes the higher wages in Virginia.

32. Edmund S. Morgan, "Slavery and Freedom: The American Paradox," *Journal of American History* 59.1 (June 1972): 18–19; Unsigned, "Jamestown and Plymouth," *The William and Mary Quarterly* 17.4 (April 1909): 307, says: "Edward Eggleston and Alexander Brown estimate the mortality among the first settlers at eighty per cent during the first year after their arrival." Captain Peter De Vries, who often visited Virginia, writing in 1632, said that "during the months of June, July and August the people who have lately arrived from England die like cats and dogs." Craven, "The Dissolution of the London Company for Virginia," 22, notes a death rate of between 45 and 75 percent, depending on the year,

between 1619 and 1623. Klein, "A Population History of the United States," 40–43, on population and natural increase in the Southern colonies.

33. Scisco, "The Plantation Type of Colony," 260–261; Diamond, "From Organization to Society," 465–466; Kukla, "Order and Chaos in Early America," 282; Morgan, "The Labor Problem at Jamestown, 1607–1618," 595–611.

34. Scisco, "The Plantation Type of Colony," 262; Jones, "Historical Development of the Law of Business Competition," 44.

35. Rabb, "Investment in English Overseas Enterprise, 1575–1630," 80, on the backgrounds of Massachusetts Bay Colony investors; J. T. Peacey, "Seasonable Treatises: A Godly Project of the 1630s," *English Historical Review* 113.452 (June 1998): 667–679. Please also see William Holmes, "Governmental Accounting in Colonial Massachusetts," *The Accounting Review* 54.1 (January 1979): 48.

36. Kulikoff, "From British Peasants to Colonial American Farmers," 53; T. H. Breen and Stephen Foster, "Moving to the New World: The Character of Early Massachusetts Immigration," *The William and Mary Quarterly* 30.2 (April 1973): 222.

37. Walter W. Woodward, "Captain John Smith and the Campaign for New England: A Study in Early Modern Identity and Promotion," *New England Quarterly* 81.1 (March 2008): 93. John Smith, "The generall historie of Virginia, New-England, and the Summer Isles" (London: Printed by I[ohn] D[awson] and I[ohn] H[aviland] for Michael Sparkes, 1624); John Smith, "Advertisements for the unexperienced planters of New-England, or any where" (London: Printed by Iohn Haviland, 1631).

38. Edward Winslow, "Good nevves from New-England" (London: I. D[awson] and Eliot's Court Press] for William Bladen and Iohn Bellamie, 1624) is a narrative account of the first few years of the Plymouth colony.

39. Edna Scofield, "The Origin of Settlement Patterns in Rural New England," *Geographical Review* 28.4 (October 1938): 657; Kulikoff, "From British Peasants to Colonial American Farmers," 53–57, 65–66.

40. Rona S. Weiss, "Primitive Accumulation in the United States: The Interaction between Capitalist and Noncapitalist Class Relations in Seventeenth-Century Massachusetts," *Journal of Economic History* 42.1, and *The Tasks of Economic History* (March 1982): 78–79.

41. H. Roy Merrens, "The Physical Environment of Early America: Images and Image Makers in Colonial South Carolina," *Geographical Review* 59.4 (October 1969): 531–532.

42. M. Eugene Sirmans, "Politics in Colonial South Carolina: The Failure of Proprietary Reform, 1682–1694," *The William and Mary Quarterly* 23.1 (January 1966): 34–36.

43. Sirmans, "Politics in Colonial South Carolina," 55; Robert E. Gallman, "Influences on the Distribution of Landholdings in Early Colonial North Carolina," *Journal of Economic History* 42.3 (September 1982): 550–551.

44. South Carolina was particularly active in this; please see Robbie Totten, "National Security and U.S. Immigration Policy, 1776–1790," *Journal of Interdisciplinary History* 39.1 (Summer 2008): 42.

45. H. Roy Merrens and George D. Terry, "Dying in Paradise: Malaria, Mortality, and the Perceptual Environment in Colonial South Carolina," *Journal of Southern History* 50.4 (November 1984): 536, quoting Samuel Wilson, 1682, "An Account of the Province of Carolina, By Samuel Wilson, 1682," 175.

46. Thomas Amy, "Carolina" (London: Printed for W.C., 1682), 4.

47. Joel Gascoin, "A true description of Carolina" (London: 1682), 1.

48. Earle, "Pioneers of Providence," 486.

49. Karen Ordahl Kupperman, "Fear of Hot Climates in the Anglo-American Colonial Experience," *The William and Mary Quarterly* 41.2 (April 1984): 213, 215–216; Karen Ordahl Kupperman, "The Puzzle of the American Climate in the Early Colonial Period," *American Historical Review* 87.5 (December 1982): 1262–1289.

50. Sirmans, "Politics in Colonial South Carolina," 34; Anon, "Carolina described more fully then [sic] heretofore" (Dublin: 1684).

51. Leon Hühner, "The Jews of South Carolina from the Earliest Settlement to the End of the American Revolution," *Publications of the American Jewish Historical Society* no. 12 (1904): 39–61, notes that John Locke helped revise Carolina's constitution in 1669; John Locke, "The fundamental constitutions of Carolina" (London: 1682).

52. Sirmans, "Politics in Colonial South Carolina," 35–36.

53. John Archdale Papers, 1690–1706, Library of Congress, Washington, D.C.

54. Philip Otterness, *Becoming German: The 1709 Palatine Migration to New York* (Ithaca, NY: Cornell University Press, 2004), 27. The copy of the "Golden Book" at the British Library was published in 1709, is 35 pages, is approximately five inches by three inches, and could easily fit into a pocket. It contains chapters about the physical environment, the political status of the colony, the fertility of the land, the air and healthfulness, peace and security, trade opportunities, the presence of other Europeans in the region, the journey from England to Carolina, and compares Pennsylvania and Carolina (to Pennsylvania's detriment: too cold to grow grapes for wine). There are also three appendices.

55. Otterness, *Becoming German*, 29–30.

56. Otterness, *Becoming German*, 27, 32–34, 37. Kocherthal, "Aussführlich- und umständlicher Bericht von der berühmten Landschafft Carolina" (Franckfurt am Mayn: zu finden bey Heorg Heinrich Oehrling, Anno M DCC IX. [1609]).

57. Benjamin Myer Brink, "The Palatine Settlements," *Proceedings of the New York State Historical Association* 11 (1912): 140; Ulrich Simmendinger, "True and authentic register of persons still living" (Baltimore: Genealogical Publishing Company, 1962); Totten, "National Security and U.S. Immigration Policy, 1776–1790," 41.

58. Otterness, *Becoming German*, 89.

59. Daniel Defoe, *A Brief History of the Poor Palatine Refugees* (London: 1709), page 20 notes the following occupations practiced by the Palatines: "husbandmen and wine dressers, 1083; school masters, 10; herdsmen, 4; wheelrights, 13; smiths, 46; cloth and linnen weavers, 66; carpenters, 90; bakers, 32; masons,

48; coopers and brewers, 48; joiners, 20; shoemakers, 40; tailors, 58; butchers, 15; millers, 27; sadlers, 7; stocking weavers, 5; tanners, 7; miners, 3; brickmakers, 6; potters, 3; hunters, 5; turners, 6; surgeons, 3; locksmiths, 2; bricklayers, 4; glasiers, 2; hatters, 3; silversmiths, 2; 1 cook; 1 student, carvers, 2."

60. Wm. J. Hinke, "Report of the Journey of Francis Louis Michel from Berne, Switzerland, to Virginia, October 2, 1701–December 1, 1702," Part III, *Virginia Magazine of History and Biography* 24.3 (June 1916): 303.

61. Merrens, "The Physical Environment of Early America," 538.

62. Merrens, "The Physical Environment of Early America," 555; Totten, "National Security and U.S. Immigration Policy, 1776–1790," 42.

63. Oswald Seidensticker, "William Penn's Travels in Holland and Germany in 1677," *Pennsylvania Magazine of History and Biography* 2.3 (1878): 237–282.

64. William Penn et al., "A Brief account of the province of East-Jersey in America" (London: Printed for Benjamin Clark, 1682).

65. William Penn, "Some Account of the Province of Pennsylvania," (1681), digital copy retrieved from http://www.swarthmore.edu/SocSci/bdorsey1/41docs /38-pen.html, April 10, 2015. Please also see William Penn, "A brief account of the province of Pennsilvania" (London: printed for Benjamin Clark, 1682). Kulikoff, "From British Peasants to Colonial American Farmers," 50.

66. Jerry William Frost, *A Perfect Freedom, Religious Liberty in Pennsylvania* (Cambridge, UK: Cambridge University Press, 2005), especially Chapter 1, "The Creation of Religious Liberty in Early Pennsylvania," 10–28; William Penn, "The frame of the government of the province of Pennsilvania" (1682).

67. Seidensticker, "William Penn's Travels in Holland and Germany in 1677," 262–264.

68. "Articles of Agreement between the Members of the Frankfort Company, 1686," *Pennsylvania Magazine of History and Biography* 15.2 (1891): 205–211.

69. The sale of land to the Krefeld group, and their passage to America, was arranged by an English friend of Penn's living in Rotterdam, Benjamin Furly. Julius Friedrich Sachse, "Benjamin Furly, 'an English merchant at Rotterdam,' who promoted the first German emigration to America," reprinted from *Pennsylvania Magazine of History and Biography* (October 1895).

70. Samuel W. Pennypacker, "The Settlement of Germantown, and the Causes Which Led to It," *Pennsylvania Magazine of History and Biography* 4.1 (1880): 5.

71. Pennypacker, "The Settlement of Germantown," 6–7, 10–11, 13, 14. The Swiss had migrated first to Kriegsheim, now in France, and then to America.

72. Irma Corcoran, "William Penn and His Purchasers: Problems in Paradise," *Proceedings of the American Philosophical Society* 138.4 (December 1994): 482, 483.

73. Other, earlier tracts by Penn include "A further account of the province of Pennsylvania and its improvements" (London: 1685); "Information and direction to such persons as are inclined to America" (London?: 1686); and "Some proposals for a second settlement in the province of Pennsylvania" (London: Printed and sold by Andrew Sowle, 1690).

74. William Penn, "Letter to the Free Society of Traders" (London: Printed and sold by Andrew Sowle, 1683), digital copy available at http://historymatters .gmu.edu/d/7440/ located on April 10, 2015.

75. "Falckner's Curieuse Nachricht von Pensylvania [sic], The Book that Stimulated the Great German Emigration to Pennsylvania in the early years of the XVIII Century, a reprint of the edition of 1702, amplified with the Text of the Original Manuscript in the Halle Archives. Together with an Introduction and English Translation of the Complete Work by Julius Friedrich Sachse" (Philadelphia, 1905), 46–229.

76. Otterness, *Becoming German*, 26.

77. Farley Grubb, "Babes in Bondage? Debt Shifting by German Immigrants in Early America," *Journal of Interdisciplinary History* 37.1 (Summer 2006): 3; Roger Daniels, *Coming to America, A History of Immigration and Ethnicity in American Life* (New York: Perennial, 1991, 2nd ed.), 77–85.

78. Daniels, *Coming to America*, 62, Table 3.1, "Estimated Slave Imports into the Americas, by Importing Region, 1451–1870 (in thousands)," citing Philip D. Curtin, *The African Slave Trade: A Census* (Madison, WI: 1969), 288.

Chapter 2

1. Theodore C. Blegen, "The Competition of the Northwestern States for Immigrants," *Wisconsin Magazine of History* 3.1 (September 1919): 3–29; Livia Appel and T. C. Blegen, "Official Encouragement of Immigration to Minnesota during the Territorial Period," *Minnesota Historical Society Magazine*, originally published August 1923, retrieved from http://collections.mnhs.org/MNHistory Magazine/articles/5/v05i03p167-203.pdf on July 30, 2015.

2. Jack Ericson Eblen, *The First and Second United States Empires, Governors and Territorial Government, 1784–1912* (Pittsburgh, PA: University of Pittsburgh Press, 1968), 55; J. Norman Heard, *Handbook of the American Frontier, Four Centuries of Indian-White Relationships, Vol. II: The Northeastern Woodlands* (Lanham, MD: Scarecrow Press, 1990), 70–71 (Chippewa Indians); 160–161 (Illinois Indians); 161–163 (Iroquois Indians); 175–176 (Kaskakia Indians); 180–181 (Kickapoo Indians); 231 (Menominee Indians); 234–235 (Miami Indians); 278 (Ottawa Indians); 300 (Potawatomi Indians); 383 (Wea Indians); 61–62 (Castor Hill, Treaties of); 69 (Chicago, Illinois, Treaties of); 71 (Chippewanaung, Indiana, Treaties of), 98 (Detroit, Michigan, Treaties of), 107 (Edwardsville, Illinois, Treaties of); 116 (Flint River, Treaty of); 230 (Meigs, Fort, Treaty of); 317 (Saginaw, Michigan, Treaties of); 319 (St. Joseph, Michigan, Treaties of); 325 (Sault Ste. Marie, Michigan, Treaty of); 371–372 (Upper Sandusky, Ohio, Treaty of); and 383 (Wayne, Fort, Treaties of).

3. Merle Curti, "The Reputation of America Overseas (1776–1860)," *American Quarterly* 1.1 (Spring, 1949): 75, quoting S. H. Collins, *The Emigrant's Guide to the United States of America* (Hull, 1830), 27.

4. Heard, *Handbook of the American Frontier, Vol. II*, 70–71 (Chippewa Indians); 117–118 (Fox Indians); 161–163 (Iroquois Indians); 180–181 (Kickapoo Indians); 223–224 (Mascouten Indians); 234–235 (Miami Indians); 278 (Ottawa Indians); 300 (Potawatomi Indians).

5. Heard, *Handbook of the American Frontier, Vol. II*, 17 (Armstrong, Fort, Treaties of); 69 (Chicago, Illinois, Treaties of); 71 (Chippewanaung, Indiana, Treaties of); 98 (Detroit, Michigan, Treaties of); 116 (Flint River, Treaty of); 230 (Meigs, Fort, Treaty of); 317 (Saginaw, Michigan, Treaties of); 319 (St. Joseph, Michigan, Treaties of); 325 (Sault Ste. Marie, Michigan, Treaty of); 371–372 (Upper Sandusky, Ohio, Treaty of).

6. John D. Haeger, *The Investment Frontier: New York Businessmen and the Economic Development of the Old Northwest* (New York: SUNY Press, 1981), 86.

7. "John Almy," United States Census, Year: *1850;* Census Place: *Grand Rapids, Kent, Michigan;* Roll: *M432_353; 186B*; Image: 366, retrieved from Ancestry.com, at http://search.ancestry.com/cgi-bin/sse.dll?indiv=1&db=1850usfedcenancestry &rank=1&new=1&MSAV=1&gss=angs-d&gsfn=John&gsln=Almy&gsln_x =XO&msrpn__ftp=Grand+Rapids%2c+Kent%2c+Michigan%2c+USA&cpxt=0 &catBucket=rstp&uidh=yd8&cp=0&msrpn__ftp_x=XO&pcat=35&fh=0&h =3095055&recoff=&ml_rpos=1 *on April 17, 2015.*

8. *Michigan: A History of the Great Lakes State* (Hoboken, NJ: John Wiley & Sons, 2014), 130–131, retrieved from Google Books at https://books.google.de /books?id=HIiTAgAAQBAJ&pg=PA130&lpg=PA130&dq=John+Almy+Michigan &source=bl&ots=ot_ShKSkZQ&sig=XJj4SABa8Rpvmoxt67-aoF_bgoM&hl=en &sa=X&ei=EOPuVO30MYyHPbmngIAH&ved=0CEMQ6AEwBw#v=onepage&q =John%20Almy%20Michigan&f=false on April 10, 2015.

9. New York's population in 1845 was 371,223, of which 236,567 were native born and 134,656 were foreign born. Of the foreign born, 96,581 were Irish, 24,416 were German, and 13,650 were other Europeans, Chart, Birthplace of New York City Population, retrieved from http://projects.ilt.columbia.edu/seneca /svcurric/images/birthplace_early.html on January 22, 2016. Immigration to the United States, most entering at the Port of New York, was 114,371 entries for 1845, as compared to 78,615 in 1844, Chart, "Immigration by Country, 1820–2007," retrieved from http://readme.bugs3.com/pdf/Immigration_1820_1840 /Immigration_By_Country_1820_2007/45_pdf on May 11, 2015; Stanley Nadel, *Little Germany, Ethnicity, Religion and Class in New York City, 1845–1880* (Urbana and Chicago: University of Illinois Press, 1990); James R. Barrett, *The Irish Way, Becoming American in the Multiethnic City* (New York: Penguin Press, 2012).

10. *Michigan: A History of the Great Lakes State*, 131, retrieved from https://books .google.de/books?id=HIiTAgAAQBAJ&pg=PA130&lpg=PA130&dq=John+Almy +Michigan&source=bl&ots=ot_ShKSkZQ&sig=XJj4SABa8Rpvmoxt67-aoF_bgoM &hl=en&sa=X&ei=EOPuVO30MYyHPbmngIAH&ved=0CEMQ6AEwBw#v =onepage&q=John%20Almy%20Michigan&f=false on April 10, 2015. Please note that this work spells Thomson's name "Thompson."

11. Edwin Orin Wood, "History of Genesee county Michigan; her people, industries and institutions, with biographical sketches of representative citizens and genealogical records of many of the old families" (Indianapolis: Federal Pub. Co., 1916), 94, retrieved from http://archive.org/stream/historyofgenesee00wood /historyofgenesee00wood_djvu.txt on April 20, 2015.

12. Overall immigration increased from 297,024 in 1849 to 369,980 in 1850, and German immigration would increase from 385,434 for the decade 1840–1849 to 976,072 for 1850–1859, Chart, "Immigration by Country, 1820–2007."

13. *Michigan: A History of the Great Lakes State*, 131, retrieved from https:// books.google.de/books?id=HIiTAgAAQBAJ&pg=PA130&lpg=PA130&dq=John +Almy+Michigan&source=bl&ots=ot_ShKSkZQ&sig=XJj4SABa8Rpvmoxt67 -aoF_bgoM&hl=en&sa=X&ei=EOPuVO30MYyHPbmngIAH&ved=0CEMQ6AE wBw#v=onepage&q=John%20Almy%20Michigan&f=false on April 10, 2015.

14. United States Bureau of the Census, Seventh Annual Census, 1850, *Statistics of Michigan, Table III, Nativities of the Population,* 897. Note: Although the Census of 1850 was the first to ask place of birth, the Michigan statistics do not break down the national origin of foreign-born residents.

15. Wood, "History of Genesee county Michigan," 94, retrieved from http:// archive.org/stream/historyofgenesee00wood/historyofgenesee00wood_djvu.txt on April 20, 2015.

16. "Edward H. Thomson, aka Edward H. Thompson," Find a Graveyard, retrieved from http://politicalgraveyard.com/bio/thompson3.html#0LI00WAMX on April 20, 2015. Thomson also served as a colonel in the Union Army during the Civil War and was mayor of Flint from 1877 to 1878. It is unclear whether Thomson was a Democrat or Whig, but since he was appointed by a Democrat, it seems likely he was one as well.

17. *Michigan: A History of the Great Lakes State*, 131, retrieved from https:// books.google.de/books?id=HIiTAgAAQBAJ&pg=PA130&lpg=PA130&dq=John +Almy+Michigan&source=bl&ots=ot_ShKSkZQ&sig=XJj4SABa8Rpvmoxt67 -aoF_bgoM&hl=en&sa=X&ei=EOPuVO30MYyHPbmngIAH&ved=0CEMQ6AE wBw#v=onepage&q=John%20Almy%20Michigan&f=false on April 10, 2015. "Rudolph Dpenpeck, [sic], United States Census, Year: *1860*; Census Place: *New York Ward 21 District 5, New York, New York*; Roll: *M653_818*; Page: *535*; Image: *536*; Family History Library Film: *803818,* and "Rudolph Diefenbeck [sic]," United States Census, Year: *1870*; Census Place: *Detroit Ward 4, Wayne, Michigan*; Roll: *M593_712*; Page: *197A*; Image: *397*; Family History Library Film: *552211,* retrieved from Ancestry.com on April 20, 2015; "George H. Veenfliet," April 26, 1856, Ancestry.com. *U.S., Appointments of U. S. Postmasters, 1832–1971* [database online]. Provo, UT, USA: Ancestry.com Operations, Inc., 2010, located on April 20, 2015; "George F. Veenfliet," S.D. Bingham, Early history of Michigan, with biographies of state officers, members of Congress, judges and legislators, Vol 2 (1887), 25, retrieved from http://www.ebooksread.com/authors-eng/s-d-stephen -d-bingham/early-history-of-michigan-with-biographies-of-state-officers -members-of-congre-gni/page-25-early-history-of-michigan-with-biographies

-of-state-officers-members-of-congre-gni.shtml on April 20, 2015; "George H. Veen-fliet," James Cooke Mills, History of Saginaw County Michigan, Historical Commercial Biographical Profusely Illustrated with Portraits of Early Pioneers Rare Pictures and Scenes of Olden Times, and Portraits of Representative Citizens of Today, Vol. 2, (Saginaw, MI: Seemann & Peters, 1918), 326, retrieved from http://quod.lib.umich.edu/m/micounty/BAD1040.0002.001?rgn=main;view=fulltext on April 20, 2015.

18. *Michigan: A History of the Great Lakes State*, 131, https://books.google.de/books?id=HIiTAgAAQBAJ&pg=PA130&lpg=PA130&dq=John+Almy+Michigan&source=bl&ots=ot_ShKSkZQ&sig=XJj4SABa8Rpvmoxt67-aoF_bgoM&hl=en&sa=X&ei=EOPuVO30MYyHPbmngIAH&ved=0CEMQ6AEwBw#v=onepage&q=John%20Almy%20Michigan&f=false accessed on April 10, 2015.

19. Heard, *Handbook of the American Frontier*, Vol. II, 70–71 (Chippewa Indians); 117–118 (Fox Indians); 160–161 (Illinois Indians); 223–224 (Mascouten Indians); 231 (Menominee Indians); 234–235 (Miami Indians); 324–325 (Sauk Indians); 395–396 (Winnebago Indians).

20. Eblen, *The First and Second United States Empires*, 5; Heard, *Handbook of the American Frontier*, Vol. II, 17 (Armstrong, Fort, Treaties of); 26–27 (Black Hawk War); 69 (Chicago, Illinois, Treaties of); 321 (St. Peter's, Wisconsin, Treaty of).

21. Heard, *Handbook of the American Frontier* Vol. II, 25 (Black Hawk); 26–27 (Black Hawk War); 324–325 (Sauk Indians);

22. United States Bureau of the Census, Seventh Annual Census, 1850, Statistics of Wisconsin, Table V, Progress of Population from 1840 to 1850, 925.

23. United States Bureau of the Census, Seventh Annual Census, 1850, Statistics of Wisconsin, Table III, Nativities of the Population, 925.

24. *Magazine of Western History, 1888*, 304–309; Men of progress. Wisconsin. A selected list of biographical sketches and portraits of the leaders in business, professional and official life. Together with short notes on the history and character of Wisconsin, Andrew J. Aikens & Lewis A. Proctor, eds. (Milwaukee: Evening Wisconsin Co., 1897), 337–339, retrieved from http://files.usgwarchives.net/wi/biographies/pg316-350.txt on April 17, 2015.

25. Blegen, "The Competition of the Northwestern States for Immigrants," 5–6. Blegen is incorrect in his assertion that Wisconsin was the first state to develop an immigration recruitment policy.

26. "Herman Haertel," Passport application, April 18, 1889, National Archives and Records Administration (NARA); Washington, DC; NARA Series: *Passport Applications, 1795–1905*; Roll #: *324*; Volume #: *Roll 324, 16 Apr 1889–22 Apr 1889*, retrieved from Ancestry.com on April 20, 2015; "Herman Haertel," United States Census, Year: 1860; Census Place: Milwaukee Ward 6, Milwaukee, Wisconsin; Roll: M653_1423; Page: 533; Image: 143; Family History Library Film: 805423 notes Haertel's real estate work; in 1870 he described himself as a coal dealer with personal property of $15,000, "Herman Haertel," United States Census, Year: 1870; Census Place: Milwaukee Ward 6, Milwaukee, Wisconsin; Roll: M593_1728; Page: 9B; Image: 22; Family History Library Film: 553227, retrieved from Ancestry.com on April 20, 2015.

27. "Haertel, Herman, mer, 89 Greenwich," Trow's New York City directory, H. Wilson compiler, for 1853–1854 (New York: John F. Trow, pub. 1854), Vol. 1, 290. Blegen, "The Competition of the Northwestern States for Immigrants," 6, 7. Haertel passed along about $3,000 to newly arrived immigrants. Please see "The Weather and the Crops," *New York Tribune*, August 11, 1853, 3 for an example of Haertel's promoting Wisconsin in Eastern newspapers.

28. Blegen, "The Competition of the Northwestern States for Immigrants," 13. Lapham had already published "A Geographical and Topographical Description of Wisconsin" in 1844.

29. "Frederick W. Horn," National Archives and Records Administration (NARA); Washington, DC; *Soundex Index to Naturalization Petitions for the United States District and Circuit Courts, Northern District of Illinois and Immigration and Naturalization Service District 9, 1840–1950 (M1285)*; Microfilm Serial: M1285; Microfilm Roll: 86, retrieved from Ancestry.com on April 20, 2015. Horn naturalized on November 10, 1842, in Wisconsin; "FW Horn," United States Census, Year: 1860; Census Place: Cedarburg, Ozaukee, Wisconsin; Roll: M653_1425; 684; Image 112; Family History Library Film 805425, retrieved from Ancestry.com on April 20, 2015.

30. Blegen, "The Competition of the Northwestern States for Immigrants," 9.

31. "Elias Stangeland," United States Census, Year: *1860*; Census Place: *Madison Ward 3, Dane, Wisconsin*; Roll: *M653_1403*; Page: *534*; Image: *546*; Family History Library Film: *805403*, retrieved from Ancestry.com on April 20, 2015; "Elias Stangeland," National Archives and Records Administration (NARA); Washington, D.C.; *Soundex Index to Naturalization Petitions for the United States District and Circuit Courts, Northern District of Illinois and Immigration and Naturalization Service District 9, 1840–1950 (M1285)*; Microfilm Serial: M1285; Microfilm Roll: *155*, retrieved from Ancestry.com on April 20, 2015.

32. Blegen, "The Competition of the Northwestern States for Immigrants," 9.

33. Appel and Blegen, "Official Encouragement of Immigration to Minnesota during the Territorial Period," 167 (original text), retrieved from http://collections .mnhs.org/MNHistoryMagazine/articles/5/v05i03p167-203.pdf on July 30, 2015.

34. United States Bureau of the Census, Eighth Annual Census, 1860, Statistics of Michigan, Table 5, Nativities of the Free Population, 544.

35. Hildegard Binder Johnson, "The Location of German Immigrants in the Middle West," *Annals of the Association of American Geographers* 41.1 (March 1951): 32–33; Herman Haertel, "The Weather and the Crops," *New York Tribune*, August 11, 1853, page 3 claims that corn in Wisconsin grew to a height of nine feet and that spring wheat, oats, and corn yields were much greater in Wisconsin than in New York, New Jersey, or Michigan, a statement the *Tribune* editor felt compelled to rebut immediately following Haertel's article.

36. Blegen, "The Competition of the Northwestern States for Immigrants," 10.

37. Eblen, The First and Second United States Empires, 229–232; Appel and Blegen, "Official Encouragement of Immigration to Minnesota during the Territorial Period," 167 (original text), retrieved from http://collections.mnhs.org /MNHistoryMagazine/articles/5/v05i03p167-203.pdf on July 30, 2015.

38. Heard, *Handbook of the American Frontier*, Vol. II, 70–71 (Chippewa Indians); J. Norman Heard, *Handbook of the American Frontier, Four Centuries of Indian-White Relationships*, Vol. III: The Great Plains (Lanham, MD: Scarecrow Press, 1993), 115–116 (Iowa Indians); 222 (Sioux Indians, Dakota, Nadouessioux and Sisseton); 162–163 (Mendota, Minnesota, Treaty of); 240 (Traverse des Sioux, Treaty of), 263 (Yankton Sioux Indians). The Treaty of Traverse des Sioux promised the Sioux $1,665,000, while the Treaty of Mendota promised $1,410,000. The United States paid the Sioux an annuity the equivalent of three cents per acre, and charged settlers $1.25 per acre when the land was sold. Please also see Kevin Hillstrom and Laurie Collier Hillstrom, American Indian Removal and the Trail to Wounded Knee (Detroit: Omnigraphics, 2010), 37.

39. Appel and Blegen, "Official Encouragement of Immigration to Minnesota during the Territorial Period," 170–171 (original text), retrieved from http://collections.mnhs.org/MNHistoryMagazine/articles/5/v05i03p167-203.pdf on July 30, 2015.

40. "New York, New York, Index to Passenger Lists, 1820–1846," database with images, FamilySearch (https://familysearch.org/ark:/61903/1:1:K843-J3X: accessed December 23, 2015), Eugene Burnand, 1844; citing NARA microfilm publication M261 (Washington, DC: National Archives and Records Administration, n.d.); FHL microfilm 350,215, retrieved from FamilySearch.org at https://familysearch.org/ark:/61903/1:1:K843-J3X on December 23, 2015. Burnand arrived on the ship *Stephen Whitney*. He naturalized in Jefferson, New York, in 1849, "New York, County Naturalization Records, 1791–1980," database with images, FamilySearch (https://familysearch.org/ark:/61903/1:1:KFXD-NGT: accessed December 23, 2015), Eugene Burnand, 1849; citing Naturalization, Jefferson, New York, United States, the offices of county clerk from various counties; FHL microfilm 1,002,841, retrieved from FamilySearch.org at https://familysearch.org/ark:/61903/1:1:KFXD-NGT on December 23, 2015.

41. "A Newspaper Editorial, March 16, 1855," *Daily Minnesotian* (St. Paul), "Agent of Immigration," reprinted in Appel and Blegen, "Official Encouragement of Immigration to Minnesota during the Territorial Period," 180 (original text), retrieved from http://collections.mnhs.org/MNHistoryMagazine/articles/5/v05i03p167-203.pdf on July 30, 2015.

42. Appel and Blegen, "Official Encouragement of Immigration to Minnesota during the Territorial Period," 170–171 and Eugene Burnand, "Annual Report to the Legislature of the Commissioner of Emigration," January 14, 1856, 192–197 (original text), retrieved from http://collections.mnhs.org/MNHistoryMagazine/articles/5/v05i03p167-203.pdf on July 30, 2015. Burand's reports for 1855, 1856, and 1857 are reprinted in Appel and Blegen, "Official Encouragement of Immigration to Minnesota during the Territorial Period," 192–203 (original text), retrieved from http://collections.mnhs.org/MNHistoryMagazine/articles/5/v05i03p167-203.pdf on July 30, 2015, and from the beginning he complained of lack of funds, late disbursement of funds, and of losing money while living in New York.

43. Appel and Blegen, "Official Encouragement of Immigration to Minnesota during the Territorial Period," 171, 198–199, footnote 24, notes Burland's failure to attract many Belgians (original text) retrieved from http://collections.mnhs.org /MNHistoryMagazine/articles/5/v05i03p167-203.pdf on July 30, 2015. Of Minnesota's 58,728 foreign-born residents in 1860, the largest number, 18,400, were from German states, mainly Prussia, Bavaria, and Baden, United States Bureau of the Census, Eighth Annual Census, 1860, Statistics of Minnesota, Table 5, Nativities of the Population, 262.

44. "Appendix to William G. Le Duc's Report to Willis A. Gorman, 1853," reprinted in Appel and Blegen, "Official Encouragement of Immigration to Minnesota during the Territorial Period," 173 (original text), retrieved from http:// collections.mnhs.org/MNHistoryMagazine/articles/5/v05i03p167-203.pdf on July 30, 2015.

45. Letter from Eugene Burnand "To his Excellency Governor W.A. Gorman, New York, May 5, 1856," reprinted in Appel and Blegen, "Official Encouragement of Immigration to Minnesota during the Territorial Period," 198 (original text), retrieved from http://collections.mnhs.org/MNHistoryMagazine/articles/5 /v05i03p167-203.pdf on July 30, 2015.

46. Nathan H. Parker, "The Minnesota Handbook for 1856–1857" (New York: Sheldon, Blakeman and Co., 1856), retrieved from http://quod.lib.umich.edu/m /moa/AJA3458.0001.001?rgn=main;view=fulltext on August 2, 2015.

47. Annual report of Eugene Burnand, Minnesota History Bulletin: 5:194, quoted in Theodore C. Blegen, Norwegian Migration to America: The American Transition (London: Ardent Media, 1940,) 385.

48. Chart, "Total Number of Immigrants by Year, 1820–2007."

49. Eugene Burnand, "Annual Report to the Legislature of the Commissioner of Emigration," January 14, 1856, 192–197 (original text), in Appel and Blegen, "Official Encouragement of Immigration to Minnesota during the Territorial Period," 192–197 (original text), retrieved from http://collections.mnhs.org /MNHistoryMagazine/articles/5/v05i03p167-203.pdf on July 30, 2015.

50. Robert Greenhalgh Albion, The Rise of New York Port, 1815–1860 (New York: Charles Scribner's Sons, 1939), 336–353.

51. New York Times, August 1, 1855, 1; August 2, 1855, 4 (no headlines for either notice); "Castle Garden, How Emigrants Are Treated," New York Times, August 4, 1855, 1; "The New Castle Garden Arrangements—Sale of Food," letter from German Society president and emigration commissioner Rudolph Garrigue, New York Times, August 6, 1855, 2; "New-York City, Emigration Depot, Castle Garden," New York Times, August 13, 1855, 8. Report of the Commissioners of Emigration of the State of New York, made to the Legislature January 23, 1850 (New York: Casper C. Childs, printer, 1850); Annual Report of the Commissioners of Emigration of the State of New York, for the year ending December 31, 1855 (New York: William C. Bryant & Co., printers, 1856).

52. "Castle Garden, How Emigrants Are Treated"; "Indignation Meeting, Demonstration of the Runners against the Commissioners of Emigration,

Tammany Quartered on the Battery, A Loud Time under Castle Garden Walls, Capt. Rynders and O'Keefe's Speeches and a Procession," *New York Times,* August 7, 1855, 1; "Adjourned Indignation Meeting, The Runners and their Friends on the Battery, Tar Barrels, Torches, Transparencies, etc., Speeches of Theodore E. Tomlinson, Capt. Turner, D.B. Taylor, and Capt. Young, Procession through the First and Second Wards," *New York Times,* August 14, 1855, 1.

53. Carl Wittke, *Refugees of Revolution: The German Forty-Eighters in America* (Philadelphia: University of Pennsylvania Press, 1952); Nadel, Little Germany; Marion L. Huffines, "Language-Maintenance Efforts Among German Immigrants and their Descendants in the United States," chapter 16 in *America and the Germans, An Assessment of a Three-Hundred-Year History,* Vol. 1: *Immigration, Language, Ethnicity,* Frank Trommler and Joseph McVeigh, eds. (Philadelphia: University of Pennsylvania, 1985), 241–269.

54. Elliot J. Gorn, "'Good-Bye Boys, I Die a True American': Homicide, Nativism, and Working-Class Culture in Antebellum New York City," *Journal of American History* 74.2 (September 1987): 388–410.

55. Bruce Levine, "Conservatism, Nativism, and Slavery: Thomas R. Whitney and the Origins of the Know-Nothing Party," *Journal of American History* 88.2 (September 2001): 455–488; William E. Gienapp, "Nativism and the Creation of a Republican Majority in the North before the Civil War," *Journal of American History* 72.3 (December 1985): 529–559.

56. John R. Van Atta, *Securing the West: Politics, Public Lands, and the Fate of the Old Republic, 1785–1850* (Baltimore: Johns Hopkins University Press, 2014), 239–240.

57. Eric Foner, *Free Soil, Free Labor, Free Men, The Ideology of the Republican Party Before the Civil War* (Oxford: Oxford University Press, 1995 ed.), 196–198 and chapter 7, "The Republicans and Nativism," 226–260; *Tyler Anbinder, Nativism and Slavery: The Northern Know Nothings and the Politics of the 1850s* (Oxford: Oxford University Press, 1992).

58. Raymond L. Cohn, *Mass Migration Under Sail, European Immigration to the Antebellum United States* (Cambridge, MA: Cambridge University Press, 2009). Hamburg-America Steamship Company converted to steam in 1857, the same year North German Lloyd Steamship Company was founded. British passenger transportation companies also quickly adopted steam power between 1850–1870.

59. Raymond L. Cohn, "Nativism and the End of the Mass Migration of the 1840s and 1850s," *Journal of Economic History* 60.2 (June 2000): 361–383; Chart, "Total Number of Immigrants by Year, 1820–2007."

60. Cohn, "Nativism and the End of the Mass Migration of the 1840s and 1850s," 374–375.

61. Ibid., 375–379.

62. Letter from Charles P. Daly, New York, to Col. D.A. Robertson, St. Paul, October 3, 1855, reprinted in Appel and Blegen, "Official Encouragement of Immigration to Minnesota during the Territorial Period," 188–190 (original

text), retrieved from http://collections.mnhs.org/MNHistoryMagazine/articles/5/v05i03p167-203.pdf on July 30, 2015.

63. Letter from Daly to Robertson, 1855, reprinted in Appel and Blegen, "Official Encouragement of Immigration to Minnesota during the Territorial Period," 188 (original text retrieved from http://collections.mnhs.org/MNHistoryMagazine/articles/5/v05i03p167-203.pdf on July 30, 2015. The Crimean War diverted English ships from the Atlantic and the British military draft in Ireland both siphoned off potential emigrant men and increased wages in Ireland, discouraging immigration.

64. Heard, *Handbook of the American Frontier* Vol. II, 25 (Black Hawk): 26–27 (Black Hawk War), 70–71 (Chippewa Indians), 117–118 (Fox Indians), 300 (Potawatomi Indians), 324–325 (Sauk Indians); Richard White, "It's Your Misfortune and None of My Own," *A History of the American West* (Norman: University of Oklahoma Press, 1991), 86–89.

65. Table, "Indian Wars, Their Cost, and Civil Expenditures," covering military expenditures from July 4, 1776 to June 30, 1890, Department of the Interior, Census Office, Report on Indians taxed and Indians not taxed in the United States (except Alaska) (Washington, DC, Government Printing Office, 1894, reprinted by Norman Ross Publishing, 1994), 641. 1843 was the only year in which less than $1 million was spent on Indian affairs, mainly military control.

66. United States Census Bureau, U.S. Censuses of Population and Housing, 1790–1990, retrieved from http://lwd.dol.state.nj.us/labor/lpa/census/1990/poptrd1.htm on January 21, 2016.

67. Foner, *Free Soil, Free Labor, Free Men*, 236. Texas and Missouri were the only slave states to receive large numbers of immigrants, mainly Germans, before the Civil War, but these immigrants generally did not practice slavery.

68. Ibid.

69. Although immigration numbers begin to rise in 1863, they do not surpass the number of entries in 1854 until 1873; Cohn, "Nativism and the End of the Mass Migration of the 1840s and 1850s," 379–380.

Chapter 3

1. Stephen V. Ward, *Selling Places: The Marketing and Promotion of Towns and Cities, 1850–2000* (New York: Routledge, 1998), especially Chapter 2, "Selling the Frontier," 9–28; Sig Mickelson, *The Northern Pacific Railroad and the Selling of the West* (Sioux Falls, SD: The Center for Western Studies, 1993); Jason Eric Pierce, "Making the White Man's West: Whiteness and the Creation of the American West" (PhD dissertation, University of Arkansas, Fayetteville, 2008), especially Chapter 6, "Promoting the White Man's West: Railroads and White Settlement," 111–145.

2. M. Jean Ferrill, "Rainfall Follows the Plow," *Encyclopedia of the Great Plains*, David J. Wishart, ed. (Lincoln: University of Nebraska Press, 2011), located at http://plainshumanities.unl.edu/encyclopedia/doc/egp.ii.049 on November 23, 2015. Paul Wallace Gates, "The Promotion of Agriculture by the Illinois Central

Railroad, 1855–1870," *Agricultural History* 5.2 (April 1931): 57–76 notes the railroads' involvement in agricultural stations and scientific farming, particularly in the early 20th century.

3. Robert M. Utley, *The Indian Frontier of the American West, 1846–1890* (Albuquerque: University of New Mexico Press, 1984); Robert Wooster, *The American Military Frontiers, The United States Army in the West, 1783–1900* (Albuquerque: University of New Mexico Press, 2009).

4. The United States also gained territory through the Louisiana Purchase of 1803 from France, the negotiation of the boundary between Great Britain and the United States at the 49th parallel in 1846 (the Oregon Territory), and the Mexican-American War. The federal government distributed public land to states, individuals, and corporations in other ways, such as through the Swamp Land Grant Act of 1850, the Homestead Act of 1862, the Land-Grant College (Morrill) Act of 1862, the Timber Culture Act of 1873, and bounties to war veterans, and to construct canals, public roads, and improve waterways.

5. David Maldwyn Ellis, comments on "The Railroad Land Grant Legend in American History Texts," David Maldwyn Ellis, Richard C. Overton, Robert E. Riegel, Herbert O. Brayer, Chester McArthur Destler, Stanley Pargellis, Fred A. Shannon, and Edward C. Kirkland, *The Mississippi Valley Historical Review* 32.4 (March 1946): 558.

6. William Richard Black, *Transportation: A Geographical Analysis* (New York: Guilford Press, 2003), 23.

7. This requirement was added to most treaties the United States negotiated with Indian nations in the late 19th century, J. Norman Heard, *Handbook of the American Frontier, Four Centuries of Indian-White Relationships,* Vol. III: The Great Plains (Lanham, MD: Scarecrow Press, 1993), 161 (Medicine Lodge Creek, Treaties of), 175 (Northern Pacific Railroad Battles), 263 (Yellowstone, Battle of); J. Norman Heard, *Handbook of the American Frontier, Four Centuries of Indian-White Relationships, Vol. IV: The Far West* (Lanham, MD: Scarecrow Press, 1997), 301 (Treaty of Tabeguache Agency), and 302 (Treaties of Table Rock, Oregon); Keith L. Bryant, Jr., *History of the Atchison, Topeka & Santa Fe Railway* (Lincoln: University of Nebraska, 1974), 13.

8. Ward, *Selling Places*, 9–28; David M. Wrobel, *Promised Lands, Promotion, Memory, and the Creation of the American West* (Lawrence, KS: University Press of Kansas, 2002), 20. This effort at "region creating" is particularly evident in the Northern Pacific Railroad's promotional work. Please see the *Northern Pacific* magazine, *Golden Northwest*, or the pamphlets "The Northern Pacific Railroad: its routes, resources, progress and business, the new northwest and its great thoroughfare" (Jay Cooke & Co., Philadelphia, 1872) and *The Northern Pacific, Its land grant, resources, traffic, and tributary country, valley route to the Pacific* (issued by Jay Cooke & Co, Philadelphia, 1873).

9. Ray Allen Billington, *Land of Savagery, Land of Promise: The European Image of the American Frontier in the Nineteenth Century* (New York: W. W. Norton & Co., 1981), 59.

10. Utley, *The Indian Frontier of the American West*, page 4 says 360,000 Indians lived west of the Mississippi and 200,000 in the Mexican Cession; Wooster, *The American Military Frontiers*, 118–119 notes 200,000 Indians and 85,000 Mexicans in the Mexican Cession. The estimate for the Chinese population is based on the total number of Chinese immigrants from 1820 to 1869, Chart, "Immigration by Country, 1820–2007," located at http://readme.bugs3.com/pdf/Immigration_1820_1840/Immigration_By_Country_1820_2007/45_pdf on May 11, 2015. Ward, *Selling Places*, 9–28; Wrobel, *Promised Lands*, 25–27; Billington, *Land of Savagery, Land of Promise*, 59–78.

11. Atchison, Topeka & Santa Fe Railroad, "A New Home in an Old Settlement: Come and See the 'New Land in an Old Country'" (May 1, 1876), located at the Kansas Historical Society and Kansas Historical Foundation, at http://www.kansasmemory.org/item/213108 on September 17, 2015; Bryant, *History of the Atchison, Topeka & Santa Fe Railway*, 13.

12. Ten whites were killed in the Meeker massacre as part of the Utes' larger resistance to segregation on the White River Agency reservation, Heard, *Handbook of the American Frontier*, Vol. IV, 301 (Treaty of Tabeguache Agency), 186 (Meeker Massacre), 190 (Battle of Milk Creek).

13. *Atchison, Topeka & Santa Fe Railroad*, "Arizona Interests via the Atchison, Topeka and Santa Fe Railroad" (1882), no page number on original, "Historical" section, page 1 on digital copy, located at Kansas Historical Society and Kansas Historical Foundation, at http://www.kansasmemory.org/item/212703 on September 17, 2015. Please also see *Atchison, Topeka & Santa Fe Railroad*, "A Glimpse of the Southwest, New Mexico, the Santa Fe Route" (1884), located at Kansas Historical Society and Kansas Historical Foundation, at http://www.kansasmemory.org/item/212705 on September 17, 2015.

14. *Atchison, Topeka & Santa Fe Railroad*, "Arizona Interests via the Atchison, Topeka and Santa Fe Railroad" (1882).

15. Heard, *Handbook of the American Frontier*, Vol. IV, 29 (Big Dry Wash, battle), 147–148 (Josanie, Chiricahua Apache warrior), 296 (George H. Stevens Ranch, raid).

16. "Land and Emigration," four-page tabloid newspaper published by the European Agency of the Land and Emigration Department of the Northern Pacific Railroad (Vols. 1–20, London, 1871–1873) made no mention of Indians in Northern Pacific territory. A sister publication, *Minnesota*, published around 1873, stated, "Do the Indians give the settlers any trouble?" "There are only a few Indians in Minnesota—the Chippewas—and they have always been friendly; they are now on reservations, living in houses, and cultivating the land. They are not troublesome." (Minnesota, undated, probably after February 1873, Questions & Answers, 4).

17. Heard, *Handbook of the American Frontier*, Vol. III, 175 (Northern Pacific Railroad Battles), 263 (Yellowstone, Battle of).

18. Elliott West, *The Contested Plains, Indians, Goldseekers, & the Rush to Colorado* (Lawrence: University Press of Kansas, 1998), 311–312; Bryant, *History of the Atchison, Topeka & Santa Fe Railway*, 56.

19. Heard, *Handbook of the American Frontier*, Vol. IV, entries for the Nez Percé are on 24–25 (Bear Paw Mountain, battle), 30 (Big Hole, battle), 49 (Camp Stevens, Washington, treaties), 51 (Canyon Creek, battle), 67–68 (Clearwater River, battle), 80 (Cow Island, battle), 163 (Lapwai Valley, treaties), 206–207 (Nez Percé), 338 (White Bird Canyon, battle).

20. Ibid., Vol. IV, 281 (Sheepeater War) and 281–282 (Shoshoni Indians).

21. Charles Nordhoff, *California for Health, Pleasure, and Residence: A Book for Travellers and Settlers* (New York: Harper & Brothers, 1874), preface. This work has been digitized and is available through the Central Pacific Railroad Museum's website: http://cprr.org/Museum/Books/I_ACCEPT_the_User_Agreement/Calif_Nordhoff_1872.pdf located on September 2, 2015. Wrobel, *Promised Lands*, 25–27.

22. Victoria E. Dye, *All Aboard for Santa Fe, Railway Promotion of the Southwest, 1890s to 1930s* (Albuquerque: University of New Mexico Press, 2005), 24–27.

23. "Land and Emigration," lists prices in every issue, usually on page 2; Stanley N. Murray, "Railroads and the Agricultural Development of the Red River Valley of the North, 1870–1890," *Agricultural History* 31.4 (October 1957): 60–62; James B. Hedges, "The Colonization Work of the Northern Pacific Railroad," *Mississippi Valley Historical Review* 13.3 (December 1926): 320–321; *Atchison, Topeka & Santa Fe Railroad*, "The Inter Ocean" (April 6, 1882), 10, 12, located at Kansas Historical Society and Kansas Historical Foundation, at http://www.kansasmemory.org/item/213102 on September 17, 2015.

24. "The Northern Pacific Railroad: its routes, resources, progress and business, the new northwest and its great thoroughfare" (Jay Cooke & Co., Philadelphia, 1872), 4.

25. *Atchison, Topeka & Santa Fe Railroad*, "A New Home in an Old Settlement: Come and See the 'New Land in an Old Country'" (May 1, 1876), located at the Kansas Historical Society and Kansas Historical Foundation, at http://www.kansasmemory.org/item/213108 on September 17, 2015. Capitalization in original.

26. Wrobel, *Promised Lands*, 20; Ronald Howell Ridgley, "Railroads and the Development of the Dakotas: 1872–1914" (PhD dissertation, Indiana University, 1967), 40–42.

27. *Atchison, Topeka & Santa Fe Railroad*, "How and Where to Get a Living, A Sketch of the "Garden of the West,'" (1876), 7, located at the Kansas Historical Society and Kansas Historical Foundation, at http://www.kansasmemory.org/item/1142 on September 17, 2015. Also, Bryant, *History of the Atchison, Topeka & Santa Fe Railway*, 67.

28. Bryant, *History of the Atchison, Topeka & Santa Fe Railway*, 56, 67.

29. Dye, *All Aboard for Santa Fe*, 3; New Mexico Bureau of Immigration, "Ho! To the Land of Sunshine, A Guide to New Mexico for the Homeseeker" (Albuquerque, New Mexico Bureau of Immigration, 1909), 39 (quote). Also please see "Santa Fe as a Health Resort" (Passenger Department Santa Fe Route, 1890), "New Mexico Health Resorts" (Passenger Department Santa Fe Route, 1897), "Resorts on the Santa Fe" (Passenger Department Santa Fe Route, 1898), "Climatology and

Mineral Springs of New Mexico—Health and Pleasure Resorts" (Santa Fe: New Mexico Printing Co., 1900).

30. "The Northern Pacific Railroad: its routes, resources, progress and business, the new northwest and its great thoroughfare" (Jay Cooke & Co., Philadelphia, 1872), 5; "Minnesota," 1, undated tabloid newspaper, published after February 1873 (Northern Pacific Railroad). See also "The Truth about the Snow-Storm," *Land and Emigration*, March 1873, 2.

31. "Health," "Minnesota," 1.

32. "What Minnesotans Say About the Climate," *Land and Emigration*, April 1873, 4.

33. "The Northern Pacific Railroad: its routes, resources, progress and business, the new northwest and its great thoroughfare" (Jay Cooke & Co., Philadelphia, 1872), 4.

34. "The Northern Pacific Railway; Its Effect Upon the Public Credit, the Public Revenues, and the Public debt, Speech of Hon. William Windom, of Minnesota, delivered in the House of Representatives, January 5, 1869," 34 and 35, included in "Northern Pacific Railroad: A Statement of Its Resources and Merits, as Presented to the Pacific Railroad Committee of Congress, March 1868" (Washington, DC: Intelligencer Printing House, 1868) (497, 498 of 785 pages of PDF, located at Google Books at https://books.google.co.uk/books?id=5zkzAQAAMAAJ &printsec=frontcover&dq=%22northern+pacific+railroad%22&hl=en&sa =X&ved=0CDUQ6AEwBGoVChMI_Kvl693ExwIVg27bCh3aOgvi#v=onepage&q =%22northern%20pacific%20railroad%22&f=false on August 25, 2015.

35. Bryant, *History of the Atchison, Topeka & Santa Fe Railway*, 70–72; "C. B. Schmidt," Kansas Historical Society and Kansas Historical Foundation, located at https://www.kshs.org/kansapedia/c-b-schmidt/17252 on September 17, 2015.

36. Ibid.; also March 23, 1875 letter from Schmidt to Colonel A. S. Johnson of the railroad's Land Commission discussing his trip to Russia and meeting with Mennonites in Prussia and Russia, located at http://www.kansasmemory.org /item/226015 on September 17, 2015. Please also see La Vern J. Rippley, "Germans from Russia," *Harvard Encyclopedia of American Ethnic Groups*, Stephan Thernstrom, ed. (Cambridge, MA: The Belknap Press of Harvard University Press, 1980), 425–430.

37. Melvin D. Epp, *The Petals of a Kansas Sunflower, A Mennonite Diaspora* (Eugene, OR: Wipf and Stock Publishers, 2012), 390.

38. *Atchison, Topeka & Santa Fe Railroad*, "The Inter Ocean," 10, 12.

39. Ridgeley, "Railroads and the Development of the Dakotas, 1872–1914"; William M. Bomash, *Guide to a Microfilm Edition of the Northern Pacific Land Department Records* (Minnesota Historical Society, 1983), 19. George Hibbard to Jay Cooke, May 19, 1873, Northern Pacific Railway Company Land Department Records, microfilm, roll 24, notes the importance that the Northern Pacific placed on recruiting Germans from Russia.

40. J. Gregory Smith, president, Northern Pacific Railroad, "Explanation of the Bill Now Before Congress," July 1866, 9, included in "Northern Pacific

Railroad: A Statement of Its Resources and Merits, as Presented to the Pacific Railroad Committee of Congress, March 1868" (Washington, DC: Intelligencer Printing House, 1868) (140 of 785 pages of PDF, located at Google Books at https://books.google.co.uk/books?id=5zkzAQAAMAAJ&printsec=frontcover &dq=%22northern+pacific+railroad%22&hl=en&sa=X&ved=0CDUQ6AEwBG oVChMI_Kvl693ExwIVg27bCh3aOgvi#v=onepage&q=%22northern%20 pacific%20railroad%22&f=false on August 25, 2015. John G. Rice, "The Effect of Land Alienation on Settlement," Annals of the Association of American Geographers 68.1 (March 1978): 61–72 focuses on Kandiyohi County in central Minnesota and notes the large number of Dutch and Swedish settlers to the region in the 1870s and 1880s.

41. George Sheppard to Frederick Billings, March 18, 1872, No. 3 in Foreign Agents I, Northern Pacific collection, Minnesota Historical Society, St. Paul, cited in Mickelson, the *Northern Pacific Railroad and the Selling of the West*, 83.

42. A. B. Nettleton to Frederick Billings, April 27, 1872, A. B. Nettleton Letters, I, cited in Mickelson, the *Northern Pacific Railroad and the Selling of the West*, 83.

43. William H. Freehling, *The Road to Disunion, Volume II: Secessionists Triumphant, 1854–1861* (Oxford: Oxford University Press, 2007), 40–41, 123–124, 128–129. Examples of this "isothermal theory of migration" can be found in *The First Report of the Board of Immigration for the State of Missouri, to the Twenty-Fourth General Assembly, for the Years 1865 and 1866* (Jefferson City, MO: Emory S. Foster, public printer, 1867), 31, located at HathiTrust Digital Library at http://catalog .hathitrust.org/Record/007936560?type[]=all&lookfor[]=Missouri%20immi gration&ft=on February 29, 2016, and Col. A. J. McWhirter speech given at Vicksburg, Mississippi, November 21, 1883, at the Cotton Planters' Association of America's annual convention, reprinted in Jason H. Silverman and Susan R. Silverman, *Immigration in the American South, 1864–1895, A Documentary History of the Southern Immigration Conventions* (Lewiston, ID: The Edwin Mellon Press, 2006), 74. Please also see John Higham, *Strangers in the Land, Patterns of American Nativism, 1860–1925* (New Brunswick, NJ: Rutgers University Press, 1994 ed.), Chapter 6, "Toward Racism: The History of an Idea," 131–157.

44. Oscar O. Winther, "Promoting the American West in England, 1865–1890," *Journal of Economic History* 16.4 (December 1956): 507–508; Bomash, *Guide to a Microfilm Edition of The Northern Pacific Land Department Records*, 17, 19, 24; Edna Monch Parker, "The Southern Pacific Railroad and Settlement in Southern California," *Pacific Historical Review* 6.2 (June 1937): 111, footnote 29, 112–113; Richard J. Orsi, *Sunset Limited, The Southern Pacific Railroad and the Development of the American West, 1850–1930* (Berkeley and Los Angeles: University of California Press, 2007), 151–152.

45. "English emigrants are in many respects peculiar and troublesome," George Sheppard wrote to Frederick Billings, December 13, 1873, No. 49, in Foreign Agents, II, cited in Mickelson, the *Northern Pacific Railroad and the Selling of the West*, 84.

46. Mickelson, *The Northern Pacific Railroad and the Selling of the West*, 84.

47. "Land and Emigration," August 1871, 3, quoting a speech by Northern Pacific land commissioner John Loomis, entitled "Land for the Landless, Free Homes for Free Men."

48. "Land and Emigration," December 1871, 2.

49. Parker, "The Southern Pacific Railroad and Settlement in Southern California," 111–112. A Mr. Schiever was the Southern Pacific's agent in New Orleans in 1883, the multilingual agent was a Mr. Meyer.

50. Orsi, Sunset Limited, 134; Parker, "The Southern Pacific Railroad and Settlement in Southern California," 108.

51. "Edwin Hawley Dead; Worth $60,000,000; Financier and Railroad Magnate Dies at His Home in His 63d Year," *New York Times*, February 2, 1912, 9; Parker, "The Southern Pacific Railroad and Settlement in Southern California," 111–112.

52. Hedges, "The Colonization Work of the Northern Pacific Railroad," 329.

53. Mickelson, *The Northern Pacific Railroad and the Selling of the West*, 12.

54. Zhou Min and Rebecca Y. Kim, "The Paradox of Ethnicization and Assimilation: The Development of Ethnic Organizations in the Chinese Immigrant Community in the United States," chapter 10 in *Voluntary Organizations in the Chinese Diaspora: Illusions of Open Space in Hong Kong, Tokyo, and Shanghai*, Khun Eng Kuah-Pearce, Evelyn Du-Dehart, eds. (Hong Kong: Hong Kong University Press, 2006), p. 232; The Central Pacific Railroad Photographic History Museum has a large collection of material online about Chinese railroad workers. Please see http://cprr.org/Museum/Chinese.html accessed on June 24, 2016.

55. Mickelson, *The Northern Pacific Railroad and the Selling of the West*, 79. This was one of the few instances in which the NP combined labor recruitment and immigration promotion and land sales.

56. Hedges, "The Colonization Work of the Northern Pacific Railroad," 330 (quote); James B. Hedges, "Promotion of Immigration to the Pacific Northwest by the Railroads," *Mississippi Valley Historical Review* 15.2 (September 1928): 198–199; Land and Emigration.

57. Orsi, *Sunset Limited*, 146, 159.

58. Billington, *Land of Savagery, Land of Promise*, 69, notes *Die Süddeutsche Auswanderung's Zeitung*, *Die Hansa*, and *Die Allgemeine Auswanderung's Zeitung* in Germany; *Die Schweizer Auswander's Zeitung* in Switzerland; *The American Settler, America, and Emigration* in England; and *Chambers' Information for the People* and *Chambers' Edinburgh Journal* in Scotland. *Die Deutsche Auswanderer-Zeitung* in Bremen, Germany, was another such newspaper.

59. Hedges, "The Colonization Work of the Northern Pacific Railroad," 315–321; Hedges, "Promotion of Immigration to the Pacific Northwest by the Railroads," 199.

60. Mickelson, *The Northern Pacific Railroad and the Selling of the West*, 14, 52.

61. Ibid., 86.

62. Ibid., 87.

63. Ibid., 87–88.

64. Hedges, "The Colonization Work of the Northern Pacific Railroad," 315, 329; Bomash, *Guide to a Microfilm Edition of the Northern Pacific Land Department Records*, 10, 17. Sheppard's name appears as an agent for the Northern Pacific in advertisements in *The American Settler "A Guide to British Emigration"* 2.13 (January 1, 1873)–2.26 (December 15, 1873), 2.27 (January 3, 1874)–4.78 (December 26, 1874), and 4.79 (January 2, 1875)–4.99 (May 22, 1875). This weekly newspaper was published by the *Anglo-American*, a pro-emigration newspaper based in London, in the 1870s, and asserted the belief that "emigration is for the benefit of the settler; and, British emigration to the United States is for the benefit of the Anglo-Saxon race" (January 3, 1874, Vol. II, No. 27, 1). Mickelson, *The Northern Pacific Railroad and the Selling of the West*, Chapter 6, "The Campaign in Europe," 73–94.

65. "Land and Emigration," July 1872, 4, and November 1872, page 4 lists agents of the railroad and the cities in which they were based. Also please see Mickelson, *The Northern Pacific Railroad and the Selling of the West*, 80.

66. Hedges, "The Colonization Work of the Northern Pacific Railroad," 329–330; Hedges, "Promotion of Immigration to the Pacific Northwest by the Railroads," 198–199.

67. Parker, "The Southern Pacific Railroad and Settlement in Southern California," 111, footnote 29, 112–113. Kingsbury was unusual among railroad agents in that he promoted immigration from Ireland.

68. Hedges, "The Colonization Work of the Northern Pacific Railroad," 316–317, 319.

69. Ibid., 317.

70. Mickelson, *The Northern Pacific Railroad and the Selling of the West*, 72–76.

71. Bryant, *History of the Atchison, Topeka & Santa Fe Railway*, 70–72; "C. B. Schmidt."

72. Parker, "The Southern Pacific Railroad and Settlement in Southern California," 115; Glenn S. Dumke, "Colony Promotion during the Southern-California Land Boom," *Huntington Library Quarterly* 6. 2 (February 1943): 244; Norton B. Stern, "Bernhard Marks: Founder of the Raising Industry, Fresno, California, 1832–1913," *Western States Jewish History* 41.4 (Summer 2009): 671.

73. Orsi, *Sunset Limited*, 149.

74. Ibid., 150–151.

75. Ibid., 136–137, 140.

76. Ibid., 158.

77. Hedges, "The Colonization Work of the Northern Pacific Railroad," 315–321.

78. Ibid., 318; also Mickelson, *The Northern Pacific Railroad and the Selling of the West*, page 80 notes that by 1882 the NP had relationships with seven steamship lines to get their passengers to the United States from Liverpool alone, but there were 41 other steamship lines with which the NP did not have special contracts.

79. Parker, "The Southern Pacific Railroad and Settlement in Southern California," 111–112; Bomash, *Guide to a Microfilm Edition of the Northern Pacific Land Department Records*, 17, 19, 24.

80. Orsi, *Sunset Limited*, 131.

81. Hedges, "The Colonization Work of the Northern Pacific Railroad," 320–321.

82. Parker, "The Southern Pacific Railroad and Settlement in Southern California," 115.

83. Ibid., 114; also Dumke, "Colony Promotion during the Southern-California Land Boom," 239.

84. Hedges, "The Colonization Work of the Northern Pacific Railroad," 315–321.

85. Parker, "The Southern Pacific Railroad and Settlement in Southern California," 114; also Dumke, "Colony Promotion during the Southern-California Land Boom," 239.

86. Ibid., 242.

87. Parker, "The Southern Pacific Railroad and Settlement in Southern California," 106–107; Dumke, "Colony Promotion during the Southern-California Land Boom," 242. Nordhoff, "California for Health, Pleasure, and Residence."

88. Dumke, "Colony Promotion during the Southern-California Land Boom," 238–239.

89. Bomash, *Guide to a Microfilm Edition of the Northern Pacific Land Department Records*, 12.

90. Ibid., 17, 19, 24; also Harold F. Peterson, "Some Colonization Projects of the Northern Pacific Railroad," a paper read at the 80th annual meeting of the Minnesota Historical Society, January 21, 1929, 138–139. *Land and Emigration* published extensive information about the Yoevil Colony and Furness Colonies as well as the organization of new colony communities in Minnesota in virtually every issue.

91. Peterson, "Some Colonization Projects of the Northern Pacific Railroad," 130, quoting Jay Cooke, in the *Duluth Minnesotian*, December 31, 1870.

92. United States Bureau of the Census, Ninth Annual Census, 1870, General Nativity and Foreign Parentage, Table IV, The United States, 299; United States Bureau of the Census, Tenth Annual Census, 1880, Population by States and Territories, Table 1a, The United States, in the Aggregate, and by Sex, Nativity, and Race, 3, and Population by Race, Sex, and Nativity, Table XIII, Showing the Nativities of the Foreign-born Population in the United States and in Each State and Territory: 1880, 492–495; United States Bureau of the Census, Eleventh Annual Census, 1890, Statistics of Population, Table 1, Population of States and Territories at Each Census: 1790 to 1890, 2–3, and Table 32, Foreign Born Population, Distributed According to Country of Birth, By States and Territories: 1890, 606–609; United States Bureau of the Census, Twelfth Annual Census, 1900, Statistics of Population, Table 9, Population by Sex, General Nativity, and Color by States and Territories: 1900, 482–483, and Table 33, Foreign Born Population, Distributed According to Country of Birth, By States and Territories: 1900, 732–735.

93. Bureau of the Census, 1870, Table IV, The United States, 299; United States Bureau of the Census, Ninth Annual Census, 1870, Table VI, Population

of the United States (by States and Territories), Classified by Race and Place of Birth, showing the Number of Persons Born in Each State and Territory and Specified Foreign Country, Dakota, 336–342; Bureau of the Census, 1880, Table 1a, The United States, 3, and Table XIII, 492–495; Bureau of the Census, 1890, Table 1, 2–3, and Table 32, 606–609; Bureau of the Census, 1900, Table 9, 482–483, and Table 33, 732–735.

94. Bureau of the Census, 1870, Table VI, 336–342; Bureau of the Census, 1880, Table 1a, The United States, 3, and Table XIII, 492–495; Bureau of the Census, 1890, Table 1, 2–3, and Table 32, 606–609; Bureau of the Census, 1900, Table 9, 482–483, and Table 33, 732–735.

95. Bureau of the Census, 1870, Table VI, 336–342; Bureau of the Census, 1880, Table 1a, 3, and Table XIII, 492–495; Bureau of the Census, 1890, Table 1, 2–3, and Table 32, 606–609; Bureau of the Census, 1900, Table 9, 482–483, and Table 33, 732–735.

96. Bryant, *History of the Atchison, Topeka & Santa Fe Railway*, 64; Bureau of the Census, 1870, Table IV, 299, and Table VI, 336–342; Bureau of the Census, 1880, Table 1a, 3, and Table XIII, 492–495; Bureau of the Census, 1890, Table 1, 2–3, and Table 32, 606–609.

97. Bureau of the Census, 1870, Table VI, 336–342; Bureau of the Census, 1880, Table 1a, 3, and Table XIII, 492–495; Bureau of the Census, 1890, Table 1, 2–3, and Table 32, 606–609; Bureau of the Census, 1900, Table 9, 482–483, and Table 33, 732–735.

98. Parker, "The Southern Pacific Railroad and Settlement in Southern California," 105–106.

99. United States Bureau of the Census, Twelfth Annual Census, 1900, Minor Civil Divisions, Table 5, Population of States and Territories by Minor Civil Division: 1890 and 1900, continued 75–80.

Chapter 4

1. Matthew Bowman, *The Mormon People, The Making of an American Faith* (New York: Random House, 2012), 108, says that 85,000 converts came to Utah between 1852 and 1887, while Richard L. Jensen, "Immigration and Emigration," *Encyclopedia of Mormonism*, retrieved from http://eom.byu.edu/index.php/Immigration_and_Emigration on December 11, 2015, says that more than 103,000 emigrated between 1840 and 1910. Edith Matteson and Jean Matteson, "Mormon Influence on Scandinavian Settlement in Nebraska," *On Distant Shores: Proceedings of the Marcus Lee Hansen Immigration Conference; Aalborg, Denmark June 29–July 1, 1992*, Birgit Flemming Larsen, Henning Bender, and Karen Veien, eds. (Denmark: Danes Worldwide Archives in collaboration with the Danish Society for Emigration History in Aalborg, 1993), 311, gives figures for Scandinavian Mormon emigration.

2. Jack Glazier, *Dispersing the Ghetto: The Relocation of Jewish Immigrants Across the United States* (Ithaca, NY: Cornell University Press, 1998), 34–37; Bernard Marinbach, *Galveston: Ellis Island of the West* (Albany, NY: SUNY Press, 1983).

3. La Vern J. Rippley, "Germans from Russia," 425–430, and John A. Hostetler, "Hutterites," 471–473, both in *Harvard Encyclopedia of American Ethnic Groups*, Stephan Thernstrom, ed. (Cambridge, MA: Belknap Press of Harvard University Press, 1980), 425–430.

4. Bowman, *The Mormon People*, xv–xvi.

5. Leonard J. Arrington, Feramorz Y. Fox, and Dean L. May, *Building the City of God, Community and Cooperation among the Mormons* (Urbana and Chicago: University of Illinois, 1992, 2nd ed.).

6. Bowman, *The Mormon People*, 67; Mindi Sitterud-McCluskey, "'Saints in the Pit,' Mormon Colliers in Britain and the Intermountain West," Chapter 10, *Immigrants in the Far West: Historical Identities and Experiences*, Jessie L. Embry and Brian Q. Cannon, eds. (Salt Lake City: University of Utah Press, 2015), 325, notes that of the 38,000 British converts who emigrated between 1840 and 1870, those who described themselves as miners, colliers, or pitmen were the single largest occupational group.

7. *Mormons in Early Victorian Britain*, Richard L. Jensen and Malcolm R. Thorp, eds. (Salt Lake City: University of Utah Press, 1989), especially Robert L. Lively, Jr., Chapter 2, "Some Sociological Reflections on the Nineteenth-Century British Mission," 17–19, note that within the first year, the missionaries had gained 1,500 converts, and by 1851, when Britain conducted a religious census, there were 35,626 Mormons in England and Wales at a time when thousands of British Mormons were emigrating. Please also see Ray Jay David, Chapter 15, "Law and the Nineteenth-Century British Mormon Migration," 243.

8. Matteson and Matteson, "Mormon Influence on Scandinavian Settlement in Nebraska."

9. Bowman, *The Mormon People*, 42–43.

10. Ibid., 108; also Jensen, "Immigration and Emigration."

11. Ibid.; also *Mormons in Early Victorian Britain*, 247, on the ports converts sailed from; Bowman, *The Mormon People*, 108, on the handcart migration in the 1850s. Also, please see John D. Unruh, *The Plains Across, Emigrants, Wagon Trains and the America West* (Urbana and Chicago: University of Illinois Press, 1979, Plimico, London, ed.), Chapter 9, "The Mormon 'Halfway House,'" 252–284.

12. Dean L. May, "Feeling Babylon: The English Mormon Migration to Alpine, Utah," Chapter 3 in *The European Immigrants in the American West, Community Histories*, Frederick Luebke, ed. (Albuquerque: University of New Mexico Press, 1998), 38.

13. "Advice to Emigrants," from Nauvoo, November 9, 1841, "Dear Brother in the new and everlasting covenant," by Francis Moon, *Latter-Day Saints' Millennial Star* 2.10 (February 1842): 151. Please note: the *Millennial Star* numbered its pages consecutively from the first issue, versus starting over with each new issue with page 1.

14. Bowman, *The Mormon People*, 113; Arrington, Fox, and May, *Building the City of God*.

15. J. Norman Heard, *Handbook of the American Frontier, Four Centuries of Indian-White Relationships, Vol. IV: The Far West* (Lanham, MD: Scarecrow Press,

1997), 317 (Tuilla Valley, treaty), 321–322 (Ute Indians); Peter R. Decker, "The Utes Must Go!" *American Expansion and the Removal of a People* (Golden, CO: Fulcrum Publishing, 2004), 27–28.

16. United States Bureau of the Census, Seventh Annual Census, 1850, Territories, Table III, Nativities of the Population, 996; United States Bureau of the Census, Tenth Annual Census, 1880, Population by Race, Sex, and Nativity, Table 7: Population, as native and foreign-born, by states and territories: 1880, 1870, 1860, 426, and Table XIII, Showing the Nativities of Foreign-born Population in the United States and in each State and Territory: 1880, 492–495.

17. Deborah E. Popper, "Great Opportunities for the Many of Small Means": New Jersey's Agricultural Colonies," *Geographical Review* 96.1 (January 2006): 27; Theodore Norman, *An Outstretched Arm, A History of the Jewish Colonization Association* (London: Routledge & Kegan Paul, 1985), 16–21.

18. Chart, Immigration by Country, 1820–2007. Note, immigration virtually ceased after the outbreak of World War I, so this mass immigration really ended in August 1914.

19. Sheldon Morris Neuringer, *American Jewry and United States Immigration Policy, 1881–1953* (New York: Arno Press, 1980); Popper, "Great Opportunities for the Many of Small Means," 28.

20. Julius Goldman, *Hebrew Emigrant Aid Society of the United States, Report of the Colonization of Russian Refugees in the West* (New York: Evening Post Job Printing Office, 1882), 22, 23.

21. Ibid., 7.

22. Popper, "Great Opportunities for the Many of Small Means," 29.

23. Ibid., 30–32.

24. Ibid., 33–34.

25. Jewish Colonization Association, entry in the *Jewish Encyclopedia* (1906), 178–181, retrieved from http://www.jewishencyclopedia.com/articles/8633-jewish -colonization-association#1068 on November 5, 2015; Norman, *An Outstretched Arm*, 16–21.

26. Norman, *An Outstretched Arm*, 108–111.

27. Samuel Joseph, *History of the Baron de Hirsch Fund: The Americanization of the Jewish Immigrant* (Augustus M. Kelley, publishers, Fairfield, 1978 ed., originally published Philadelphia: Jewish Publication Society for the Baron De Hirsch Fund, 1935), 50.

28. Ibid., 53.

29. Ibid., 48–51.

30. Ibid., 53–54.

31. Ibid., 52–53, 55. Of the original 60 families, only 41 eventually signed leases, the other 19 were given refunds and evicted from the colony.

32. Ibid., 55.

33. Ibid., 62–63.

34. Ibid., 64–65.

35. Popper, "Great Opportunities for the Many of Small Means," 34–35; Joseph, *History of the Baron de Hirsch Fund*, 48–115; Norman, *An Outstretched Arm*, 109.

36. Popper, "Great Opportunities for the Many of Small Means," 37.

37. United States Bureau of the Census, Twenty-third Annual Census, 2010, New Jersey, Table 9, "Population and Housing Units: 1990 to 2010; and Area Measurements and Density: 2010," retrieved from https://www.census.gov/prod /cen2010/cph-2-32.pdf on November 5, 2015. There is a movement to preserve Alliance's synagogue building, which still exists, and the Jewish Cemetery, "Preserving the History of a Colony," *New York Times*, September 23, 2007, p.14NJ1, retrieved from http://www.nytimes.com/2007/09/23/nyregion/nyregionspecial2 /23colnj.html?_r=0 on November 12, 2015.

38. Popper, "Great Opportunities for the Many of Small Means," 28–29.

39. Marinbach, *Galveston*, 3; Glazier, *Dispersing the Ghetto*, 15; David M. Bressler, "Results and Significance of the Galveston Movement," *Bulletin of the National Conference of Jewish Charities, Jewish Communal Service Association of North America* (JCSA) 5.1 (August 1914): 4–5, retrieved from http://www.bjpa.org/Publications /details.cfm?PublicationID=1449, and Morris D. Waldman, "The Galveston Movement," *Jewish Social Services Quarterly* 4.3 (March 1928): 197–205, retrieved from http://www.bjpa.org/Publications/details.cfm?PublicationID=3343, on November 5, 2015.

40. Marinbach, *Galveston*, 13–15. Waldman remained in Galveston for a little more than a year, when he was replaced by Henry Berman as manager of the JIIB in the summer of 1909, 52; Berman left the JIIB in late 1913, and he was replaced by Maurice Epstein, 166.

41. Marinbach, *Galveston*, 12; Glazier, *Dispersing the Ghetto*, 59–61.

42. Marinbach, *Galveston*, 14, 121.

43. Ibid., 21–23; Glazier, *Dispersing the Ghetto*, 145–146.

44. Marinbach, *Galveston*, 11.

45. Ibid., 23.

46. Ibid., 58–60, 116 on 1910 deportations.

47. Bressler, "Immigration Distribution" (September 1914): 32.

48. Glazier, *Dispersing the Ghetto*, 60–61.

49. Bressler, "*Results and Significance of the Galveston Movement*" (August 1914): 4–5.

50. Glazier, *Dispersing the Ghetto*, 15; David M. Bressler, "The Removal Work, Including Galveston: Presentation and Discussion," *Proceedings of the Sixth National Conference of Jewish Charities* (Jewish Communal Service Association of North America [JCSA], Kohn & Pollock, May 1910), 111–140, retrieved from http://www .bjpa.org/Publications/details.cfm?PublicationID=1401 on November 5, 2015.

51. Glazier, *Dispersing the Ghetto*, 18.

52. Ibid., 19, 24.

53. Bressler, "Immigration Distribution" (September 1914): 34; Glazier, *Dispersing the Ghetto*, appendix, Table 1.

54. Glazier, *Dispersing the Ghetto*, 28.

Chapter 5

1. John Gerring, *Party Ideologies in America, 1828–1996* (Cambridge, MA: Cambridge University Press, 2001).

2. Merle Curti and Kendall Birr, "The Immigrant and the American Image in Europe, 1860–1914," *Mississippi Valley Historical Review* 37.2 (September 1950): 203–230; Ray Allen Billington, *Land of Savagery, Land of Promise: The European Image of the American Frontier in the Nineteenth Century* (New York: W. W. Norton & Co., 1981).

3. CHAP. LXXV. —An Act to secure Homesteads to actual Settlers on the Public Domain (1862). Text of the Homestead Act can be read here, retrieved from Our Documents.gov at http://www.ourdocuments.gov/doc.php?flash=true &doc=31&page=transcript on March 2, 2016.

4. Folke Dovring, "European Reactions to the Homestead Act," *Journal of Economic History* 22.4 (December 1962): 464–468.

5. Robert Wooster, *The American Military Frontiers: The United States Army in the West, 1783–1900* (Albuquerque: University of New Mexico Press, 2009), 255.

6. J. Norman Heard, *Handbook of the American Frontier, Four Centuries of Indian-White Relationships, Vol. III: The Great Plains* (Lanham, MD: Scarecrow Press, 1993), 2 (Acton, Minnesota, Murders), 6 (Amidon, Joseph B., Murder of), 20 (Beaver Creek, Minnesota, Massacre), 31–32 (Birch Coulee, Battle of), 89 (Forest City, Minnesota, Raid), 114 (Hutchinson, Minnesota, Raid), 211 (Sacred Heart Creek, Minnesota, Massacre), 166 (Minnesota Sioux Uprising), 172 (New Ulm, Minnesota, Battle of), 200 (Redwood Agency Massacre), 201 (Redwood Ferry, Battle of), 258–259 (Wood Lake, Minnesota, Battle of), 161 (Mdewakanton Sioux Indians), 222 (Sioux Indians and Sisseton Sioux Indians); Kevin Hillstrom and Laurie Collier Hillstrom, *American Indian Removal and the Trail to Wounded Knee* (Detroit: Omnigraphics, 2010), 42–43.

7. Heard, *Handbook of the American Frontier*, Vol. III, 395–396 (Winnebago Indians).

8. Ibid., 29 (Big Mound, Battle of), 43–44 (Buffalo Lake, Battle of), 231 (Stony Lake, Battle of), 255 (Whitestone Hill, Battle of), 127 (Killdeer Mountain, Battle of), 238 (Teton Indian Tribes).

9. Ibid., 30 (Big Sandy Creek, Battle of), 100–101 (Hancock's War), 169–170 (Mud Springs Ranch Fight), 212 (Saline River, Kansas Raid).

10. Iowa Board of Immigration, *First Biennial Report of the Board of Immigration to the Fourteenth General Assembly of the State of Iowa* (Des Moines: G. W. Edwards, State Printer, 1872), 33, "Report of Louis A. Ochs," retrieved from Harvard University Library Open Collections Program at http://nrs.harvard.edu/urn-3:FHCL :922652 on October 16, 2015.

11. Theodore C. Blegen, "The Competition of the Northwestern States for Immigrants," *Wisconsin Magazine of History* 3.1 (September 1919): 11–12.

12. *First Annual Report of the Commissioner of Immigration of the State of Wisconsin*, for the Year 1871 (1872), 9.

13. Minnesota State Board of Immigration, "Minnesota, the empire state of the new North-west, the commercial, manufacturing and geographical centre of the American continent," (St. Paul, MN: H. M. Smyth & co., 1878), 6–8, 4, 5 for quotes (images 5–9 of 89). The probable author was the secretary, John Wesley Bond. A digitized copy of this pamphlet is retrieved from the Library of Congress, located http://memory.loc.gov/cgi-bin/ampage?collId=lhbum&fileName =09183/lhbum09183.db&recNum=4&itemLink=r?ammem/lhbum:@field %28DOCID+@lit%28lhbum09183div5%29%29:%23091830007&linkText=1 on December 8, 2015.

14. Minnesota State Board of Immigration, "Minnesota, the empire state of the new North-west" (1878), 61 (image 62 of 89), italics in original.

15. Nell Irvin *Painter, Exodusters (New York: W. W. Norton & Co., 1976)*.

16. Blegen, "The Competition of the Northwestern States for Immigrants," 26–27; Maurice G. Baxter, "Encouragement of Immigration to the Middle West During the Era of the Civil War," *Indiana Magazine of History* 46.1 (1950): 25–38, "A Circular from the Commissioner of Emigration to the Agriculturalists, Manufacturers and Capitalists of Indiana, prepared by John A. Wilstach, Commissioner" (Indianapolis: Samuel M. Douglass, state printer, 1866), 3; Message of Governor Oliver P. Morton, Delivered January 11, 1867, Documents of the General Assembly of Indiana at the Forty-Five General Session, Begun on the Tenth of January, A.D. 1867 (Annual Reports of the Officers of State of the State of Indiana), Part 1 (Indianapolis: Samuel M. Douglass, state printer, 1867), 18–20; "John Augustine Wilstach," R. E. Banta, *Indiana Authors and Their Books 1816– 1916: Biographical Sketches of Authors Who Published During the First Century of Indiana Statehood with Lists of Their Books*, Vol. 343 (Crawfordsville, IN: Wabash College, 1949), 343. *History of Nebraska*, Ronald C. Naugle, James C. Olson, John J. Montag, eds. (Lincoln: University of Nebraska Press, 2014, 4th edition), 194, 217; The revised statutes of the Territory of Nebraska, in force July 1, 1866, with marginal notes, showing the contents of each section, and a full and complete index; to which is added an appendix, embracing all of the special and local laws passed at the 11th session of the Legislative Assembly of the Territory of Nebraska, revised by E. Estabrook (E. B. Taylor, 1866), 738; Nebraska State Board of Immigration, "Nebraska: a Sketch of Its History, Resources and Advantages It Offers to Settlers" (Nebraska City, 1870).

17. William E. Lass, *Minnesota: A History* (New York: W. W. Norton & Company, 2000, 2nd ed.), 142. Mattson also did immigration recruitment for the Northern Pacific Railroad in the 1870s, James B. Hedges, "The Colonization Work of the Northern Pacific Railroad," *Mississippi Valley Historical Review* 13.3 (December 1926): 317. The Republican Party controlled Minnesota state politics between 1860 and 1895, when a Democrat was elected for one two-year term, and afterward the party was competitive in Minnesota state politics until 1931.

18. Blegen, "The Competition of the Northwestern States for Immigrants," 23–24; Lars Ljungmark, *For sale—Minnesota: Organized promotion of Scandinavian immigration 1866–1873* (Göteborg: Läromedelsförl, 1971), 87, 149; John G. Rice,

"The Effect of Land Alienation on Settlement," *Annals of the Association of American Geographers* 68.1 (March 1978): 70; Hans Mattson, *Reminiscences: The Story of an Emigrant* (St. Paul, MN: 1892), 98–102.

19. Blegen, "The Competition of the Northwestern States for Immigrants," 23–25.

20. "Davis Edwin Page, commr, 153 B'way, h B'klyn," Trow's New York City Directory, compiled by H. Wilson, vol. LXXXV for the year ending May 1, 1872 (New York: John F. Trow, pub), vol. 1, A–L, 268; Blegen, "The Competition of the Northwestern States for Immigrants," 25–26.

21. Blegen, "The Competition of the Northwestern States for Immigrants," 11–12. The Republican Party controlled Wisconsin state politics between 1856 and 1931, with only one Democrat serving as governor for two two-year terms from 1891–1895.

22. Laws of Wisconsin, Chapter 171, March 14, 1868, "An Act to amend Chapter 126, general laws of 1867, entitled, "An act authorizing the establishment of a board of immigration," retrieved from http://docs.legis.wisconsin.gov/1868/related/acts/171.pdf on April 12, 2015; Wisconsin State Board of Immigration, *Statistics: Exhibiting the History, Climate and Productions of the State of Wisconsin* (Madison, WI: Atwood & Rublee, State Printers, 1869), 74–76, retrieved from https://books.google.co.uk/books?id=OlNZAAAAcAAJ&pg=PA75&dq=J.A.+Becher+Wisconsin+Immigration&hl=en&sa=X&redir_esc=y#v=onepage&q=J.A.%20Becher%20Wisconsin%20Immigration&f=false on October 22, 2015.

23. Blegen, "The Competition of the Northwestern States for Immigrants," 11–12; Wisconsin State Board of Immigration, *Statistics* (1869), 74–76.

24. Wisconsin State Board of Immigration, *Statistics* (1869), 75.

25. Ibid. For examples of Wisconsin's foreign-language publications, please see Wisconsin State Commission of Immigration, "Wisconsin. Ein Bericht über Bevölkerung, Boden, Klima, Handel, und die industriellen Verhältnisse dieses Staates im Nordwesten der Nordamerikanischen Union (Milwaukee, 1870), a digital copy is available through the British Library at http://access.bl.uk/item/viewer/ark:/81055/vdc_100022786868.0x000001#ark:/81055/vdc_100022789929.0x000004 accessed on October 22, 2015.

26. Blegen, "The Competition of the Northwestern States for Immigrants," 12, citing *General Laws of Wisconsin*, 1870, Chapter 50.

27. Iowa Board of Immigration, *First Biennial Report* (1872), 29, "Report of Carl Jaaks."

28. *Michigan: A History of the Great Lakes State* (Hoboken, NJ: John Wiley & Sons, 2014), 131–132, https://books.google.de/books?id=HIiTAgAAQBAJ&pg=PA130&lpg=PA130&dq=John+Almy+Michigan&source=bl&ots=ot_ShKSkZQ&sig=XJj4SABa8Rpvmoxt67-aoF_bgoM&hl=en&sa=X&ei=EOPuVO30MYyHPbmngIAH&ved=0CEMQ6AEwBw#v=onepage&q=John%20Almy%20Michigan&f=false accessed on April 10, 2015. The Republican Party controlled Michigan politics between 1855 and 1933, but Democrats were elected governor in 1883, 1891, and 1913.

29. Blegen, "The Competition of the Northwestern States for Immigrants," 26. Blegen says the appropriation was $10,000, but the 1872 Biennial Report of the Board of Immigration states that the appropriation was $5,000.

30. Iowa Board of Immigration, *Iowa: The Home of Immigrants* (Des Moines: Mills & Co, State Printers, 1870), 3, retrieved from Google Books at https://books.google.co.uk/books?id=rIYUAAAAYAAJ&dq=iowa+home+for+immigrants&pg=PA1&redir_esc=y#v=onepage&q&f=false on October 16, 2015; Iowa Board of Immigration, *First Biennial Report* (1872), 4. The Republican Party controlled Iowa politics between 1858 and 1933, with one Democrat being elected governor in 1890.

31. This happened in 1870. J. Norman Heard, *Handbook of the American Frontier, Four Centuries of Indian-White Relationships, Vol. II: The Northeastern Woodlands* (Lanham, MD: Scarecrow Press, 1990), 300 (Potawatomi Indians).

32. Iowa Board of Immigration, *First Biennial Report* (1872), 27, "Report of Carl Jaaks."

33. Ibid., 32–33, "Report of Louis A. Ochs."

34. Blegen, "The Competition of the Northwestern States for Immigrants," 26; Iowa Board of Immigration, *First Biennial Report* (1872), 7 (quote), 9–10, 15 notes that E. T. Edginton and Hospers were paid one hundred dollars as agents for one month each.

35. Iowa Board of Immigration, *Iowa: The Home of Immigrants* (1870); Iowa Board of Immigration, *First Biennial Report* (1872), 5–6.

36. Iowa Board of Immigration, *First Biennial Report* (1872), 3.

37. Heard, *Handbook of the American Frontier*, Vol. II, 70–71 (Chippewa Indians); Heard, *Handbook of the American Frontier*, Vol. III, 114 (Hunkpatina Indians), 176 (Ogala Sioux Indians), 177 (Oohenopa Sioux Indians); "Treaty with the Sioux—Brulé, Oglala, Miniconjou, Yanktonai, Hunkpapa, Blackfeet, Cuthead, Two Kettle, Sans Arcs, and Santee—and Arapaho, 1868" (Treaty of Fort Laramie, 1868), 15 Stat. 635, Indian Affairs: Laws and Treaties—Vol. II: Treaties, Charles J. Kappler, compiler and ed. (Washington, DC: Government Printing Office, 1904), 998–1007, retrieved from the Oklahoma State University Library, Electronic Publishing Center, retrieved from http://digital.library.okstate.edu/kappler/Vol2/treaties/sio0998.htm on March 4, 2016; Hillstrom and Collier Hillstrom, *American Indian Removal and the Trail to Wounded Knee*, 45–48.

38. United States Bureau of the Census, Ninth Annual Census, 1870, General Nativity and Foreign Parentage, Table IV, 299.

39. U.S. Bureau of the Census, 1870, Table VI, 336–342. The breakdown of the foreign-born in 1870 was 1,218 British, 888 Irish, 705 Canadian, 1,179 Norwegian, 563 German, 383 Swedish, and 115 Danish.

40. Herbert S. Schell, *History of South Dakota* (Lincoln: University of Nebraska Press, 1961), 117–118; John Hudson, "Two Dakota Homestead Frontiers," *Annals of the Association of American Geographers* 63.4 (December 1973): 445.

41. Schell, *History of South Dakota*, 117–118; "Dakota Territory Promotion," *South Dakota Historical Collections and Report* (Pierre, SD: State Publishing Co., 1953), 435–436; Hudson, "Two Dakota Homestead Frontiers," 445.

42. James S. Foster, *Outlines of the History of the Territory of Dakota, and Emigrant's Guide to the Free Lands of the Northwest* (Yankton, Dakota Territory: M'Intyre and Foster, 1870).

43. Blegen, "The Competition of the Northwestern States for Immigrants," 16–17.

44. Wisconsin Immigration Commissioner, *First Annual Report* (1872), 10; Blegen, "The Competition of the Northwestern States for Immigrants," 18–19; for examples, please see the Danish booklet, Wisconsin State Board of Immigration, Beskrivelse over Staten Wisconsin (La Crosse, WI: 1870), and the Welsh pamphlet, Wisconsin State Board of Immigration, Ystadegau o adnoddau, cynyrchion, a phoblogaeth Talaeth Wisconsin (Madison, WI: 1870).

45. Wisconsin Immigration Commissioner, *First Annual Report* (1872), 10, 12; "Collections of the State Historical Society of Wisconsin," Vol. XII, Reuben Gold Thwaites, ed. (Madison, WI: Democrat Printing Co, State Printers, 1892), 328, retrieved from http://www.mocavo.com/Collections-of-the-State-Historical-Society-of-Wisconsin-Volume-Xii/795658/10#357 on October 22, 2015.

46. Ibid., 12.

47. Ibid., 13.

48. Ibid., 13.

49. Blegen, "The Competition of the Northwestern States for Immigrants," 19; "Collections of the State Historical Society of Wisconsin," Vol. XII, 328. The Wisconsin state legislature was controlled by Republicans in 1874 but briefly by Democrats for 1875, before returning to a Republican majority in 1876.

50. Heard, *Handbook of the American Frontier*, Vol. III, 34 (Black Hills Expedition), 67–68 (Crazy Horse, Ogala Sioux Chief), 224–225 (Slim Buttes, Battle of); Hillstrom and Collier Hillstrom, *American Indian Removal and the Trail to Wounded Knee*, especially Chapter 3, "Standing in the Way of Westward Expansion," 35–48.

51. Schell, *History of South Dakota*, 118; Hudson, "Two Dakota Homestead Frontiers," 445.

52. Heard, *Handbook of the American Frontier*, Vol. III, 67–68 (Crazy Horse, Ogala Sioux Chief), 143–144 (Little Bighorn, Battle of), 208 (Rosebud, Battle of), 224–225 (Slim Buttes, Battle of).

53. Marc Reisner, *Cadillac Desert: The American West and Its Disappearing Water* (New York: Viking Penguin, 1986), 109–111.

54. Blegen, "The Competition of the Northwestern States for Immigrants," 20; *Laws of Wisconsin*, Chapter 176, March 7, 1879, "An act to establish a board of immigration," retrieved from http://docs.legis.wisconsin.gov/1879/related/acts/176.pdf on April 12, 2015; "Collections of the State Historical Society of Wisconsin," Vol. XII, 328–329.

55. State Board of Immigration of Wisconsin, "Wisconsin, what it Offers to the Immigrant: An Official Report Published by the State Board of Immigration of Wisconsin," retrieved from Google Books at https://books.google.co.uk/books?id=f0tEAQAAMAAJ&q=J.A.+Becher+Wisconsin+Immigration&dq=J.A.+Becher+Wisconsin+Immigration&hl=en&sa=X&redir_esc=y on October 22, 2015.

56. Blegen, "The Competition of the Northwestern States for Immigrants," 21–22. 25,000 pamphlets were printed in 1881; nearly 30,000 were distributed in 1882; 19,884 maps and pamphlets were distributed in 1883; 17,016 in 1884; 23,032 in 1885–1886.

57. Ibid., 22. Kennan supposedly received and responded to 20,000 letters during his time in Basel. "Collections of the State Historical Society of Wisconsin," Vol. XII, 329.

58. *Report of the Iowa Commissioner of Immigration to the Governor, From May 1, 1880 to Nov. 1, 1881* (Des Moines: F. M. Mills, State Printer, 1880), retrieved from Hathitrust Digital Library at http://babel.hathitrust.org/cgi/pt?id=iau.3185805 1999112 on October 16, 2015.

59. George D. Perkins, *Biographical Directory of the United States Congress*, retrieved from http://bioguide.congress.gov/scripts/biodisplay.pl?index=P000233 on October 16, 2015.

60. *Iowa Commissioner of Immigration, Report* (1880), 3–4. Whether these agents were employed by the state, or more likely, freelancers who were also working for the railroads, is unknown. Given the small size of the appropriation, it is doubtful that any of Perkins's agents were paid for their work by the state.

61. Ibid., 3.

62. *Michigan: A History of the Great Lakes State*, 132; Frederick Morley, *Michigan and Its Resources: Sketches of the Growth of the State, Its Industries, Agricultural Productions, Institutions, and Means of Transportation; Description of Its Soil, Climate, Timber, Financial Condition, and the Situation of Its Unoccupied Lands; and a Review of Its General Characteristics as a Home* (Lansing, MI: W. S. George & Co., State Printers and Binders, 1881). There were at least two editions of this book published.

63. Michigan Compiled Laws, Archives of Commissioner of Immigration, Act 31 of 1885, retrieved from https://www.legislature.mi.gov/%28S%28edp5ksreyg qzku55yjiss2ju%29%29/documents/mcl/pdf/mcl-Act-31-of-1885.pdf and http://www.legislature.mi.gov/%28S%28rr152nu1w1zxckcyqg1hskio%29%29/mileg .aspx?page=getObject&objectName=mcl-Act-31-of-1885 on April 12, 2015. The Republican Party controlled the Michigan state legislature between 1881 and 1885.

64. Blegen, "The Competition of the Northwestern States for Immigrants," 27. Also see Laws of Wisconsin, Chapter 235, "An act to establish a board of immigration," April 25, 1895, retrieved from https://docs.legis.wisconsin.gov/1895 /related/acts/235.pdf on April 12, 2015. The Democratic Party controlled the Wisconsin state legislature and the governorship from 1891 to 1894.

65. Laws of Wisconsin, Chapter 279, May 1, 1899, "An Act to establish a board of immigration, and making an appropriation to provide for the cost of maintenance thereof," retrieved from https://docs.legis.wisconsin.gov/1899/related /acts/279.pdf on April 12, 2015.

66. Blegen, "The Competition of the Northwestern States for Immigrants," 27.

67. Hudson, "Two Dakota Homestead Frontiers," 458.

68. Heard, *Handbook of the American Frontier*, Vol. III, 259–260 (Wounded Knee, Battle of); Hillstrom and Collier Hillstrom, *American Indian Removal and the Trail to Wounded Knee*, especially Chapter 5, "The Massacre at Wounded Knee," 63–78, and Biographies of Big Foot, 121–124; Sitting Bull, 147–151; Wovoka, 152–156.

69. *Second Biennial report of the Commissioner of Immigration for the state of South Dakota* (Pierre, SD: Commissioner of Immigration, 1914), 7–8, retrieved from HathiTrust Digital Library at http://catalog.hathitrust.org/Record/100566014 on March 7, 2016. The first commissioner of immigration was John M. Deets, who served from 1910–1913, and then Charles M. McCaffree. The Republican Party held most offices in South Dakota state government between 1889 and 1933, with Democrats and Populists occasionally being elected to the governorship.

70. *The European Immigrants in the American West: Community Histories*, Frederick Luebke, ed. (University of New Mexico Press, 1998), x.

71. Blegen, "The Competition of the Northwestern States for Immigrants," 13–14; Wisconsin State Board of Immigration, Statistics (1869).

72. Frederick Morley, *Michigan and Its Resources: Sketches of the Growth of the State, Its Industries, Agricultural Productions, Institutions, and Means of Transportation; Description of Its Soil, Climate, Timber, Financial Condition, and the Situation of Its Unoccupied Lands; and a Review of Its General Characteristics as a Home* (Lansing, MI: W. S. George & Co., State Printers and Binders, 1882, 2nd ed.), 146.

73. Iowa State Board of Immigration, *Iowa: The Home of Immigrants* (1870), Chapter IX, "General Information and Practical Suggestions, Character of Population," 68.

74. The list continues to praise Wisconsin's postal facilities, markets, and water power, among other things, Wisconsin State Board of Immigration, *Statistics* (1869), 29.

75. Minnesota State Board of Immigration, "Minnesota, the empire state of the new North-west" (1878), 63 (image 64 of 89).

76. Minnesota State Board of Immigration, "Minnesota, Her Agricultural Resources, Commercial Advantages, and Manufacturing Capabilities, being a concise description of Minnesota, and the inducements she offers to those seeking homes in a new country" (St. Paul, MN: H. M. Smith, printers, 1879), 28.

77. Iowa State Board of Immigration, "Iowa: The Home of Immigrants" (1870), Chapter IX, "General Information and Practical Suggestions, Character of Population," 66.

78. Minnesota State Board of Immigration, "Minnesota, the empire state of the new North-west" (1878), 55 (image 56 of 89).

79. Minnesota State Board of Immigration, "Minnesota, Her Agricultural Resources, Commercial Advantages, and Manufacturing Capabilities" (1879), 9.

80. Foster, *Outlines of the History of the Territory of Dakota* (1870); Stephen V. Ward, *Selling Places: The Marketing and Promotion of Towns and Cities, 1850–2000* (New York: Routledge, 1998), 20.

81. David M. Wrobel, *Promised Lands: Promotion, Memory, and the Creation of the American West* (Lawrence: University Press of Kansas, 2002), 42, quoting

George Alexander Batchelder, *A Sketch of the History and Resources of Dakota Territory* (Yanckton, Dakota territory: Press Stream Power Printing Co. 1870, 25–26).

82. Blegen, "The Competition of the Northwestern States for Immigrants," 16–17.

83. "Edward Mumm," *Portrait and Biographical Album of Lee County, Iowa* (Chicago, IL: Chapman Brothers, 1887), retrieved from http://www.rootsweb.ancestry .com/~iabiog/lee/pbh1887/pbh1887-klm.htm on October 21, 2015.

84. "Rohlfs, Matias J.," Joseph Eiboeck, Die Deutschen von Iowa und deren Errungenschaften ("The Germans of Iowa and Their Achievements"), 428 (Des Moines: des Iowa Staats-Anzeiger, 1900), extract of biographical sketches transcribed by Jim W. Faulkinbury and retrieved from http://www.jwfgenresearch .com/IowaGermans.htm on October 21, 2015; History of Scott County, Iowa; together with sketches of its cities, villages and townships and biographies of representative citizens (Chicago: Inter-State Publishing, 1882), retrieved from https://archive.org/stream/historyofscottco00inte/historyofscottco00inte_djvu .txt on October 21, 2015.

85. "Claus L. Clausen: Pioneer Pastor and Settlement Promoter," translated and edited by Carlton C. Qualey, *Norwegian American Historical Association*, Volume VI, 12, retrieved from http://www.naha.stolaf.edu/pubs/nas/volume06 /vol06_2.htm on October 21, 2015.

86. "Rhynsburger, C.," *The History of Marion County, Iowa: Containing a History of the County, Its Cities, Towns, & C., Biographical Sketches of Its Citizens* (Des Moines: Union Historical Company, 1881) 669, retrieved from Iowa Genealogy at http://www.beforetime.net/iowagenealogy/marion/HistoryOfMarionCounty1881 /P669.html on October 21, 2015. Rhynsburger's home in Pella is on the National Registry of Historic Places, Sarah *Oltrogge, "Properties Listed on National Register of Historic Places Earn Recognition," State Historical Society of Iowa,* retrieved from http://www.iowahistory.org/contacts/news_release/2004/nrhp_properties.htm on October 21, 2015.

87. Iowa Board of Immigration, *First Biennial Report* (1872), 19–22, "Report of Henry Hospers," and 8 (quote). Hospers immigrated around 1846.

88. "S. F. Spofford," *The History of Polk County, Iowa* (Union Historical Company, Birdsall, Williams & Co. 1880), 869–870, retrieved from http://files .usgwarchives.net/ia/polk/bios/plkdmbio5.txt on October 21, 2015; Centennial History of Polk County, Iowa, J. M. Dixon, ed. (Des Moines: State Register Printer, 1876), 44, 108, retrieved from https://archive.org/stream/centennialhistor 01dixo/centennialhistor01dixo_djvu.txt on October 21, 2015.

89. "Marcus Tuttle," *Iowa Territorial and State Legislators Collection* compiled by volunteers and staff at the State Historical Society of Iowa Library, Des Moines, Iowa, retrieved from https://www.legis.iowa.gov/docs/History_Docs/13th%20 GA/13_tuttle_marcus_cerrogordo.pdf on October 21, 2015.

90. "Alexander Robert 'A. R.' Fulton," Find a Grave, retrieved from http://www .findagrave.com/cgi-bin/fg.cgi?page=gr&GRid=38978473 on October 21, 2015.

91. Joseph L. Gavett, *North Dakota: Counties, Towns, and People* (Seaside, OR: Watchmaker Publishing, Ltd, 2008), 82–83; The Federal Writers Project, *The WPA Guide to South Dakota: The Prairie State* (reprinted by Trinity University Press, San Antonio, TX: 2013), 58. Foster died in 1890 in a gun accident at the age of 62.

92. Reisner, *Cadillac Desert*, 109–111; Wrobel, *Promised Lands*, 52; Elliott West, *The Contested Plains, Indians, Goldseekers, & the Rush to Colorado* (Lawrence: University Press of Kansas, 1998), 329.

93. "The Truth about the Snow-Storm," *Land and Emigration* (newspaper published by the Northern Pacific Railroad in London), March 1873, 2.

94. United States Bureau of the Census, *Twelfth Annual Census, 1900, Statistics of Population*, Table 9, Population by Sex, General Nativity, and Color by States and Territories: 1900, 482–483, and Table 33, Foreign Born Population, Distributed According to Country of Birth, By States and Territories: 1900, 732–735; The European Immigrants in the American West, Community Histories, Frederick Luebke, ed. (Albuquerque: University of New Mexico Press, 1998), x.

Chapter 6

1. Frank Van Nuys, *Americanizing the West: Race, Immigrants, and Citizenship, 1890–1930* (Lawrence: University Press of Kansas, 2002); James B. Hedges, "The Colonization Work of the Northern Pacific Railroad," *Mississippi Valley Historical Review* 13.3 (December 1926): 341.

2. Richard J. Orsi, Sunset Limited, *The Southern Pacific Railroad and the Development of the American West, 1850–1930* (Berkeley and Los Angeles: University of California Press, 2007), 147.

3. Jack Ericson Eblen, *The First and Second United States Empires, Governors and Territorial Government, 1784–1912* (Pittsburgh, PA: University of Pittsburgh Press, 1968), 31, 49, 51.

4. Hedges, "The Colonization Work of the Northern Pacific Railroad," 341; J. Norman Heard, *Handbook of the American Frontier, Four Centuries of Indian-White Relationships, Vol. III: The Great Plains* (Lanham, MD: Scarecrow Press, 1993); Kevin Hillstrom and Laurie Collier Hillstrom, *American Indian Removal and the Trail to Wounded Knee* (Detroit, MI: Omnigraphics, 2010).

5. M. Jean Ferrill, "Rainfall Follows the Plow," *Encyclopedia of the Great Plains*, David J. Wishart, ed. (Lincoln: University of Nebraska, Lincoln, 2011), retrieved from http://plainshumanities.unl.edu/encyclopedia/doc/egp.ii.049 on November 23, 2015; Marc Reisner, *Cadillac Desert: The American West and Its Disappearing Water* (New York: Viking Penguin, 1986), 118–120; Donald Worster, *Rivers of Empire: Water, Aridity, and the Growth of the American West* (New York: Pantheon Books, 1985), 160–161.

6. Reisner, *Cadillac Desert*, 109–111.

7. *The European Immigrants in the American West, Community Histories*, Frederick Luebke, ed. (Albuquerque: University of New Mexico Press, 1998), x–xi.

8. Wyoming Board of Immigration, "The Territory of Wyoming, History, Soil, Climate, Resources, Etc." (Laramie City, WY: Daily Sentinel, Printers, 1874).

9. Oregon State Board of Immigration, "Oregon. Facts Regarding Its Climate, Soil, Mineral and Agricultural Resources, Means of Communication, Commerce and Industry, Laws, Etc., Etc., for Use of Immigrants, with Map," (Boston, MA: Rand, Avery and Company, 1876), located through HathiTrust Digital Library at http://catalog.hathitrust.org/Record/100735011 on March 1, 2015; Oregon State Board of Immigration, "Der Staat Oregon, Eine Schilderung von Klima, Boden- und Mineral-Reichtum, Handel und Industrie, Berkehrsmitteln, Gesetzen, usw., usw., Mit Karten" (1876), located through Google Books at https://books.google .co.uk/books?id=GnMP4IQfBl0C&pg=PA3&dq=%22Oregon+State+Board+of +immigration%22&hl=en&sa=X&ved=0CD8Q6AEwBDgKahUKEwj68vb0zrDI AhUJPxQKHdIeBhI#v=onepage&q=%22Oregon%20State%20Board%20of%20 immigration%22&f=false on October 7, 2015.

10. Washington Bureau of Statistics, Labor, Agriculture, and Immigration, "Agricultural, manufacturing and commercial resource and capabilities of Washington" (Olympia, WA: Gwinn Hicks, state printers, 1901), 175, retrieved from HathiTrust Digital Library at http://catalog.hathitrust.org/Record/100347848 on January 18, 2016.

11. *Report of the Board of Immigration of Colorado Territory*, for the two years ending December 31, 1873 (Denver, CO: William N. Byers, Public Printer, 1874), 15.

12. David M. Wrobel, *Promised Lands, Promotion, Memory, and the Creation of the American West* (Lawrence: University Press of Kansas, 2002), 45; Victoria E. Dye, *All Aboard for Santa Fe: Railway Promotion of the Southwest, 1890s to 1930s* (Albuquerque: University of New Mexico Press, 2005), 21–22.

13. Heard, *Handbook of the American Frontier*, Vol. III, 40 (Box Elder Creek Raid), 114 (Hungate Family Massacre), 212–213 (Sand Creek Massacre), also please see 21–22 (Beecher's Island, Battle of) and 232–233 (Summit Springs, Battle of). Elliott West, *The Contested Plains: Indians, Goldseekers & the Rush to Colorado* (Lawrence: University Press of Kansas, 1998); Peter R. Decker, "The Utes Must Go!" *American Expansion and the Removal of a People* (Golden, CO: Fulcrum Publishing, 2004).

14. Heard, *Handbook of the American Frontier*, Vol. III, 189-190 (Platte Bridge, Battle of), 240 (Tongue River, Battle of), also see 86–87 (Fetterman Massacre).

15. T. A. Larson, *History of Wyoming* (Lincoln: University of Nebraska Press, 1990, 2nd edition), 117, retrieved from https://books.google.co.uk/books?id =9zVKYtdsUDEC&pg=RA1-PA118&dq=Territory+of+Wyoming,+History,+Soil, +Climate,+Resources&hl=en&sa=X&ved=0ahUKEwi6gdm_gL3JAhUDPhQKH SzSCJQQ6AEINjAB#v=onepage&q=Territory%20of%20Wyoming%2C% 20History%2C%20Soil%2C%20Climate%2C%20Resources&f=false on December 2, 2015.

16. Heard, *Handbook of the American Frontier, Four Centuries of Indian-White Relationships, Vol. IV: The Far West* (Lanham, MD: Scarecrow Press, 1997), 302 (Treaties of Table Rock), 336 (Waleshead Oregon massacre), 23 (Battle Creek

massacre), 161 (Battles of Lake Albert), 178 (Battle of Malheur River), 295 (Battle of Stein's Mountain), 97 (Battles of Donner and Blitzen Creek), 31–32 (Battle of Birch Creek).

17. *Report of the Board of Immigration of Colorado Territory* (1874), 5.

18. Elliott West, *The Contested Plains*, 126; Richard White, "It's Your Misfortune and None of My Own," *A History of the American West* (Norman: University of Oklahoma Press, 1991), 196; Keith L. Bryant, Jr., *History of the Atchison, Topeka & Santa Fe Railway* (Lincoln, NB: University of Nebraska, 1974), 39.

19. *Report of the Board of Immigration of Colorado Territory* (1874), 16.

20. United States Bureau of the Census, Ninth Annual Census, 1870, Table VI, Population of the United States (by States and Territories), Classified by Race and Place of Birth, Showing the Number of Persons Born in Each State and Territory and Specified Foreign Country, 336–342; Larson, *History of Wyoming*, 117.

21. Heard, *Handbook of the American Frontier*, Vol. III, 17 (Bates, Battle of), 263 (Yellowstone, Battle of), 199 (Red Fork, Battle of), 67–68 (Crazy Horse, Ogala Sioux Chief), also please see 225 (Smith, Bill, Massacre); Richard White, "It's Your Misfortune and None of My Own," *A History of the American West*, 94–99, 104–106; Hillstrom and Collier Hillstrom, *American Indian Removal and the Trail to Wounded Knee*.

22. Larson, *History of Wyoming*, 118.

23. Wyoming Board of Immigration, "The Territory of Wyoming," 48.

24. U.S. Census Bureau, 1870, Table VI, 336–342; United States Bureau of the Census, Tenth Annual Census, 1880, Population by States and Territories, Table 1a, The United States, in the Aggregate, and by Sex, Nativity, and Race, 3, and Population by Race, Sex, and Nativity, Table XIII, Showing the Nativities of the Foreign-Born Population in the United States and in Each State and Territory: 1880, 492–495; United States Bureau of the Census, Eleventh Annual Census, 1890, Statistics of Population, Table 1, Population of States and Territories at Each Census: 1790 to 1890, 2–3, and Table 32, Foreign Born Population, Distributed According to Country of Birth, by States and Territories: 1890, 606–609.

25. James B. Hedges, "Promotion of Immigration to the Pacific Northwest by the Railroads," *Mississippi Valley Historical Review* 15.2 (September 1928): 183–184; Oregon State Board of Immigration, "Oregon"; Oregon State Board of Immigration, "Der Staat Oregon" (1876).

26. Oregon State Board of Immigration, "Oregon. Facts Regarding Its Climate, Soil, Mineral and Agricultural Resources, Means of Communication, Commerce and Industry, Laws, Etc., Etc., for Use of Immigrants, with Map" (Boston: Franklin Press: Rand, Avery and Company, 1877 and 1880 editions).

27. Oregon State Board of Immigration, "Oregon" (1876), 47 (electronic version, in appendix).

28. 1875 Page Law (An *act supplementary to the acts in relation to immigration*), Sess. II, Chap. 141; 18 Stat. 477, 43rd Congress; adopted March 3, 1875.

29. Arthur J. Brown, "The Promotion of Emigration to Washington: 1854–1909," *Pacific Northwest Quarterly* 36.1 (January 1945): 11–12.

30. Heard, *Handbook of the American Frontier*, Vol. IV, 49 (June 9–11, 1855 Camp Stevens, WA treaties), 163 (Treaties of Lapwai Valley), 206–207 (Nez Perce Indians), 338 (Battle of White Bird Canyon).

31. Ibid., 281–282 (Sheepeater War, Shoshoni Indians).

32. Janet McDonnell, *The Dispossession of the American Indian* (Indianapolis: Indiana University Press, 1991); Leonard A. Carlson, *Indians, Bureaucrats, and Land* (Santa Barbara, CT: Greenwood Press, 1981); 25 U.S.C. Section 71 (Future treaties with Indian tribes), 42nd Congress; approved March 3, 1871; Dawes Severalty Act (An act to provide for the allotment of lands in severalty to Indians on the various reservations, and to extend the protection of the laws of the United States and the Territories over the Indians, and for other purposes), Stat. 388, Sess. II, Chap. 119, 24 Stat. 387 aka 24. 49th Congress; approved February 8, 1887.

33. 1882 Chinese Exclusion Act *(An act to inaugurate certain treaty stipulations relating to Chinese)*, Sess. I, Chap. 126; 22 Stat. 58. 47th Congress; approved May 6, 1882. The Republican Party controlled both houses of Congress, by a slim majority, and the president was Republican James Garfield.

34. Between 1870 and 1879, 133,139 Chinese immigrants entered the United States; between 1880 and 1889, only 65,797 entered, and between 1890 and 1899, only 15,268 Chinese entered, Chart, "Immigration by Country, 1820–2007," retrieved from http://readme.bugs3.com/pdf/Immigration_1820_1840 /Immigration_By_Country_1820_2007/45_pdf on May 11, 2015.

35. C. J. Smith, "Early Development of Railroads in the Pacific Northwest," *Washington Historical Quarterly* 13.4 (October 1922): 243–250; Hedges, "Promotion of Immigration to the Pacific Northwest by the Railroads," 184.

36. Hedges, "The Colonization Work of the Northern Pacific Railroad," 329–330; Hedges, "Promotion of Immigration to the Pacific Northwest by the Railroads," 198.

37. Hedges, "Promotion of Immigration to the Pacific Northwest by the Railroads," 183–186; Scott M. Cutlip, *Public Relations History: From the 17th to the 20th Century: The Antecedents* (New York: Routledge, 2013).

38. Hedges, "Promotion of Immigration to the Pacific Northwest by the Railroads," 186. This pamphlet was probably "Oregon as It Is, Solid Facts and Actual Results, for the Use and Information of Immigrants," Oregon State Board of Immigration (Portland, OR: Lewis & Dryden Printing Co., 1886), retrieved from HathiTrust Digital Library at http://catalog.hathitrust.org/Record/100735567 on March 1, 2015.

39. Oregon State Board of Immigration, "Oregon as It Is."

40. *Peopling the High Plains: Wyoming's European Heritage*, Gordon Olaf Hendrickson, ed. (Cheyenne: Wyoming State Archives and Historical Department, 1977).

41. U.S. Census Bureau, 1890, Statistics of Population, Table 1, 2–3, and Table 32, 606–609. Most of these Chinese immigrants fled to San Francisco.

42. Brown, "The Promotion of Emigration to Washington: 1854–1909," 10–12.

43. Public Documents, Inaugural Address of Sylvester Pennoyer to the Legislative Assembly, 1887, Salem, Oregon, W. H. Byars, State Printer, 1886, digital transcript retrieved from http://arcweb.sos.state.or.us/pages/records/governors/guides/state/pennoyer/inaugural.html on April 23, 2016; Oregon Historical Society, "Sylvester Pennoyer," *The Oregon Encyclopedia*, retrieved from http://www.oregonencyclopedia.org/articles/pennoyer_sylvester_1831_1902_/#.VlMit79buVc on November 23, 2015.

44. Heard, *Handbook of the American Frontier*, Vol. IV, 48 (Camp Grant Massacre), 342 (Wickenburg Massacre), 318 (Turret Mountain attack), 29 (Battle of Big Dry Wash Chevelon's Fork), 296 (George H. Stevens ranch raid), 147–148 (Josanie, Chiricahua Apache warrior).

45. William H. Lyon, "'Live, Active Men, with Plenty of Push': Arizona's Territorial Immigration Commissioners," *Journal of Arizona History* 37.2 (Summer 1996): 150, 154, citing Act #53, Acts and Resolutions of the Eleventh Legislative Assembly (Prescott: Office of the Arizona Miner, 1881), 90–92.

46. Lyon, "'Live, Active Men, with Plenty of Push," 154.

47. Ibid., 151–155.

48. Ibid., 156–157.

49. Colorado Bureau of Immigration and Statistics, *The Natural Resources and Industrial Development and Condition of Colorado* (Denver: The Collier Cleveland Lith Co., State Printers, 1889), 120, retrieved from the HathiTrust Digital Library at http://catalog.hathitrust.org/Record/009587169 on January 16, 2016.

50. Wrobel, *Promised Lands*, 52–53; Reisner, *Cadillac Desert*, 111.

51. Brown, "The Promotion of Emigration to Washington: 1854–1909," 11–12; J. H. Price, *First Annual Report of the State of Washington Bureau of Statistics, Agriculture, and Immigration on the Agricultural, Industrial and Commercial Conditions of the State, up to and including January 1, 1896* (Olympia, WA: O. C. White, Printers, 1896), retrieved from HathiTrust Digital Library at http://babel.hathitrust.org/cgi/pt?id=mdp.39015067870413 on January 19, 2016.

52. "The State of Idaho," *Biennial Report, Bureau of Immigration, Labor, and Statistics* (Boise, ID: 1903), v–vi, retrieved from HathiTrust Digital Library at http://catalog.hathitrust.org/Record/009008867?type[]=all&lookfor[]=Idaho%20immigration&ft= on March 8, 2016.

53. Brown, "The Promotion of Emigration to Washington: 1854–1909," 13. By 1920, "The Resources and Industries of Washington," was up to 152 pages. Washington Bureau of Statistics, Labor, Agriculture, and Immigration, "Agricultural, Manufacturing and Commercial Resource and Capabilities of Washington," (1901).

54. Washington (State). Bureau of Statistics, Agriculture and Immigration: "A Review of the Resources and Industries of Washington 1905. Published Under Authority of the Legislature, for Gratuitous Distribution" (Olympia, WA: C. W. Gorham, Public Printer, 1905), retrieved from HathiTrust Digital Library at http://catalog.hathitrust.org/Record/009037201 on January 19, 2016. Please see Washington (State). Bureau of Statistics and Immigration, "*The Irrigated Lands of the State of*

Washington" (Olympia, WA: E.L. Boardman, Public Printer, 1910), retrieved from HathiTrust Digital Library at http://catalog.hathitrust.org/Record/000455541 on January 19, 2016; Washington (State) Bureau of statistics and immigration, "*Homeseekers' Guide to the State of Washington*" (Olympia, WA: F. M. Lamborn, Public Printer, 1914), also by Harry F. Giles, retrieved from HathiTrust Digital Library at http://catalog.hathitrust.org/Record/001444310 on January 19, 2016; Washington (State). Bureau of Statistics and Immigration, "*The Beauties of the State of Washington: A Book for Tourists*" (Olympia, WA: F.M. Lamborn, Public Printer, 1915), also by Harry F. Giles, retrieved from HathiTrust Digital Library at http://catalog.hathitrust.org/Record/008653227 on January 19, 2016; Washington (State). Bureau of Statistics and Immigration, "*Manufacturing Opportunities in the State of Washington*" (Olympia, WA: F. M. Lamborn, Public Printer, 1918), also by Harry F. Giles and University of Washington, retrieved from HathiTrust Digital Library at http://catalog.hathitrust.org/Record/000967339 on January 19, 2016; Washington (State). Bureau of Statistics and Immigration, "*The Advantages and Opportunities of the State of Washington for Homebuilders, Investors and Travelers*" (Olympia, 1920), also by Harry F. Giles, retrieved from HathiTrust Digital Library at http://catalog.hathitrust.org/Record/000199775 on January 19, 2016.

55. Gayle Kathleen Beradi, "Colorado," *Contemporary Immigration in America: A State-by-State Encyclopedia*, Vol. 1, Kathleen R. Arnold, ed. (Santa Barbara, CA: Greenwood Press, 2015), 93–98, retrieved from https://books.google.co.uk/books?id=5L8oBgAAQBAJ&printsec=frontcover&dq=contemporary+Immigration+in+America:+A+State-by-State+Encyclopedia&hl=en&sa=X&ved=0ahUKEwjyor-on73JAhWCVRoKHbxDDwcQ6AEIKTAA#v=onepage&q=contemporary%20Immigration%20in%20America%3A%20A%20State-by-State%20Encyclopedia&f=false on December 2, 2015.

56. Kristofer Allerfeldt, *Race, Radicalism, Religion, and Restriction: Immigration in the Pacific Northwest, 1890–1924* (Santa Barbara, CA: Praeger, 2003), 12.

57. White, "It's Your Misfortune and None of My Own," 147–148;

58. Oregon State Board of Immigration, "Oregon," 47 (electronic version, in appendix); Allerfeldt, *Race, Radicalism, Religion, and Restriction*, 20; John D. Unruh, *The Plains Across: Emigrants, Wagon Trains and the America West* (Champaign, IL: University of Illinois Press, 1979), 61.

59. Oregon State Board of Immigration, "The Pacific Northwest: Facts Relating to the History, Topography, Climate, Soil, and Agriculture . . . Etc., of Oregon and Washington Territory . . . Also an Appendix Containing Suggestions to Emigrants, a Short Description of the Several Counties . . . Issued for the Information and Guidance of Settlers and Others" (1882), 4, retrieved from HathiTrust Digital Library at https://catalog.hathitrust.org/Record/008653387 on March 1, 2015; Oregon State Board of Immigration, "Oregon as It Is" (1886); Wrobel, *Promised Lands*, 27.

60. Washington (State). Bureau of Statistics, Agriculture and Immigration, "*A Review of the Resources and Industries of Washington*" (1905). Please see Washington (State). Bureau of Statistics and Immigration, "*The Irrigated Lands of the State of*

Washington" (1910); Washington (State) Bureau of Statistics and Immigration, "*Homeseekers' Guide to the State of Washington*" (1914); Washington (State). Bureau of Statistics and Immigration, "*The Beauties of the State of Washington*" (1915); Washington (State). Bureau of Statistics and Immigration, "*Manufacturing Opportunities in the State of Washington*" (1918); Washington (State). Bureau of Statistics and Immigration, "*The Advantages and Opportunities of the State of Washington for Homebuilders, Investors and Travelers*" (1920).

61. Report of the Board of Immigration of Colorado Territory (1874), 19–24. Please also see Colorado Bureau of Immigration and Statistics, "The Natural Resources and Industrial Development and Condition of Colorado" (1889), 24.

62. *Report of the Board of Immigration of Colorado Territory* (1874), 6–7.

63. Wyoming Board of Immigration, "The Territory of Wyoming" (1874), 48.

64. Wrobel, *Promised Lands*, 56.

65. Robert P. Fuller, "Wonderful Wyoming, The Undeveloped Empire" (Cheyenne, WY: State Board of Immigration, 1910?), retrieved from HathiTrust Digital Library at http://catalog.hathitrust.org/Record/009008932 on March 10, 2016.

66. Marienka J. Sokol, *Illusions of Abundance: Culture and Urban Water Use in the Arid Southwest* (Ann Arbor, MI: Proquest, 2008), 60.

67. Lyon, "'Live, Active Men, with Plenty of Push," 156; Sokol, *Illusions of Abundance*, 45, quoting John Black, "Arizona: The Land of Sunshine and Silver, Health and Prosperity, the Place for Ideal Homes" (Phoenix: Republican Book and Job Print, 1890), 7; Wrobel, *Promised Lands*, 42 on boosters of Arizona downplaying the heat.

68. An L. Abrams, born in Baden, Germany, in 1839, is listed in the 1880 Census for Laramie, Albany County, retrieved from https://www.censusrecords .com/Search?CensusYear=1880&County=ada,albany&o=State&d=desc&pages ize=40 on December 2, 2015.

69. Wyoming Board of Immigration, "The Territory of Wyoming" (1874), 48 lists the board members. "Erasmus Nagle," *Progressive Men of the State of Wyoming* (Chicago, IL: A. W. Bowen & Co., 1903), 562, retrieved from HathiTrust Digital Library at http://babel.hathitrust.org/cgi/pt?ql=Post%20%26%20Nagle;id=loc .ark%3A%2F13960%2Ft4nk4mblk;view=image;seq=392;start=1;sz=10;page=searc h;num=354 on December 2, 2015, for Post; "Carbon County," Wyoming State Archives, retrieved from https://wyomingstatearchives.wikispaces.com/Carbon +County on December 2, 2015 for Smith; "Uinta County," retrieved from http:// www.courthouses.co/us-states/v-z/wyoming/uinta-county/ on December 2, 2015 for McDonald; "James Kime," *Progressive Men of the State of Wyoming* (Chicago, IL: A. W. Bowen & Co., 1903), 562, retrieved from HathiTrust Digital Library at http:// babel.hathitrust.org/cgi/pt?ql=Kime;id=loc.ark%3A%2F13960%2Ft4nk4mblk;vie w=image;seq=626;start=1;sz=10;page=search;num=562 on December 2, 2015.

70. *Report of the Board of Immigration of Colorado Territory* (1874), 4.

71. Caroline Bancroft, *Gulch of Gold: A History of Central City, Colorado* (Boulder, CO: Big Earth Publishing, 2003), 120 for Collier's background; "David M.

Byers," *Portrait and Biographical Record of Denver and Vicinity Colorado* (Chicago, IL: Chapman Publishing Co., 1898), 145–147.

72. "David M. Byers," 145–147.

73. Ansel Watrous, *History of Larimer County, Colorado* (1911, reprint. London: Forgotten Books, 2013), 485–486.

74. Harriet Rochlin and Fred Rochlin, *Pioneer Jews: A New Life in the Far West* (Boston, MA: Houghton Mifflin Harcourt, 2000), 58–59.

75. Lyon, "'Live, Active Men, with Plenty of Push," 149–162. Arizona Democratic governor Louis Hughes, the former editor of the *Tucson Star*, appointed Herbert Brown of the Republican *Tucson Citizen* to represent Pima County; George Kelly of the *Solomon Valley Bulletin* for Graham County; Aaron Hackney of the *Globe Silver-Belt* for Gila County; Orville Jackson of the Prescott Journal-Miner, for Yavapai County; F. J. Wallace for Coconino County; F. S. O'Brien of the Phoenix Republican, for Maricopa County; J.W. Dorrington of the Sentinel, for Yuma County, and Anson Smith, of the Kingman Miner, for Mohave County. The commissioners were a mix of Republicans and Democrats

76. Lyon, "'Live, Active Men, with Plenty of Push," 158–159.

77. Oregon State Board of Immigration, "Oregon" (1876), 47 (electronic version, in appendix).

78. Although the document "Oregon. Facts Regarding Its Climate, Soil, Mineral and Agricultural Resources, Means of Communication, Commerce and Industry, Laws, Etc., Etc., for Use of Immigrants, with Map" lists Leinenweber as "A. Leinenweber," other documents suggest his name was Christian A. Leinenweber. Please see Christian Leinenweber House, National Register for Historic Places application, 1999, retrieved from http://focus.nps.gov/pdfhost/docs/NRHP/Text/99000604.pdf on November 23, 2015.

79. "Bernard Goldsmith," Joseph Gaston, *Portland, Oregon: Its History and Builders*, Vol. 3 (Chicago, Portland: S. J. Clarke Publishing Co., 1911), 167, retrieved from http://freepages.genealogy.rootsweb.ancestry.com/~jtenlen/ORBios/bgoldsmith2.txt on November 23, 2015.

80. A biography of Reid is in *The Works of Hubert Howe Bancroft*, Volume XXIX, *History of Oregon*, Vol. 1, 1834–1848 (San Francisco, CA: The History Company, 1886), Vol. 29, Chapter XXIV, "Oregon's Envoys Erection of a Territorial Government, 1848," retrieved from http://freepages.history.rootsweb.ancestry.com/~jkidd/books/bancroft/29/26.htm on November 23, 2015.

81. Oregon Historical Society, "William S. Ladd," *Oregon Encyclopedia*, retrieved from http://www.oregonencyclopedia.org/articles/ladd_william_s_1826_1893_/#.VlMEur9buVc on November 23, 2015.

82. Henry Winslow Corbett papers, retrieved from Oregon Historical Society, Davies Family Research Library, biography retrieved from http://archiveswest.orbiscascade.org/ark:/80444/xv43136 on November 18, 2015.

83. The other members were William M. Ladue of Salem, vice president; Henry Winslow Corbett of Portland (who had served on the first Board of Commissioners); H. R. Miller of Grant's Pass, and S. Rothschild of Pendleton. Oregon

State Board of Immigration, "Oregon as It Is," (1886). The cover of the booklist lists the board members. Please also see Biennial Message of Gov. Z. F. Moody to the Legislative Assembly, Fourteenth Regular Session, 1887, as part of *The Journal of the House of the Legislative Assembly of the State of Oregon* (W. H. Byars, state printers, Salem, OR, 1886), Appendix, 16, retrieved from http://www.mocavo .co.uk/The-Journal-of-the-House-of-the-Legislative-Assembly-of-the-State-of -Oregon-6/907880/860 on November 18, 2015.

84. "Dodd, Charles H.," *Republican League Register of Oregon* (The Register Publishing Company, 1896), 200, transcribed at Genealogy.com and retrieved from http://www.genealogy.com/forum/regional/states/topics/or/10127/ on November 18, 2015.

85. In 1890, the census announced that for the first time the line beyond which the population density was under two inhabitants per square mile (0.8 inhabitants per square kilometer) no longer existed and so the West as a region was considered settled. Wrobel, *Promised Lands*, 56–57. About 1.4 million homestead claims were filed between 1862 and 1900.

86. U.S. Census Bureau, 1890, Statistics of Population, Table 1, 2–3, and Table 32, 606–609; United States Bureau of the Census, Twelfth Annual Census, 1900, Statistics of Population, Table 9, Population by Sex, General Nativity, and Color by States and Territories: 1900, 482–483, and Table 33, Foreign Born Population, Distributed According to Country of Birth, by States and Territories: 1900, 732–735.

87. U.S. Census Bureau, 1870, General Nativity and Foreign Parentage, Table IV, 299 and Table VI, 336–342; U.S. Census Bureau, 1880, Population by States and Territories, Table 1a, 3, and Table XIII, 492–495. Note: in Table 1a, the Chinese population is listed as 3,186, while in Table XIII it is listed as 3,166; U.S. Census Bureau, 1890, Statistics of Population, Table 1, 2–3, and Table 32, 606–609; U.S. Census Bureau, 1900, Statistics of Population, Table 9, 482–483, and Table 33, 732–735.

88. U.S. Census Bureau, 1870, Table VI, 336–342; U.S. Census Bureau, 1890, Statistics of Population, Table 1, 2–3, and Table 32, 606–609; U.S. Census Bureau, 1900, Statistics of Population, Table 9, 482–483, and Table 33, 732–735.

89. U.S. Census Bureau, 1870, Table VI, 336–342; U.S. Census Bureau, 1900, Statistics of Population, Table 9, 482–483, and Table 33, 732–735.

90. *Peopling the High Plains: Wyoming's European Heritage*, Gordon Olaf Hendrickson, ed. (Cheyenne, WY: Wyoming State Archives and Historical Department, 1977).

Chapter 7

1. The Page Act of 1885 prohibited advertising for workers or encouraging immigration by promising employment, and the 1891 Immigration Act that created Ellis Island and other immigration inspection stations also prohibited steamship and other transportation companies from advertising or otherwise

encouraging immigration beyond the posting of basic transportation information such as sailing times and places, please see Section 4, 1891 Immigration Act
(*An act in amendment to the various acts relative to immigration and the importation
of aliens under contract or agreement to perform labor*), Sess. II Chap. 551; 26 Stat.
1084, 51st Congress, March 3, 1891, text of the law can be found at U.S. Immigration Legislation On-line, retrieved from http://library.uwb.edu/static/USimmigration
/26%20stat%201084.pdf on February 16, 2016; Department of Commerce and
Labor, Bureau of Immigration and Naturalization, "Immigration Laws and Regula-
tions of July 1, 1907," Section 6, (Washington, DC: Government Printing Office,
1910), retrieved from Archive.org at https://archive.org/details/cu31924021131101
on February 16, 2016.

2. Winston Lee Kinsey, "The Immigrant in Texas Agriculture during Reconstruction," *Agricultural History* 53.1 (Southern Agriculture Since the Civil War: A
Symposium, January 1979): 129–134.

3. *The First Report of the Board of Immigration for the State of Missouri, to the
Twenty-Fourth General Assembly, for the Years 1865 and 1866* (Jefferson City, MO:
Emory S. Foster, public printer, 1867), 31, retrieved from HathiTrust Digital
Library at http://catalog.hathitrust.org/Record/007936560?type[]=all&lookfor[]
=Missouri%20immigration&ft= on February 29, 2016.

4. Elizabeth Cometti, "Swiss Immigration to West Virginia, 1864–1884: A
Case Study," *Mississippi Valley Historical Review* 47.1 (June 1960): 67 (quote);
Maryland Bureau of Immigration, Seventh Biennial Report, v. 7–8 (Chestertown,
MD: Kent Nevvs Print, 1909–1911), 9, retrieved from HathiTrust Digital Library
at http://catalog.hathitrust.org/Record/100234562?type[]=all&lookfor[]=maryland
%20immigration&filter[]=language%3AEnglish&ft= on February 29, 2016. Note,
the report was submitted on October 31, 1909, and covers the period from April
1907 to October 1909.

5. Jason H. Silverman and Susan R. Silverman, *Immigration in the American
South, 1864–1895: A Documentary History of the Southern Immigration Conventions*
(Lewiston, NY: The Edwin Mellon Press, 2006), 25–26, reprinting *The Constitu-
tion*, January 5, 1869, which reprinted Tennessee's immigration commissioner
Hermann Bokum's report.

6. Richard Griggs, Commissioner of Immigration and Agriculture, "Guide to
Mississippi" (Jackson, MS: Pilot Publishing Co, state printers, 1874), 6.

7. Seth French, commissioner of the Bureau of Immigration, "Semi-Tropical
Florida; Its Climate, Soil, and Productions, with a Sketch of Its History, Natural
Features, and Social Condition, Being a Manual of Reliable Information Concerning
the Resources of the State and the Inducements Which It Offers to Persons Seeking
New Homes and Profitable Investments" (Jacksonville, FL: Published for the State
by S. French, 1879), 20, retrieved from HathiTrust Digital Library at http://catalog
.hathitrust.org/Record/009609351?type[]=all&lookfor[]=Florida%20immigration
&filter[]=authorStr%3AFlorida.%20Bureau%20of%20Immigration&ft= on February 29, 2016.

8. Mark Wahlgren, *Summers, Railroads, Reconstruction, and the Gospel of Prosperity: Aid Under the Radical Republicans, 1865–1877* (Princeton, NJ: Princeton University Press, 2014), 147–148.

9. "Commissioner of Emigration" was Debar's official title. Cometti, "Swiss Immigration to West Virginia, 1864–1884," 70; Kenneth R. Bailey, "A Temptation to Lawlessness: Peonage in West Virginia, 1903–1908," *West Virginia History* 50 (1991), 215, reprinted by West Virginia Division of Culture and History, retrieved from http://www.wvculture.org/history/journal_wvh/wvh50-2.html on October 28, 2015.

10. "Story About One of the State's Most Interesting Characters," *West Union Record*, January 28, 1941, reprinted by West Virginia Division of Culture and History, retrieved from http://www.wvculture.org/history/notewv/dissdebr1.html on October 28, 2015; Cometti, "Swiss Immigration to West Virginia, 1864–1884," 70–71.

11. *Sixth Annual Report of the Commissioner of Immigration of the State of West Virginia for the Year 1869* (Wheeling, WV: John Frew, public printer, 1870), 3–4, retrieved from HathiTrust Digital Library at http://catalog.hathitrust.org/Record /008913319?type[]=all&lookfor[]=virginia%20immigration&ft= on February 29, 2016; Cometti, "Swiss Immigration to West Virginia, 1864–1884," 72.

12. *Sixth Annual Report of the Commissioner of Immigration of the State of West Virginia (1870)*, 4. The Republican Party dominated West Virginia state politics from 1863 to 1870.

13. *Sixth Annual Report of the Commissioner of Immigration of the State of West Virginia (1870)*, 15–19.

14. Most of the contributors to the "immigration fund" were naturalized citizens, most of them German-born. *The First Report of the Board of Immigration for the State of Missouri (1867)*, 7–8, 12, 52–53 ("Quarterly Report of the Special Agent," J. H. Schinkowsky), 75–82 ("List of Honorary Members and of Contributors to the Immigration Fund"). The Republican Party dominated Missouri state politics between 1862 and 1871, when the Democratic Party gained control and held it until 1896.

15. Muench was the board's German agent, although he did not leave Missouri; the Rev. Martin W. Willis was the board's "general agent" and traveled around the northern United States and Canada; J. H. Schinkowsky was the board's "soliciting agent" and was responsible for raising money. *The First Report of the Board of Immigration for the State of Missouri (1867)*, 7–8, 20–21, 48 (Report of Martin W. Willis), 52 ("Report of the General Agent").

16. *The First Report of the Board of Immigration for the State of Missouri (1867)*, 38, 40, 18, 54–55 (report of John Ruedi).

17. Ibid., 8, 11.

18. Ibid., 7–8, 36, 41. Note, Hertle's book is titled "Germans in North America and the War in Missouri," on 41 but called "The Germans in North America and the Struggle of Freedom in Missouri" on 36. In addition, S. Waterhouse,

"The Resources of Missouri" are included in the biennial report, but the numbering begins with page 1.

19. Ibid., 25.

20. Ibid., 24.

21. Silverman and Silverman, *Immigration in the American South, 1864–1895*, 95.

22. E. Russ Williams Jr., "Louisiana's Public and Private Immigration Endeavors: 1866–1893," *Louisiana History: The Journal of the Louisiana Historical Association* 15. 2 (Spring 1974): 153–173; Rowland T. Berthoff, "Southern Attitudes toward Immigration, 1865–1914," *Journal of Southern History* 17.3 (August 1951): 337; J. C. Kathman, "Information for Immigrants into the State of Louisiana" (New Orleans: Bureau of Immigration, 1868), 3, Section 3 of "An Act to Organize a Bureau of Immigration," retrieved from Google Books at https://books.google.de/books?id =zmdZAAAAcAAJ&pg=PA9&dq=Information+for+immigrants+into+the+state+of +louisiana&hl=en&sa=X&ei=lmvwVOafOcm-PI3OgMAK&ved=0CDQQ 6AEwAA#v=onepage&q=Information%20for%20immigrants%20into%20the%20 state%20of%20louisiana&f=false on August 3, 2015.

23. Alan G. Gauthreaux, *Italian Louisiana: History, Heritage, and Tradition* (Charleston, SC: The History Press, 2014), 24–25. Gauthreaux says that Dr. Thomas Cottman, a noted surgeon, replaced Kathman as immigration commissioner in 1866, yet Kathman's name is on the 1868 report "Information for Immigrants in the State of Louisiana." Kathman's feud with James Noyes and his accusation that Noyes was slandering his character can be seen in his letter to the editor in the *Times-Picayune*, February 15, 1870, 6. *The Times-Picayune*, December 3, 1869, 5, notes that Kathman dealt in coke and charcoal. Moon-Ho Jung, *Coolies and Cane: Race, Labor, and Sugar in the Age of Emancipation* (Baltimore, MD: Johns Hopkins University Press, 2009), 174, and footnote 52, citing the *West Baton Rouge Sugar Planter*, May 4, 1867.

24. Kathman, "Information for Immigrants into the State of Louisiana" (1868), 41–55; Letter from B. F. White to J. C. Kathman, June 11, 1867, excerpt from *Debow's Review*, "Department of Immigration and Labor," 1867, Roy Rosenzweig Center for History and New Media, George Mason University, retrieved from https://chnm.gmu.edu/courses/122/recon/debows.html on September 30, 2015.

25. Kathman, "Information for Immigrants into the State of Louisiana" (1868), 9, Preface.

26. Jung, *Coolies and Cane*, 174.

27. Ibid.; also James O. Noyes, *Report of the Bureau of Immigration to the General Assembly of Louisiana* (New Orleans: A. L. Lee, State Printer, 1869), 28–29. Louisiana had two sitting state legislatures, one Democratic, the other Republican, between November 1872 and 1874, and it is not clear which legislature defunded the Bureau of Immigration.

28. Silverman and Silverman, *Immigration in the American South*, 39–43. South Carolina had a military governor from 1866 to 1868, when it was readmitted to the Union. The Republican Party controlled South Carolina politics between 1868 and 1875, when the Democratic Party regained control.

29. R. H. Woody, "The Labor and Immigration Problem of South Carolina during Reconstruction," *Mississippi Valley Historical Review* 18.2 (September 1931): 202–203; Berthoff, "Southern Attitudes toward Immigration, 1865–1914," 336; Silverman and Silverman, *Immigration in the American South, 1864–1895*, 39–43.

30. Woody, "The Labor and Immigration Problem of South Carolina during Reconstruction," 202–203; "An Act for the Encouragement and Protection of European Immigration, and for the Appointment of a Commissioner and Agents and for Other Purposes therein Expressed," December 20, 1866, *Reports and Resolutions of South Carolina to the General Assembly*, 310, retrieved from Google Books at https://books.google.de/books?id=K3NDAQAAMAAJ&pg=RA1-PA319&dq =south+carolina+an+Act+for+the+Encouragement+and+Protection+of+European +Immigration&hl=en&sa=X&ei=yWvwVMPDC4TJPN76gKgP&ved=0CCAQ6 AEwAA#v=onepage&q=south%20carolina%20an%20Act%20for%20the%20 Encouragement%20and%20Protection%20of%20European%20Immigration &f=false on August 4, 2015; Silverman and Silverman, *Immigration in the American South, 1864–1895*, 39–43.

31. Berthoff, "Southern Attitudes toward Immigration, 1865–1914," 336–337.

32. Hermann Bokum, "The Tennessee Hand-Book and Immigrant's Guide: Giving a Description of the State of Tennessee; Its Agricultural and Mineralogical Character: Its Waterpower, Timber, Soil, and Climate; Its Various Railroad Lines . . . Its Adaptation for Stockraising, Grape Culture, Etc., Etc., with Special Reference to the Subject of Immigration" (Philadelphia: J. B. Lippincott & Co., 1868), 130–135, 151–152, retrieved from HathiTrust Digital Library at http:// catalog.hathitrust.org/Record/008652448?type[]=all&lookfor[]=tennessee %20immigration&ft= on February 29, 2016; Silverman and Silverman, *Immigration in the American South, 1864–1895*, 25–26. Tennessee did not experience military occupation under Reconstruction, and the Republican Party controlled Tennessee state politics between 1868 and 1875, when the Democratic Party regained control.

33. The Bureau of Immigration was created in February 1869. Florida was under military occupation between 1867 and 1877, and the Republican Party dominated Florida state politics between 1868 and 1877, when the Democratic Party regained control of state politics. J. S. Adams, commissioner of immigration, "Florida: Its Climate, Soil, and Productions, with a Sketch of Its History, Natural Features and Social Condition: A Manual of Reliable Information Concerning the Resources of the State and the Inducements to Immigrants" (Jacksonville, FL: E. M. Cheney, 1869), retrieved from HathiTrust Digital Library at http://catalog.hathitrust.org/Record/008652208?type[]=all&lookfor[]=Florida %20immigration&ft= on February 29, 2016; Dennis Eagan, commissioner of lands and immigration, "Sixth Annual Report of the Commissioner of Lands and Immigration of the State of Florida, for the Year Ending December 31, 1874, Together with Reports from the Several Counties . . . Descriptive of the Soil, Products and General Characteristics, Thus Forming a Complete Manual of

Information for Immigrants," also entitled, "The Florida Settler; or, Immigrants' guide" (Tallahassee, FL: Charles H. Walton, printer, 1874, 2nd ed.), retrieved from HathiTrust Digital Library at http://catalog.hathitrust.org/Record/009779275 on February 29, 2016. Note: the listing for the document says this is the sixth annual report, but the document itself says it is the second annual report.

34. Eagan, *Sixth Annual Report of the Commissioner of Lands and Immigration of the State of Florida (1874)*, 5, 18, 22–24.

35. Barbara J. Rozek, *Come to Texas: Attracting Immigrants, 1865–1915* (College Station, TX: Texas A&M University Press, 2003), 22–25. Texas was under military occupation between 1867 and 1870, when it was readmitted to the Union. The Republican Party controlled Texas state politics between 1867 and 1873, when the Democratic Party regained control.

36. Ibid., 25.

37. Ibid., 24, 27.

38. Chapter 156, "An Act to Encourage Immigration into the State of West Virginia," passed February 28, 1871, *Acts of the Legislature of West Virginia* (Wheeling, WV: J. Frew, Public Printer, 1871), 208, retrieved from Google Books at https://books.google.co.uk/books?id=loFIAAAAYAAJ&pg=PA208&dq=an+Act +to+Encourage+Immigration+into+the+State+of+West+Virginia&hl=en&sa=X &ved=0CB8Q6AEwAGoVChMIyavkw4zlyAIVBOkUCh2d6AWL#v=onepage&q =an%20Act%20to%20Encourage%20Immigration%20into%20the%20State%20 of%20West%20Virginia&f=false on October 28, 2015.

39. Berthoff, "Southern Attitudes toward Immigration, 1865–1914," 338; Eric Foner, *Forever Free: The Story of Emancipation and Reconstruction* (New York: Knopf Doubleday, 2013), 136.

40. Griggs, "Guide to Mississippi" (1874).

41. Rozek, *Come to Texas*, 22. The Texas Bureau of Immigration published 11 editions of "Texas, the Home for the Emigrant, from Everywhere," between 1873 and 1875 in both English and German, Texas Bureau of Immigration, "Texas, the Home for the Emigrant, from Everywhere" (Houston: A. C. Gray, State Printers, 1875), retrieved from The Portal to Texas History, University of North Texas Libraries' Digital Project Unit, retrieved from http://texashistory .unt.edu/ark:/67531/metapth28586/?q=Texas%2C%20the%20home%20for %20the%20emigrant%2C%20from%20everywhere on February 29, 2016. Please also see "The Home for the Emigrant: Texas, Her Vast Extent of Territory, Fertility of Soil, Diversity of Productions, Geniality of Climate, and the Facilities She Affords Emigrants for Acquiring Homes; the Land of Promise, to Which All Eyes Are Turned" (Austin: Institution for the Deaf and Dumb, 1877), retrieved from HathiTrust Digital Library at http://catalog.hathitrust.org/Record/009024564 ?type[]=all&lookfor[]=texas%20the%20home%20for%20the%20emigrant&ft= on February 29, 2016.

42. Laura K. Bennett, "Rural and Urban Boosterism in Texas, 1880s to 1930s" (MA thesis, University of Texas, Arlington, 2008), 6–7.

43. Bennett, "Rural and Urban Boosterism in Texas, 1880s to 1930s," 7; J. Norman Heard, *Handbook of the American Frontier: Four Centuries of Indian-White*

Relationships, Vol. III: The Great Plains (Lanham, MD: Scarecrow Press, 1993), 112 (Howard Wells, Texas, Massacre), 151 (McClellan Creek Fight), 43 (Buell, George, Campaigns), 200 (Red River Indian War).

44. Thomas J. Janes, Georgia Department of Agriculture, "A Manual of Georgia for the Use of Immigrants and Capitalists" (Atlanta: J. P. Harrison & Co., 1878), 51–52, retrieved from HathiTrust Digital Library at http://catalog.hathitrust.org/Record/011441102?type[]=all&lookfor[]=georgia%20immigration&filter[]=topicStr%3AGeorgia%20Description%20and%20travel&ft= on February 29, 2016; Thomas Janes, Georgia Department of Agriculture, "Georgia, from the Immigrant Settler's Stand-Point: Giving the Results of the Experience of Actual Settlers from Other States and Countries, Prefaced with an Account of the Natural Resources of Georgia, and the Inducements to Immigrants and Capitalists" (Georgia: Dept. of Agriculture, 1879), retrieved from HathiTrust Digital Library at http://catalog.hathitrust.org/Record/100735430?type[]=all&lookfor[]=georgia%20immigration&filter[]=topicStr%3AGeorgia%20Description%20and%20travel&ft= on February 29, 2016; Francis Fontaine, "The State of Georgia; What It Offers to Immigrants, Capitalists, Producers and Manufacturers, Fruit and Vegetable Growers, and Those Desiring to Better Their Condition" (Atlanta: 1880), retrieved from HathiTrust Digital Library at http://catalog.hathitrust.org/Record/009571547?type[]=all&lookfor[]=georgia%20immigration&filter[]=topicStr%3AGeorgia%20Description%20and%20travel&ft= on February 29, 2016.

45. Janes, "Georgia, from the Immigrant Settler's Stand-Point" (1879), 61–64.

46. Westley F. Busbee Jr., *Mississippi: A History* (Hoboken, NJ: John Wiley & Sons, 2014), 165–166, 171; E. G. Wall, "The State of Mississippi, Resources, Condition and Wants" (Jackson, MS: Clarion Steam Printing, 1879).

47. Nell Irvin Painter, *Exodusters* (New York: W. W. Norton, 1976); E. G. Wall, *Wall's Manual of Agriculture, for the Southern United States* (Memphis: Southwestern Publishing Co., 1870).

48. Chapter 90, "An Act Authorizing the Appointment of a State Agent on Immigration, and Appropriating Money for Immigration Purposes," passed March 10, 1879, *Acts of the Legislature of West Virginia* (Wheeling, WV: J. Frew, Public Printer, 1879), 170, retrieved from Forgotten Books at http://www.forgottenbooks.com/readbook_text/Acts_of_the_Legislature_of_West_Virginia_1000730562/173 on October 28, 2015. Eugene Daetwyler, Annie Teuscher, and E. Metzner, "The Story of Helvetia Community," West Virginia Division of Culture and History, located at http://www.wvculture.org/history/agrext/helvetia.html on October 28, 2015.

49. Jean Ann Scarpaci, *Italian Immigrants in Louisiana's Sugar Parishes, Recruitment, Labor Conditions, and Community Relations, 1880–1910* (New York: Arno Press, 1980), 68–69; *Painter, Exodusters*.

50. Charles Shanabruch, "The Louisiana Immigration Movement 1891–1907: An Analysis of Efforts, Attitudes, and Opportunities," *Louisiana History* 18.2 (Spring 1977): 208.

51. Although Wagener's position was eliminated in 1868, the legislature passed an act in 1882 formally abolishing the office of the superintendent of

immigration and transferring its responsibilities to the state's Department of Agriculture. "South Carolina," *Reports of the Immigration Commission, Immigration Legislation* (Washington, DC: Government Printing Office, 1911), 501, retrieved from http://www.mocavo.com/Reports-of-the-Immigration-Commission-Immigration -Legislation/872786/515 on September 29, 2015, also please see *Fourth Annual Report of the Commissioner of Agriculture of South Carolina*, for the fiscal year ending October 31, 1883 (Columbia, SC: Charles A. Calvo, state printer, 1883), 59–61, retrieved from https://archive.org/details/annualreport01carogoog on October 26, 2015, and South Carolina Department of Agriculture, Commerce, and Immigration, *Handbook of South Carolina, Resources, Institutions and Industries of the State; a Summary of the Statistics of Agriculture, Manufactures, Geography, Climate, Geology and Physiography, Minerals and Mining, Education, Transportation, Commerce, Government, Etc.* (Columbia, SC: 1908, 2nd ed.), 513, for discussion of Boykin's work, retrieved from https://archive .org/details/handbookofsouthc00sout on October 26, 2015.

52. *Fourth Annual Report of the Commissioner of Agriculture of South Carolina (1883)*, 59–61.

53. Silverman and Silverman, *Immigration in the American South, 1864–1895*, 23.

54. Butler was from an old South Carolina family and was a cotton planter, Theodore D. Jervey, "The Butlers of South Carolina," *South Carolina Historical and Genealogical Magazine* 4.4 (October 1903): 296–311. This Andrew Pickens Butler should not be confused with Senator Andrew Pickens Butler (1796–1857), who was the agricultural commissioner's great-grandson.

55. Berthoff, "Southern Attitudes toward Immigration, 1865–1914," 336–337.

56. Beth Anne English, *A Common Thread: Labor, Politics, and Capital Mobility in the Textile Industry* (Athens, GA: University of Georgia, 2010), 41–43.

57. This agency was renamed the Board of Agriculture and Immigration by the early 1900s. *Report of the State Board of Agriculture of Virginia* (Richmond, VA: J. W. Fergusson & Son, State Printers, 1888) also listed as *Bulletin, Virginia Department of Immigration and Agriculture (1888)*, 4, retrieved from HathiTrust Digital Library at http://babel.hathitrust.org/cgi/pt?id=uiug.30112105783564 on March 16, 2016.

58. 1. 891 Immigration Act *(An Act in Amendment to the Various Acts Relative to Immigration and the Importation of Aliens Under Contract or Agreement to Perform Labor)*, Sess. II Chap. 551; 26 Stat. 1084, 51st Congress; March 3, 1891, Section 3, digital copy of text retrieved from http://library.uwb.edu/static/USimmigration /26%20stat%201084.pdf on April 25, 2016.

59. South Carolina Department of Agriculture, Commerce, and Immigration, *Handbook of South Carolina (1908)*, 518. Note: in this document, Watson's name is incorrectly noted as "A. J. Watson."

60. Scarpaci, *Italian Immigrants in Louisiana's Sugar Parishes*, 74. This league was sometimes also called the Louisiana Immigration Association and was created in July 1905 by leaders of the Sugar Planters Association, several of whom had been active in the State Immigration Association.

61. South Carolina Department of Agriculture, Commerce, and Immigration, *Handbook of South Carolina* (1908), 520–521.

62. Joseph Goldberg and William T. Moye, *The First One Hundred Years of the Bureau of Labor Statistics* (Washington, DC: U.S. Department of Labor, 1985), 50–51 (original text, 60–61 in digital reader), retrieved from Google Books at https://books.google.de/books?id=LskaPobqNyEC&dq=south+carolina+an+Act +to+Establish+a+Department+of+Agriculture,+Commerce,+and+Immigration &source=gbs_navlinks_s on August 4, 2015; Berthoff, "Southern Attitudes toward Immigration, 1865–1914," 341, please also see Cong. Record, 59 Cong., 2 Sess., 2944–3083 (February 15, 1907) for Bonaparte's ruling.

63. Scarpaci, *Italian Immigrants in Louisiana's Sugar Parishes*, 77–78.

64. Gunther Peck, *Reinventing Free Labor, Padrones and Immigrant Workers in the North American West, 1880–1930* (Cambridge, UK: Cambridge University Press, 2000), 105.

65. Maryland Bureau of Immigration, *Seventh Biennial Report (1909–1911)*, 7–9.

66. Maryland Bureau of Immigration, *Seventh Biennial Report (1909–1911)*, 9, 13, (about the Midwestern tour), 17–20 (about the Europe trip). Please also see Maryland Bureau of Immigration, "The State of Maryland and Its Advantages for Immigrants, Especially Farmers, Manufacturers and Capitalists" (Baltimore: 1904), retrieved from HathiTrust Digital Library at http://catalog.hathitrust.org /Record/009574336?type[]=all&lookfor[]=maryland%20immigration&filter[] =language%3AEnglish&ft= on February 29, 2016.

67. Wall, "The State of Mississippi, Resources, Condition and Wants" (1879) 21, quoting letter from C. Menelas of Brookhaven, MS. Menelas immigrated to the United States around 1871–1872 and bought a plantation in Brookhaven. He is described as a "merchant farmer" who had had no farming experience prior to moving to Mississippi, 22.

68. John R. Procter, "Information for Emigrants: The Climate, Soils, Timbers, & C., of Kentucky, Contrasted with Those of the Northwest" (Frankfort, KY: S. I. M. Major, public printer, 1881), 1–21, 10 (quote), retrieved from HathiTrust Digital Library http://catalog.hathitrust.org/Record/000237387?type[]=all&lookfor[]=k entucky%20immigration&filter[]=publishDateRange%3A1881&ft= on February 29, 2016. Note: Procter was the director of the Kentucky Geological Survey and Bureau of Immigration.

69. A. A. Robinson, commissioner of state Bureau of Immigration, "Florida: A Pamphlet Descriptive of Its History, Topography, Climate, Soil, Resources and Natural Advantage" (Tallahassee, FL: Printed at the Floridian book and job office, 1882), 8, retrieved from HathiTrust Digital Library at http://catalog .hathitrust.org/Record/009591095 on February 29, 2016, italics in original text.

70. Janes, "A Manual of Georgia for the Use of Immigrants and Capitalists" (1878), 7 (quote), 8.

71. Robinson, "Florida" (1882), 3.

72. Janes, "A Manual of Georgia for the Use of Immigrants and Capitalists" (1878), 7 (quote), 8.

73. Texas Bureau of Immigration, "Texas, the Home for the Emigrant, from Everywhere" (1875), 4.

74. Silverman and Silverman, *Immigration in the American South, 1864–1895*, 39–43.

75. French, "Semi-tropical Florida" (1879).

76. John Sullivan Adams, "Florida Colonist, or The Settler's Guide" (Jacksonville, FL: Florida union job printing rooms, December 1871, 2nd ed.), 3–5, 6, retrieved from HathiTrust Digital Library at http://catalog.hathitrust.org/Record /005879997 on February 29, 2016.

77. B. F. Riley, "Alabama as It Is: Or, the Immigrant's and Capitalist's Guide Book to Alabama" (Atlanta: Constitution Publishing Company, 1888, 2nd ed.), retrieved from HathiTrust Digital Library at http://catalog.hathitrust.org/Record /008885310?type[]=all&lookfor[]=alabama%20immigration&ft= on February 29, 2016; and South Alabama Immigration Bureau, "Farm Lands for Sale in the South," (Dothan, AL: The Wire-grass Siftings, 1895), retrieved from HathiTrust Digital Library at http://catalog.hathitrust.org/Record/009600690?type[]=all &lookfor[]=alabama%20immigration&ft= on February 29, 2016.

78. Joseph H. Diss Debar, "The West Virginia Hand Book and Immigrant's Guide" (Parkersburg, WV: 1870), 172, 185; Adams, "Florida" (1869), 1.

79. Kathman, "Information for Immigrants into the State of Louisiana" (1868), 41–55.

80. Shanabruch, "The Louisiana Immigration Movement 1891–1907," 208.

81. Griggs, "Guide to Mississippi" (1874), 1–118; Texas Bureau of Immigration, "Texas, the Home for the Emigrant, from Everywhere" (1875), 15–21.

82. Woody, "The Labor and Immigration Problem of South Carolina during Reconstruction," 202–203; Silverman and Silverman, *Immigration in the American South, 1864–1895*, 41.

83. Shanabruch, "The Louisiana Immigration Movement 1891–1907," 222, 212.

84. Janes, "A Manual of Georgia for the Use of Immigrants and Capitalists" (1878), 25.

85. Robinson, "Florida" (1882), 14. Saul Green, "Oxygenation Therapy: Unproven Treatments for Cancer and AIDS," *Scientific Review of Alternative Medicine* (Spring/Summer 1998), retrieved from QuackWatch at http://www.quackwatch .org/01QuackeryRelatedTopics/Cancer/oxygen.html on March 21, 2016.

86. Texas Bureau of Immigration, "Texas, the Home for the Emigrant, from Everywhere" (1875), 35.

87. Kathman, "Information for Immigrants into the State of Louisiana" (1868), 15–16.

88. French, "Semi-tropical Florida" (1879), 44; Adams, "Florida" (1869), 18–28.

89. Griggs, "Guide to Mississippi" (1874), 32.

90. Wall, "The State of Mississippi, Resources, Condition and Wants" (1879) 12.

91. Bokum, *The Tennessee Hand-Book and Immigrant's Guide* (1868), 109, 126 (quote).

92. Silverman and Silverman, *Immigration in the American South, 1864–1895*, 56.

93. Kathman, "Information for Immigrants into the State of Louisiana" (1868), Preface, 13.

94. Shanabruch, "The Louisiana Immigration Movement 1891–1907," 217–218; Edward F. Haas, "Guns, Goats, and Italians: The Tallulah Lynching of 1899," *North Louisiana Historical Association* 13.1 and 13.2 (1982); Berthoff, "Southern Attitudes toward Immigration, 1865–1914," 343.

95. Maryland Bureau of Immigration, "The State of Maryland and Its Advantages for Immigrants, Especially Farmers, Manufacturers and Capitalists" (Baltimore, 1904), 3, retrieved from HathiTrust Digital Library at http://catalog.hathitrust.org/Record/009574336?type[]=all&lookfor[]=maryland%20immigration&filter[]=language%3AEnglish&ft= on February 29, 2016.

96. Karl L. Franke, "Die materiellen verhältnisse und vortheile für einwanderer im staate Kentucky, Ver. Staaten v. Amerika," "Kentucky bureau für geologie und immigration, John R. Procter, direktor" (Frankfort, KY: Electrotypirl-von Major, Johnston + Barrett, 1880), retrieved from HathiTrust Digital Library at http://catalog.hathitrust.org/Record/100554338?type[]=all&lookfor[]=kentucky%20immigration&filter[]=language%3AGerman&ft= on February 29, 2016; John R. Procter, "Mittheilungen für Auswanderer : Klima, Boden, Wälder u.s.w. von Kentucky, verglichen mit denen des Nordwestens / von John R. Procter" (Frankfort, KY: Major, Johnston & Barrett, 1881), retrieved from HathiTrust Digital Library at http://catalog.hathitrust.org/Record/100215829?type[]=all&lookfor[]=kentucky%20immigration&filter[]=language%3AGerman&ft= on February 29, 2016. Also, Procter, "Information for Emigrants" (1881).

97. "Story about One of the State's Most Interesting Characters"; Cometti, "Swiss Immigration to West Virginia, 1864–1884: A Case Study," 70–71.

98. "Charleston Man Founded Walhalla," *Charleston News & Courier*, May 31, 1954, 14; "Gen. John A. Wagener," *Charleston News & Courier*, August 28, 1876, 2; Jeffrey Strickland, "Federick W. Wagener," *Immigrant Entrepreneurship, German-American Business Biographies* (Washington, DC: German Historical Institute, 2011), retrieved from http://www.immigrantentrepreneurship.org/entry.php?rec=24 on September 29, 2015, focuses on Wagener's brother, Frederick, but also discusses John A. Wagener.

99. Water B. Stevens, "Frederick (Friedrich) Muench," *Centennial History of Missouri (The Center State), One Hundred Years in the Union, 1820–1921*, Vol. 2. (St. Louis-Chicago: The S. J. Clarke Publishing Company, 1921). Missouri Germans Consortium, retrieved from http://mo-germans.com/friedrich-muench/ on March 22, 2016.

100. Cyrus Adler, Cohen, "Bush (Busch), Isidor," *Jewish Encyclopedia* (New York: Funk and Wagnalls, 1901), digital copy retrieved from http://www.jewishencyclopedia.com/articles/3850-bush-busch-isidor on March 22, 2016.

101. Bokum, *The Tennessee Hand-Book and Immigrant's Guide* (1868), 3 (Introduction).

102. Rozek, *Come to Texas*, 23.

103. Ibid., 31–33.

104. "Riley, Benjamin Franklin, 1849–1925," *Alabama Authors*, The University of Alabama University Libraries, retrieved from http://www.lib.ua.edu /Alabama_Authors/?p=1955 on March 17, 2016.

105. United States Bureau of the Census, Twelfth Annual Census, 1900, Statistics of Population, Table 9, Population by Sex, General Nativity, and Color by States and Territories: 1900, 482–483, and Table 33, Foreign Born Population, Distributed According to Country of Birth, by States and Territories: 1900, 732–735.

106. Silverman and Silverman, *Immigration in the American South, 1864–1895*, 2–3.

107. Cometti, "Swiss Immigration to West Virginia, 1864–1884," 73.

108. Col. A. J. McWhirter, speech given November 21, 1883, at the Cotton Planters' Association of America's annual convention in Vicksburg, Mississippi, reprinted in Silverman and Silverman, *Immigration in the American South, 1864–1895*, 73.

109. Letter from B. F. White to J. C. Kathman, June 11, 1867.

Further Reading

Appel, Livia, and T. C. Blegen. "Official Encouragement of Immigration to Minnesota during the Territorial Period." *Minnesota Historical Society Magazine* (originally published August 1923), retrieved from http://collections.mnhs.org/MNHistoryMagazine/articles/5/v05i03p167-203.pdf, July 30, 2015.

Berthoff, Rowland T. "Southern Attitudes toward Immigration, 1865–1914." *Journal of Southern History* 17.3 (August 1951): 328–360.

Billington, Ray Allen. *Land of Savagery, Land of Promise: The European Image of the American Frontier in the Nineteenth Century* (New York: W. W. Norton & Co., 1981).

Blegen, Theodore C. "The Competition of the Northwestern States for Immigrants." *Wisconsin Magazine of History* 3.1 (September 1919): 3–29.

Cometti, Elizabeth. "Swiss Immigration to West Virginia, 1864–1884: A Case Study." *Mississippi Valley Historical Review* 47.1 (June 1960): 67–88.

Curti, Merle. "The Reputation of America Overseas (1776–1860)." *American Quarterly* 1.1 (Spring 1949): 58–82.

Cutlip, Scott M. *Public Relations History: From the 17th to the 20th Century: The Antecedents* (New York: Routledge, 2013).

Dovring, Folke. "European Reactions to the Homestead Act." *Journal of Economic History* 22.4 (December 1962): 464–468.

Dumke, Glenn S. "Colony Promotion during the Southern-California Land Boom." *Huntington Library Quarterly* 6.2 (February 1943): 238–249.

Dye, Victoria E. *All Aboard for Santa Fe: Railway Promotion of the Southwest, 1890s to 1930s* (Albuquerque: University of New Mexico Press, 2005).

Fox, Stephen R. *The Mirror Makers: A History of American Advertising and Its Creators* (Chicago: University of Illinois Press, 1997).

Glazier, Jack. *Dispersing the Ghetto: The Relocation of Jewish Immigrants across the United States* (Ithaca, NY: Cornell University Press, 1998).

Hedges, James B. "The Colonization Work of the Northern Pacific Railroad." *Mississippi Valley Historical Review* 13.3 (December 1926): 311–342.

Jung, Moon-Ho. *Coolies and Cane: Race, Labor, and Sugar in the Age of Emancipation* (Baltimore, MD: Johns Hopkins University Press, 2009).

Kinsey, Winston Lee. "The Immigrant in Texas Agriculture during Reconstruction." *Agricultural History* 53.1 (Southern Agriculture Since the Civil War: A Symposium, January 1979): 129–134.

Klebaner, Benjamin J. "State and Local Immigration Regulation in the United States Before 1882." *International Review of Social History* 3.2 (August 1958): 269–295.

Kupperman, Karen Ordahl. "Fear of Hot Climates in the Anglo-American Colonial Experience." *The William and Mary Quarterly* 41.2 (April 1984): 213–240.

"The Labor Problem at Jamestown, 1607–1618." *American Historical Review* 76.3 (June 1971): 595–611.

Larsen, Birgit Flemming, Henning Bender, and Karen Veien, eds. *On Distant Shores: Proceedings of the Marcus Lee Hansen Immigration Conference; Aalborg, Denmark June 29–July 1, 1992* (Danes Worldwide Archives in collaboration with the Danish Society for Emigration History in Aalborg, Denmark, 1993).

Ljungmark, Lars. *For Sale—Minnesota: Organized Promotion of Scandinavian Immigration 1866–1873* (Göteborg, Läromedelsförl, 1971).

Luebke, Frederick, ed. *The European Immigrants in the American West, Community Histories* (Albuquerque: University of New Mexico Press, 1998).

Lyon, William H. "'Live, Active Men, with Plenty of Push': Arizona's Territorial Immigration Commissioners." *Journal of Arizona History* 37.2 (Summer 1996): 149–162.

Marinbach, Bernard. *Galveston: Ellis Island of the West* (Albany, NY: SUNY Press, 1983).

McDonnell, Janet. *The Dispossession of the American Indian* (Indianapolis: Indiana University Press, 1991).

Mickelson, Sig. *The Northern Pacific Railroad and the Selling of the West* (Sioux Falls, SD: The Center for Western Studies, 1993).

Morgan, Edmund S. "The First American Boom: Virginia 1618 to 1630." *The William and Mary Quarterly* 28.2 (April 1971): 169–198.

Murray, Stanley N. "Railroads and the Agricultural Development of the Red River Valley of the North, 1870–1890." *Agricultural History* 31.4 (October 1957): 57–66.

Norman, Theodore. *An Outstretched Arm: A History of the Jewish Colonization Association* (London: Routledge & Kegan Paul, 1985).

Orsi, Richard J. *Sunset Limited: The Southern Pacific Railroad and the Development of the American West, 1850–1930* (Berkeley and Los Angeles: University of California Press, 2007).

Otterness, Philip. *Becoming German: The 1709 Palatine Migration to New York* (Ithaca, NY: Cornell University Press, 2004).

Painter, Nell Irvin. *Exodusters* (New York: W. W. Norton & Co., 1976).

Parker, Edna Monch. "The Southern Pacific Railroad and Settlement in Southern California." *Pacific Historical Review* 6.2 (June 1937): 103–119.

Peck, Gunther. *Reinventing Free Labor: Padrones and Immigrant Workers in the North American West, 1880–1930* (Cambridge, UK: Cambridge University Press, 2000).

Popper, Deborah E. "Great Opportunities for the Many of Small Means: New Jersey's Agricultural Colonies." *Geographical Review* 96.1 (January 2006): 24–49.

"Promotion of Immigration to the Pacific Northwest by the Railroads." *Mississippi Valley Historical Review* 15.2 (September 1928): 183–203.

"The Puzzle of the American Climate in the Early Colonial Period." *The American Historical Review* 87.5 (December 1982): 1262–1289.

Reisner, Marc. *Cadillac Desert: The American West and Its Disappearing Water* (New York: Viking Penguin, 1986).

Rozek, Barbara J. *Come to Texas: Attracting Immigrants, 1865–1915* (College Station: Texas A&M University Press, 2003).

Scarpaci, Jean Ann. *Italian Immigrants in Louisiana's Sugar Parishes, Recruitment, Labor Conditions, and Community Relations, 1880–1910* (New York: Arno Press, 1980).

Shanabruch, Charles. "The Louisiana Immigration Movement 1891–1907: An Analysis of Efforts, Attitudes, and Opportunities." *Louisiana History* 18.2 (Spring 1977): 213–218.

Silverman, Jason H., and Susan R. Silverman. *Immigration in the American South, 1864–1895: A Documentary History of the Southern Immigration Conventions* (Lewiston, ME: Edwin Mellon Press, 2006).

"Slavery and Freedom: The American Paradox." *Journal of American History* 59.1 (June 1972): 5–29.

Sokol, Marienka J. *Illusions of Abundance: Culture and Urban Water Use in the Arid Southwest* (Ann Arbor, MI: Proquest, 2008).

Summers, Mark Wahlgren. *Railroads, Reconstruction, and the Gospel of Prosperity: Aid Under the Radical Republicans, 1865–1877* (Princeton, NJ: Princeton University Press, 2014).

Unruh, John D. *The Plains Across: Emigrants, Wagon Trains and the America West* (Urbana and Chicago: University of Illinois Press, 1979, Plimico, London, ed.).

Utley, Robert M. *The Indian Frontier of the American West, 1846–1890* (Albuquerque: University of New Mexico Press, 1984).

Van Atta, John R. *Securing the West: Politics, Public Lands, and the Fate of the Old Republic, 1785–1850* (Baltimore, MD: Johns Hopkins University Press, 2014).

Ward, Stephen V. *Selling Places, the Marketing and Promotion of Towns and Cities, 1850–2000* (New York: Routledge, 1998).

West, Elliott. *The Contested Plains: Indians, Goldseekers, & the Rush to Colorado* (Lawrence: University Press of Kansas, 1998).

White, Richard. *"It's Your Misfortune and None of My Own": A History of the American West* (Norman: University of Oklahoma Press, 1991).

Williams, E. Russ, Jr. "Louisiana's Public and Private Immigration Endeavors: 1866–1893." *Louisiana History* 15.2 (Spring 1974): 153–173.

Winther, Oscar O. "Promoting the American West in England, 1865–1890." *Journal of Economic History* 16.4 (December 1956): 506–513.

Wooster, Robert. *The American Military Frontiers: The United States Army in the West, 1783–1900* (Albuquerque: University of New Mexico Press, 2009).

Worster, Donald. *Rivers of Empire, Water, Aridity, and the Growth of the American West* (New York: Pantheon Books, 1985).

Wrobel, David M. *Promised Lands: Promotion, Memory, and the Creation of the American West* (Lawrence: University Press of Kansas, 2002).

Index

Note: Page numbers followed by a *t* indicate tables.

About the Author

Christina A. Ziegler-McPherson is a public historian specializing in United States migration history. She earned a PhD in history from the University of California, Santa Barbara, in 2000 and was a Fulbright Scholar at the University of Bremen, Bremen, Germany in 2014–2015.

www.ingramcontent.com/pod-product-compliance
Lightning Source LLC
Chambersburg PA
CBHW050420280326
41932CB00013BA/1935